PARTNERSHIPS IN EDUCATION
TEACHER EDUCATION YEARBOOK II

PARTNERSHIPS IN EDUCATION
TEACHER EDUCATION YEARBOOK II

EDITORS

MARY JOHN O'HAIR
Texas Tech University

SANDRA J. ODELL
Western Michigan University

under sponsorship of the Association of Teacher Educators

HARCOURT BRACE COLLEGE PUBLISHERS
Fort Worth   Philadelphia   San Diego   New York   Orlando   Austin   San Antonio
Toronto   Montreal   London   Sydney   Tokyo

Publisher	Ted Buchholz
Acquisitions Editor	Jo-Anne Weaver
Project Editor	Laura Hanna
Production Manager	Tom Urquhart
Art Director	Jim Taylor
Cover Illustration	Gloria Ross

Address Editorial Correspondence To: Harcourt Brace College Publishers, 301 Commerce Street, Suite 3700, Fort Worth, TX 76102

Address Orders To: Harcourt Brace & Company, 6277 Sea Harbor Drive, Orlando, FL 32887-6777. 1-800-782-4479, or 1-800-433-0001 (in Florida)

Printed in the United States of America

Library of Congress Catalogue Number: 93-78425

ISBN: 0-15-501221-5

3 4 5 6 7 8 9 0 1 2   066   9 8 7 6 5 4 3 2 1

TABLE OF CONTENTS

DEDICATION

This book is dedicated to Mildred Cherry and the memory of John V. Cherry, who modeled successful partnerships; to Dan O'Hair, who is a constant reminder of a successful partnership; and to Erica and Jonathan, who struggle daily with partnership concepts involving sharing and giving.

M.J.O.

This book is dedicated to Douglas P. Ferraro who continues to be my most important partner, personally and professionally, and to F. Keith Auger who taught me to understand the complex dimensions of university/public school partnerships.

S.J.O.

PARTNERSHIPS IN SUPPORT OF TEACHER EDUCATION

FOREWORD

A fourteen-year-old boy was killed recently on his way to school because two young thugs wanted his jacket. When the murderers were caught, they justified their actions by blaming their victim. If he had just given them the jacket without resistance, this never would have happened (the soundness of this logic escapes me). Such an act of violence is tragic. The report of the incident in the newspapers brought some indignation, but not very much, and it ceased being a topic of interest in only a few days. Have we as a society become so accustomed to these senseless acts of violence that the family and friends of the boy grieve alone? If so, this is the greatest tragedy of all.

The English teacher of the murdered boy called me a few days after the event in tears. As one of my former students, she felt the need to talk. Keep in mind that this teacher is a terrific person and an excellent professional. In our discussion she said that she was totally unprepared to deal with this problem. We had prepared her to teach English, not to counsel angry and confused classmates. She wanted somehow to console the parents but felt ill-prepared. Is this her role? Would it be better to turn to the social worker in the school (assuming there is one available)? Does the teacher have the principal, guidance counselor, or psychologist to deal with this? Who helps the teacher as she struggles with her own sense of helplessness? One colleague suggested that she do what she was hired to do, teach English. What does a teacher do in human situations when her preparation falls short of assisting her to cope with the whole student? How can we garner the expertise of many professionals working together to address the immense challenges we face in our schools?

I do not envision the day when teachers alone are prepared to be all things for all people. However, I can foresee, and in the very near future, a time when we will be better educated and prepared to work closely in partnership with many professionals who together know how to deal with complex aspects of the whole child. Presently we do not have expertise in working effectively and collaboratively with other professionals.

Schools are one place where all children congregate. It follows, therefore, that the school will be the locale where all services—social, medical, psychological, and legal—will be administered. As educators we must be ready not only to assist in this process, but take leadership. This will require the development of a "new" educator ready to work in partnership with many others. These educators need to work not only as facilitators, but as working professionals, knowledgeable in the language and skills of all those participating. Passing off to other professionals the affective and physical needs of our students will simply no longer do.

Over the past few years the Association of Teacher Educators (A.T.E.) has undertaken the responsibility to address these issues. Our past conference themes centering on family, diversity, and in 1993–94 "Education and Human Services: Putting the Pieces Together," focus our attention on students as people rather than as mere receivers of information. Knowledge of subject matter and knowledge of self are not incompatible. In A.T.E. we have formed commissions charged with helping us to better understand the educator's role in working with the total package. We anticipate being able to assist those charged with preparing all helping professions with guidelines, principles, and a new knowledge base. Obviously, we must continue to recruit into our profession those with "heart." The challenges presented by today's society demand that a wide variety of partnerships be created. We need to have universities, public schools, businesses, and health and human services work as partners in preparing future teachers to create schools that truly address the physical, emotional, and learning needs of today's children.

This yearbook plays a major part in helping A.T.E. live up to its commitment of partnership. Bringing together the ideas of important scholars who do see the relevance of "putting the pieces together" is one way of putting resources where currently only words exist. I feel a personal sense of delight being able to participate. The idea of all of us working together for kids is not only important, it is correct.

Leonard Kaplan
1993–94 President
Association of Teacher Educators

INTRODUCTION:
LINKING RESEARCH AND PRACTICE THROUGH PARTNERSHIPS

SANDRA J. ODELL
Western Michigan University

MARY JOHN O'HAIR
Texas Tech University

SANDRA J. ODELL is Professor of Education and Professional Development and Director of Undergraduate Studies at Western Michigan University. She has published articles on teacher induction, mentoring, and teacher development. She maintains a career-long research interest in teacher development in the context of collaborative university/school district programs.

MARY JOHN O'HAIR is Associate Professor in the Department of Educational Leadership at Texas Tech University. Her research interests include preparing teachers and administrators for changing roles in restructured schools and cooperative interdisciplinary studies on interpersonal and organizational communication. Recent publications include *The Challenge of Reflective Field Experiences* (in press, with D. J. McIntyre), *HarperCollins Handbook of Business Communication* (in press, with D. O'Hair and J. O'Rourke) and journal articles on improving communication in teacher education and educational leadership programs.

The current volume, *Partnerships in Education: Teacher Education Yearbook II*, is the second in a planned series of yearbooks under the sponsorship of the Association of Teacher Educators (A.T.E.). The design of this Yearbook series is to assist teachers, teacher educators, and administrators, whether school or college based, to link theory and research about the educational process to the classroom practice of teaching.

This linkage is intended to be multidimensional. To be sure, there is the dimension of linking educational theory and research, methodology, and specialized knowledge to the preparation of new teachers and to the real world applications executed by the classroom practitioner on a day-to-day basis; but of at least equal importance is the dimension of having the schooling experiences of college teachers, student teachers, first-year teachers, experienced teachers, master teachers, and especially students in classrooms inform the articulation of curricula for preparing teachers, the development of new teaching strategies, the design of learning environments, and basic research on the processes that theoretically underlie meaningful schooling. Still other dimensions obviously exist. As but one example, there are those that provide linkages between research on teacher preparation or classroom teaching practices and university/school administration. Indeed, linking research and practice seems to be such a desideratum that it is worth asking why the Association of Teacher Educators sees the need for a yearbook series to facilitate such linkages. Why are such linkages not fully in place already?

IMPEDIMENTS

Some years ago C. P. Snow (1959, p.4) wrote a powerful book which described the polarized cultures (extant even today) of the humanities intellectual and the physical scientist: "Between the two a gulf of mutual incomprehension—sometimes (particularly among the young) hostility and dislike, but most of all lack of understanding. They have a curious distorted image of each other. Their attitudes are so different that, even on the level of emotion, they can't find much common ground."

C. P. Snow might just as well have been describing the gulf that in the past has broadly characterized the two cultures of the educational researcher and the educational practitioner or, for that matter, a host of other subcultures within the domain of education. This has nowhere been more evident, perhaps, than in the cultures of our schools and universities.

As Barth (1984, 1990) has noted, the school classroom culture and the teacher preparation culture have often lacked a mutual respect. Schoolteachers have many times been demeaned or condescended toward by universities, while schools have often been hostile environments for academics. Universities have too often attempted to be prescriptive about classroom teaching, while classroom teachers as often have rejected the research of their academic counterparts. Dialogue did not occur, mainly because the voice of school teachers and administrators was suppressed. People who attempted to cross from one culture to the next were suspect and unlikely to be rewarded for the diversity of their interests. Eyes were closed to the reality that classroom teachers are educational theorists and teacher educators are classroom practitioners.

Gulfs as wide as these pose real impediments when one wishes to construct a linkage between the polarities. It seems obvious then that recent urgings for educational reform (e.g. Goodlad, 1990) have been clarion calls for the formation of cooperatives, collaboratives, and partnerships among the up to now too distant cultures of education.

TERMINOLOGY

First a word regarding terminology in this book. We have not asked the authors to distinguish among the terms cooperation, collaboration, and partnerships, although we are aware that such distinctions can be made (e.g. Lasley, Matezynski, & Williams, 1992). Both cooperation, in which separate authorities are maintained while working toward a common goal, and collaboration, in which a shared authority is enjoyed, yield desired linkages. And while partnerships may be either cooperative or collaborative, both are valued models that can serve the purpose of enhancing education. By and large these more subtle distinctions between terms are blurred in what follows. The terms tend to regress to a common meaning of a situation in which all parties are empowered with authority and share in the responsibilities of planning, implementation, and evaluation. Our choice of the word *partnerships* for the title of this book is a personal one in that for us it is the most visual description of what we hope to convey.

PARTNERSHIPS

There is no gainsaying that despite the impediments to forming partnerships that link research and practice, successful educational partnerships have been formed in the past that antedate the calls for school reform (e.g. Auger & Odell, 1992; Smith, 1992). For the most part these successes have involved university/school partnerships in providing preservice and inservice teacher preparation, although more recently teacher induction partnerships have been described (e.g. Odell, 1986).

While these partnerships encompass the full diversity of relationships envisioned for the future of education or attested to in the chapters of the Yearbook which are to follow, there have been some conceptualizations derived from these partnerships that may be applicable to the formation of educational partnerships in general. First, the formation of an education partnership appears to involve a progression through a number of developmental stages (e.g. Trubowitz, 1986) that may take up to ten years to achieve institutionalization (Fullan, 1991). Even at that, the final developmental stage is best perceived as unstable with the partnership needing to undergo continuing renewal.

Educational partnerships that have succeeded seem to share a set of common characteristics from which can be derived principles of effective partnerships. Foremost among these seem to be that partnerships should: engender mutual trust and ownership among the partners (Smith & Auger, 1985–1986); foster collegiality of relationships among the partners (James, McNiece, & Broyles, 1991–1992); focus on school-based problems (Ward & Pascarelli, 1987); provide consumer satisfaction (DeBevoise, 1986); and create a structure that opportunistically potentiates grass roots ideas (Auger & Odell, 1992).

GENRES

In the past educational partnerships that have linked research and practice have largely existed in preservice, inservice, or induction contexts. In order for educational reform to result from the formation of educational partnerships, the full array of partnership genres will need to be realized.

Recently, school/university partnerships have been expanded to include cluster or center schools and, more comprehensively, professional development schools. The success of this latter partnership genre is not yet determined but seems to hinge on the status of the partners in the school settings and whether all school and university partners will be equally advantaged in restructured schools. Paramount here are the degree to which teachers are truly empowered as partners and the previously attenuated voices of teachers and students are amplified.

Today's school is no longer a place for students, teachers, and principals alone. Indeed, in the ideal contemporary school there will be a host of non-teaching personnel who provide support to students and teachers alike in the health and human services areas. A new genre of educational partnership needs to be defined that will link teaching and support personnel in the schools.

Education/health and human service partnerships will also be a part of a macro partnership genre that joins our schools and universities to the broader community. An important instance of this genre will be educational partnerships with business. The challenge here will be to construct partnerships that deal with school-based problems while providing consumer satisfaction to all partners.

Anyone who has been involved in establishing an educational partnership has come face-to-face with the reality that a partnership cannot be mandated but instead must emerge from a context that is ready for collaboration. To date, few educational partnerships have emerged from within university settings. There is a dire need for a contextual change in our universities. Partnerships that focus on the education of teachers between colleges of arts and sciences and education, and between these and colleges of business and fine arts, are essential to improved schooling and the ultimate success of school reform.

Another underdeveloped genre of educational partnerships is worth emphasis here. It is a genre for which the context for partnering is prime, and the potential for mutual gain is high. We refer to micro partnerships involving individual school or university settings of the following types: student/teacher, student/student, and teacher/teacher. Take the teacher/teacher partnership for instance. Such partnerships seem almost inevitable in schools and yet they are somewhat rare, suggesting that a pervasive impediment probably exists that limits this genre of partnerships. We hypothesize that this impediment consists of inadequate communication among the participants in schools. In part for this reason we have included a separate section on partnerships in defining and improving communication in schools.

A final, clearly underdeveloped, genre is cultural partnerships; forming partnerships among culturally diverse people in our schools, universities, and communities as a means of improving schooling for our Nation's children. In truth, cultural partnerships will need to become integral to all other education partnerships, no matter how micro or macro, if educational partnering is ultimately to achieve its goal of accomplishing true excellence in all educational endeavors.

STRUCTURE

This Yearbook's structure is designed to assist the reader to form linkages from the research presented to school-based problems. Each of four major sections of the book addresses educational partnerships in different contexts: schools and teacher education programs, preparation of teachers, communication in schools, and curriculum development and evaluation. Moreover, several of the chapters incorporate the voices of university academicians in partnership with teachers in the schools.

Preceding the presentation of individual research chapters in each section, a topic overview and framework of existing knowledge for the section are provided by recognized experts in educational partnerships. These same individuals serve as respondents to the research chapters and provide a subsequent interpretation, synthesis, and application of the research. In this manner it is hoped that each major section will stand on its own so that the reader may enter the Yearbook at any major section and not suffer any discontinuity.

A final major contribution to the Yearbook makes up the fifth section and is devoted to school, university, and human service systems partnerships. As with the other, this section conforms to the theme of the 1994 Association of

Teacher Educators annual meeting theme of "Education and Human Resources: Putting the Pieces Together."

ACKNOWLEDGMENT

As editors we wish to acknowledge the support of the Association of Teacher Educators and particularly the A.T.E. Executive Board, communication's committee, and research committee. We are indebted to many university, school, and business colleagues who have assisted in the conceptualization and reviewing processes, namely: David Byrd, Dean C. Corrigan, Renee Dillard, Carl D. Glickman, Ann Graves, Terry James, D. John McIntyre, H. James McLaughlin, Elaine McNiece, Michael Morehead, and Richard Purvis. Finally, we acknowledge Jo-Anne Weaver, acquisition's editor, and Laura Hanna, project editor, at Harcourt Brace who, as for the first Yearbook, have made valuable contributions.

REFERENCES

Auger, F.K., & Odell, S.J. (1992). Three school-university partnerships in teacher development. *Journal of Teacher Education, 43*(4), 262–268.

Barth, R.S. (1990). *Improving schools from within: Teachers, parents, and principals can make the difference.* San Francisco: Jossey-Bass.

Barth, R.S. (1984). Can we make a match of schools and universities? *Education Week* (November), 16 and last page.

De Bevoise, W. (1986). Collaboration: Some principles of bridgework. *Educational Leadership, 43*(5), 9–12.

Fullan, M.G. (1991). *The new meaning of education change.* 2nd ed. New York: Teachers College Press, Columbia University.

Goodlad, J. (1990). *Teachers for our nation's schools.* San Francisco: Jossey-Bass.

James, T.L., McNiece, E.M., & Broyles, I. (1991–1992). Developing collaborative arrangements between higher education institutions and school districts. *SRATE Journal, 1*(1), 19–23.

Lasley, T.J., Matczynski, T.J., & Williams, J.A. (1992). Collaborative and non-collaborative partnership structures in teacher education. *Journal of Teacher Education, 43*(4), 257–261.

Odell, S.J. (1986). A model university-school system collaboration in teacher induction. *Kappa Delta Pi Record, 22*(4), 120–122.

Smith, S.D. (1992). Professional partnerships and educational change: Effective collaboration over time. *Journal of Teacher Education, 43*(4), 243–256.

Smith, S.D., & Auger, K.A. (1985–1986). Conflict or cooperation? Keys to success in partnerships in teacher education. *Action in Teacher Education,* 7(4). 1–9.

Snow, C.P. (1959). *The two cultures.* New York: Cambridge University Press, p. 4.

Trubowitz, S. (1986). Stages in the development of school-college collaboration. *Educational Leadership, 43*(5), 9–12.

Ward, B.A., & Pascarelli, J.I. (1987). Networking for school improvement. In J.I. Goodlad (Ed.), *The ecology of school renewal* (pp. 192–209). Chicago: University of Chicago Press.

Partnerships and Collaboration in the Contexts of Schools and Teacher Education Programs

Contexts: Overview and Framework

D. JOHN MCINTYRE
Southern Illinois University at Carbondale

D. JOHN MCINTYRE is Professor of Curriculum and Instruction and Director of the Teaching Skills Laboratory at Southern Illinois University at Carbondale. He has authored or co-authored approximately 70 publications in the area of teacher education. He was president of the Association of Teacher Educators in 1992–1993, received the Association's Distinguished Research Award in 1986, and was named one of 70 Outstanding Leaders in Teacher Education.

INTRODUCTION

The terms *partnership* and *collaboration* have become educational buzzwords of the past decade. Almost all reform efforts mention the need for partnerships and

1

collaboration as keys to reforming schooling and teacher education. This section examines partnerships and collaboration between and within schools and teacher education programs. The purpose of this overview and framework is to provide a foundation for understanding the key elements required for successful partnerships/collaboration in a variety of school settings and to set the stage for the three articles that address partnerships/collaboration in this division.

PARTNERSHIPS/COLLABORATION WITHIN SCHOOLS

The ultimate goal of encouraging collaboration and establishing partnerships is to improve the educational opportunities and outcomes for school-age children and to improve the initial and continuing preparation of their teachers. Typically, collaboration and partnerships have been discussed in the context of a variety of arrangements including public/private schools, universities and/or business and industry. Too often, we have ignored the collaboration among teachers and between teachers and administrators that must occur within a school to be effective.

Our public and private elementary and secondary schools are living, dynamic communities whose purpose is to educate all students who pass through their doors. Each school has a formal and informal structure that governs its behavior and plays an important role in determining its environment and success. Owens (1970) states that each school has a "fabric of roles" that constitutes its formal structure. People within the school—administrators, teachers, students, and support staff—occupy these roles and behave in a manner prescribed for them. However, he also asserts that an informal group structure exists within every organization that determines how individuals interact within and between their groups.

This informal structure consists of primary groups of teachers and revolves around such variables as "old-timers," "new teachers," "grade level," "content," "age," "sex," "marital status," etc. How these primary groups relate within and between groups is crucial to the potential of successful collaboration within any particular school. Iannacconne (1964) believes that informal primary groups are linked in two ways. First, when a teacher is a member of two primary groups (that is, grade level and gender), the linkage between the two groups through that teacher is *articulation*. Second, when two teachers, each belonging to a different primary group (that is, primary and intermediate grades), regularly interact, they provide a *bridge* between the two groups.

Unfortunately, collaboration among teachers and between teachers and administrators appears to be rare. The heavy demands on teachers' time and energy do not permit much reciprocal conversation among colleagues. In addition, the school's milieu tends to stifle teachers talking to each other or to any other professional because a norm for listening to teachers does not exist within the professional community. Mechanisms such as overwork, low status, and an externally defined standard of performance contribute to silencing teachers (Richert, 1992). Collaboration between teachers and with their administrators is a relatively new, revolutionary position for our profession.

Teachers' isolation within the current school structure discourages change and transformation of the schools' environment and conditions (Britzman, 1991). This isolationism results in an overreliance on oneself and an undue preoccupation with personal school history, or institutional biography. Teachers, isolated from one another and from new ideas, tend to reproduce the system experienced as students. Thus, the status quo becomes a major roadblock to any notion of reform.

Interestingly, Koerner (1992) reports that experienced elementary teachers view themselves as "collaborators" having important relationships with parents, colleagues, and students. Common elements exist in schools where teachers successfully collaborate with one another and with their administrators. These elements include: (1) a belief that the quality of education is largely determined by what happens at the school site; (2) a conviction that instruction is most effective in a school environment characterized by norms of collegiality and continuous improvement; (3) a use of a wide range of practices and structures that enable administrators and teachers to work together on school improvement, and; (4) the involvement of teachers in decisions about school goals and the means for implementing them (Smith, 1987).

Collaboration between teachers is important because much of what they need to learn is procedural. Johnson and Johnson (1987) define procedural knowledge as that which relies heavily on receiving feedback about performance and then modifying performance until errors are eliminated. They advocate collegial support groups consisting of three to five teachers who work together to improve one another's performance and to ensure one another's professional growth. They further report that research comparing teachers' collaborative efforts with individual efforts reveals that collaboration promotes higher achievement, greater social support and higher self-esteem than a teacher's isolated efforts.

Although it is clear that collaboration among teachers can be a cornerstone of school improvement, efforts toward that goal appear to be scarce. Before any successful collaboration among university and school faculty and administrators can occur, teachers must learn and be encouraged to talk among themselves. As Richert (1992) states, "It is also essential that we prepare teachers to claim their own voice and in so doing, claim access to their own power and consequently the power to change" (p. 197).

SCHOOL/UNIVERSITY COLLABORATION

Collaboration and the forming of partnerships between schools and universities is frequently viewed as a primary thrust in any program to improve teacher education and, ultimately, the education of students. Working together toward a common goal requires much planning, commitment, and effort. One of the main obstacles to collaboration is that working toward a shared vision often confronts the conflicting organizational values of both institutions. The university community tends to esteem the scientific; the schools are steeped in practice (Reiman, Head & Thies-Sprinthall, 1992). As a result, programmatic approaches to teacher education require an extra effort to merge diverse opinions and frames of reference in order to reach agreement on the best of professional practice (Smith, 1991).

Several educators have written about their perceptions regarding the essential characteristics needed for successful collaboration between schools and universities. For example, McDaniel (1988–89) describes four interrelated themes that help define the nature of collaboration and school/university interactions. First, the university collaborators, with a reform agenda in mind, enter into a collaborative relationship with a school. Second, the agenda inevitably confronts the conventional practices that are deeply embedded in the belief systems of teachers. Third, the collaborators work through these interpersonal tensions; and, finally, new models of interaction and a different perspective emerge as the collaborators realize their potential and work toward common goals. It is important to anticipate the clashes between the theoretical and idealistic notions of the university and the more realistic and practical orientations of the school. Recognition of these potential pitfalls will result in less discouragement and more of a commitment to a long-term relationship between the partners. Clemson (1990) implies that failure to recognize these potential pitfalls can often lead to "divorce."

In addition to these characteristics, McGowan (1990) argues that several essential elements must exist for successful collaboration. These elements include: the willingness to commit the appropriate amount of time to the effort; the ability to provide perks or payoffs to the collaborators; support from the administration of all agencies or institutions; a core group of committed people; collegiality; and a common mission.

The partnerships that evolve from the collaborative efforts between universities and schools can be highly rewarding. However, McGowan (1990) asserts that the potential partners must enter their relationship with a shared set of assumptions. First, a partnership is a highly personal proposition. No partnership can function without the participants interacting positively. Second, partnerships are "messy" propositions. In other words, existing roles and structures may need to be modified. Third, a partnership is a long-term operation and the participants must enlist for the duration. Finally, the partners must be committed to the notion that their efforts can be a powerful change agent.

Collaborative arrangements for improving the preparation of teachers at the preservice and staff development levels is perhaps the most common and oldest type of partnership between schools and universities. The opportunities and benefits of collaborative arrangements between schools and universities are many, including fellowship, mentorship, assistance in attaining personal and professional goals, and the accomplishment of large-scale, broad-based renewal (Clemson, 1990). As early as 1881 the normal school at Providence, Rhode Island, had an arrangement with the local public school district whereby the normal school students did their practice teaching in the public school (Johnson, 1968). However, it was not until the mid-1900's that the preparation of preservice teachers moved from university laboratory schools to the public schools. The move toward these collaborative arrangements with the public schools was instigated by the decimation of laboratory schools because of economic conditions and the call for preservice teachers to experience real teaching and learning situations with real students in real classrooms.

Griffin (1986) believes that the defining property of any effective collaborative clinical teacher education program is having the program embedded in a school context. In addition, he states that there are certain crucial features of these collaborative efforts. First, the collaborative effort must be context-sensitive. This implies that the field experience is focused, employs supportive guidance and supervision, and develops approaches to seeing and understanding the classroom context. By understanding the context, the preservice teacher is more likely to understand the social and political ramifications of teaching and schooling. Second, the collaborative effort must be purposeful and articulated. Because universities and schools often have different agendas, the purpose and goals of the collaborative effort must be clearly stated, understood, and accepted by all agencies. Third, the collaborative effort must be participatory. In this case, participation means active involvement in the project by all parties. Fourth, the collaborative effort must be knowledge-based. There is a growing body of knowledge concerning not only effective clinical teacher education programs and the skills, knowledge and attitudes desired of beginning teachers but also concerning effective collaborative partnerships. This knowledge base must be employed if the program is to be meaningful and successful. Fifth, the collaborative effort must be ongoing. If the collaborative clinical teacher education program is to be effective, it must address the continuum of teacher development so that the needs of novice as well as experienced teachers are met. Sixth, the collaborative effort must be developmental. Griffin states that "by designing clinical teacher education programs that are responsive to the developmental levels (pedagogical and institutional rather than psychological and physical) of teachers, the program can capitalize upon vested interests and realize the true nature of its human capital" (p. 21). Finally, the program must be analytic and reflective. Classrooms and schools are complex environments. Facilitating teachers' abilities to be reflective and analytic aids them in understanding their environment and allows them to control it.

Collaborative efforts for preparing preservice teachers can be placed on a wide continuum. The least intensive collaboration arrangement involves only a contractual agreement between a school district and university granting permission to place preservice teachers in their schools for early field experiences and student teaching. In such situations, the university supervisor travels to the school to observe the preservice teacher. The degree of involvement of the cooperating teachers often depends on their own initiative.

The teacher education center, or teaching center, is at the midpoint of this continuum. The teacher education center concept clusters the placement of preservice teachers in several school districts. The university assigns a coordinator or clinical professor to the center to coordinate the placement, classroom observations, and evaluations of all preservice teachers. Since the coordinators are based in the school district, they are better able to communicate the philosophy of the teacher education program to the teachers and administrators and can also relay the concerns of teachers regarding the preparation of preservice teachers to university instructors. Center coordinators may assist in developing or facilitating staff development programs for teachers.

Gardner (1979) listed the advantages of teaching centers. These included (a) placing relatively large numbers of preservice teachers in schools dramatically alters the teacher–pupil ratio and makes possible classroom activities that otherwise would not be possible; (b) the enriched student-teacher mix frees teachers for planning, evaluating, or other tasks during the school day; and (c) the presence of university faculty in the school provides extra skill and knowledge, as well as access to campus resources. McIntyre (1979) suggests that the preparation of preservice teachers based in teacher education centers facilitates the integration of theory and practice by meshing preservice and practice programs. However, the success of the center concept often relies mainly on university faculty who are committed to working with teachers (Quisenberry, McIntyre, & Byrd, 1990).

Oja (1990–91) describes a project involving a collaborative effort of university and school faculty and administrators to "develop, refine, and extend the repertoire of supervisory skills of participating principals, teachers and university supervisors" (p. 11). Teacher supervision groups were organized within each participating school. These groups met biweekly to discuss alternative approaches to supervision and adult development stages and to discuss using this knowledge base in their supervisory practice with university students and peers. Not only did the participants benefit from this collaborative approach to supervision, but the school sites themselves were influenced positively. Data indicated that time was made available for cooperating teachers to meet together; the university supervisor, cooperating teachers, and principal collaborated in making supervisory decisions; more emphasis was placed on making a good match between the cooperating teacher and intern in the placement process; and the university supervisor acted as an organizing, mobilizing force among the cooperating teachers, principal and interns at the school as well as a liaison connecting the school with the university's teacher education program.

Finally, the most intensive type of collaboration between schools and universities is the professional development school. Although professional development schools have existed in several forms for more than a century, they can currently be defined as school settings focused on the professional development of teachers and the development of pedagogy (Stallings & Kowalski, 1990). These partnerships serve to prepare preservice teachers, induct novice teachers, and support experienced teachers as well as to experiment with new ideas and conduct research in the study of teaching. Stallings and Kowalski (1990) state that the goal of this partnership is to create schools and teacher education programs in which participants will acquire essential (a) subject-area knowledge; (b) reflective, analytic, problem-solving skills; and (c) social skills, so that the educational needs of society now and in the twenty-first century are met. In professional development schools, the practitioner or cooperating teacher plays a much bigger role in the preparation of the preservice teacher, often teaching methods courses on-site. In addition, university faculty provide teachers with consistent support for staff development needs.

The collaborative approach to staff development is a major focus of teaching centers and professional development schools. University faculty work with school staff to develop approaches that enable teachers to feel good about themselves, enhance feelings of comepetence and empowerment, and push them to peak performance (Koll, Herzog, and Burke, 1988–89). The most effective staff development programs provide options for participation so that choices facilitate a match between motivation and activity. Alternative opportunities and delivery systems that can be integrated into a staff development program in order to respond to motivational considerations are pivotal.

One of the collaborative efforts between university and school faculty and administrators in professional development schools is research to improve understanding of one's classroom or the teaching-learning act. Oja and Pine (1987) assert that collaborative action-research, whether within the confines of a professional development school or not, can have long-term benefits.

Their research indicates that collaborative action research groups often exhibit the following characteristics: (1) school-university participants join together with the goals of improving practice, contributing to educational theory, and providing staff development; (2) often meet on school site; (3) reach consensus on goals that address each person's immediate concerns; (4) use cycles of action research to investigate and apply research findings; (5) coauthor and/or co-present reports of their work; and (6) over time develop a collegial, trusting relationship and communication network between schools and university. Such collaborative efforts not only contribute to knowledge about one's classroom or school and the profession but also help these professionals reexamine their traditional roles.

THREE RESEARCH REPORTS

This section of the yearbook includes three studies that examine partnerships and collaboration from varying points of view. Dana investigates the lack of teacher voice in educational reform efforts. Her chapter tells the story of two novice teachers and describes their feelings of isolation and seclusion within the school culture. The story of Kit and Pam illustrates the importance of collegiality within the school culture and the need for partnerships between teachers and teachers and administrators.

White, Rainer, Clift, and Benson examine a collaborative teacher education program. This chapter brings to life the professional literature supporting the areas of partnerships and collaboration. The issues reviewed earlier in the introduction—such as conflicting institutional agendas, changing roles, and so forth—are sometimes vividly portrayed by the comments of the teachers and university faculty who participated in the project. Their chapter illustrates that partnerships are often fluid and demand commitment and time if they are to succeed.

Finally, Harris and Harris provide insight into the actual costs and benefits, tangible and intangible, of a university/school partnership. They examine such variables as time, services, facilities, pressure, communication, control, educational quality, and empowerment. Theirs is an interesting analysis of what one gains from, and contributes to, a partnership. Each of these studies contributes to our better understanding of partnerships and the collaborative process.

REFERENCES

Britzman, D. (1991). *Practice makes practice: A critical study of learning to teach.* Albany, NY: State University of New York Press.

Clemson, S. (1990). Four models of collaborative teacher education: A comparison of success factors and maturation. *Action in Teacher Education, 12* (2), 31–37.

Gardner, W. (1979). Dean's perspective of support for teachers in the beginning years. In K. Howey & R. Bents, eds. *Toward meeting the needs of the beginning teacher* (pp. 95–110). Minneapolis, MN: Midwest Teacher Corps Network and University of Minnesota/St. Paul Schools Teacher Corps Project.

Griffin, G. (1986). Clinical teacher education. In J. Hoffman & S. Edwards, eds. *Reality and reform in clinical teacher education* (pp. 1–23). New York: Random House.

Iannacconne, L. (1964). An approach to the informal organization of the school. In D. E. Griffiths, ed. *Behavioral science and educational administration, The sixty-third yearbook of the national society for the study of education, Part II.* Chicago, IL: University of Chicago Press.

Johnson, D., & Johnson, R. (1987). Research shows the benefits of adult cooperation. *Educational Leadership, 45* (3), 27–30.

Johnson, J. (1968). *A brief history of student teaching.* DeKalb, IL: Creative Educational Materials.

Koerner, M. (1992). Teachers images: Reflections of themselves. In W. Shubert and W. Ayers, ed. *Teacher lore: Learning from our own experience* (pp. 44–60). New York: Longman.

Koll, P., Herzog, B., & Burke, P. (1988–89). Continuing professional development: Implications for professional development. *Action in Teacher Education, 10* (4), 24–31.

McDaniel, E. (1988–89). Collaboration for What? Sharpening the Focus. *Action in Teacher Education, 10* (4), 1–8.

McGowan, T. (1990). Reflections of an experienced collaborator. In H. Schwartz, ed. *Collaboration: Building common agendas* (pp. 41–47). Washington, DC: ERIC Clearinghouse for Teacher Education and the American Association for Colleges of Teacher Education.

McIntyre, J. (1979). Integrating theory and practice via the teaching center. *Contemporary Education, 50* (3), 146–149.

Oja, S. (1990–91). The dynamics of collaboration: A collaborative approach to supervision in a five year teacher education program. *Action in Teacher Education, 12* (4), 11–20.

Oja, S., & Pine, G. (1987). Collaborative action research. *Peabody Journal of Education, 64* (1), 96–113.

Owen, R. (1970). *Organizational behavior in schools.* Englewood Cliffs, NJ: Prentice Hall.

Quisenberry, N., McIntyre, J. & Byrd, D. (1990). Collaboration and reflectivity: Cornerstones of a teacher education program. In H. Schwartz (ed.).

Collaboration: Building common agendas. Washington, DC: ERIC Clearinghouse for Teacher Education and American Association of Colleges for Teacher Education.

Reiman, A., Head, F., & Thies-Sprinthall, L. (1992). Collaboration and mentoring. In T. Bey & T. Holmes, (eds.). *Mentoring: Contemporary principles and views* (pp. 79–94). Reston, VA: Association of Teacher Educators.

Richert, A. (1992). Voice and power in teaching and learning to teach. In L. Valli, ed. *Reflective teacher education: Cases and critiques* (pp. 187–197). Albany, NY: State University of New York Press.

Smith, S. (1987). The collaborative school takes shape. *Educational Leadership, 45* (3), 4–6.

Smith, S. D. (1991). Educational change and social context, 1977–1989. In S. D. Smith, ed. *Distinguished company: Distinguished program in teacher education awards,* 1977–1989. Reston, VA: Association of Teacher Educators.

Stallings, J., & Kowalski, T. (1990). Research on professional development schools. In R. Houston (ed.). *Handbook of research on teacher education* (pp. 251–263). New York: Macmillan.

CHAPTER 1

Building Partnerships to Effect Educational Change: School Culture and the Finding of Teacher Voice

NANCY FICHTMAN DANA

The Pennsylvania State University

NANCY FICHTMAN DANA is Assistant Professor of Early Childhood and Elementary Education, Department of Curriculum and Instruction, The Pennsylvania State University, University Park, Pennsylvania. Her research interests include issues in teacher education including reflective practice, alternative assessment, and teaching cases.

ABSTRACT

The purpose of this ethnographic study was to examine the process of teacher-initiated change through collaborative research in one elementary school. Traditionally, a culture of seclusion and isolation has served to contain teachers' voices within the four walls of their classrooms and has limited teacher voice in educational change. Teachers yearn for their voices to be heard beyond their four walls. This assertion is supported by the stories of two novice teachers. Their stories describe the socialization of teachers into a culture of isolation and seclusion, a culture that silences teachers' voices and prevents visions of educational change from being implemented. Not until a school culture becomes collegial will teachers begin to build meaningful partnerships with one another and become empowered to create and sustain educational change in their classrooms.

OBJECTIVE/PURPOSE

The field of education continues to be inundated with cries for reform, restructure, and change (Bacharach, 1990; Culver & Hoban, 1973; Fullan, 1991; Goodlad, 1975). Many major reform efforts, however, have not included the voices of those who will be expected to implement and thus, perhaps, be most affected by change: classroom teachers. For example, in the 1980s, the voices of teachers were silenced by the cries for reform from education, government, and business leaders (Carnegie Forum on Education and the Economy, 1986) and a consortium of education deans (The Holmes Group, 1986). Additionally, educational researchers have historically silenced teachers by defining change as implementations of innovations from outside the classroom and subsequently characterizing teachers as "recalcitrant and resistant to change" (Richardson, 1990). Moreover, researchers have silenced teachers through the methodological approaches to their work. Gitlin (1990) writes:

> Educational research is still a process that for the most part silences those studied, ignores their personal knowledge, and strengthens the assumption that researchers are the producers of knowledge (p. 444). . . . Just as teachers may silence students to get on with learning, so may researchers silence those studied to get on with their research. (p. 446)

Scholars now recognize the failure of top-down approaches to educational reform, a failure that may in part be due to the omission of teacher voice from reform efforts (Barth, 1990; Deal, 1984; McDonald, 1989). According to these scholars, for school reform, restructuring and change to take place, the impetus must also come from the classroom teacher. Therefore, practitioners and researchers have begun to cooperate to effect educational change. In contrast to previous attempts at school change, collaborative endeavors have had promising results (Gitlin, 1990; Miller, 1990).

The purpose of this study was to examine the process of teacher-initiated change through collaborative research in one elementary school. The need to incorporate teacher voice in educational change efforts is the focus of the study.

Theoretical Framework: The Voice Metaphor

Stimulated largely by the work of Lakoff and Johnson (1980), many educational researchers are making sense of educational practices through the use of metaphor (e.g., Marshall, 1990). The metaphor of voice, prevalent in feminist literature (Belenky, Clinchy, Goldberger, & Tarule, 1986; Gilligan, 1982), has been adopted by some educational theorists as a way to understand schooling.

The use of the voice metaphor in feminist theory can be largely attributed to the groundbreaking work on moral and psychological development completed by Carol Gilligan. Gilligan (1982) asserted that the theory of morality grounded in the work of Kohlberg (1984) presented a narrow view of morality for numerous reasons: (a) The theories were based solely on a component of justice; (b) Kohlberg selected only male subjects to develop his theory; and (c) The measurement of moral judgments was based on hypothetical situations that presented only limited options for resolution (Scott, 1987). From Gilligan's interviews and analyses of the stories women told of the resolutions of personal, moral dilemmas, we learned that women speak "in a different voice," that is, a voice of care, responsibility, and connectedness.

Following Gilligan's work on women's moral development, Belenky, Clinchy, Goldberger, and Tarule (1986) studied female epistemology and development. From in-depth life history interviews of 135 women, Belenky and her co-authors concluded that "women repeatedly used the metaphor of voice to depict their intellectual and ethical development; and that the development of a sense of voice, mind, and self were intricately intertwined" (p. 18).

In critical education literature, the voice metaphor has been employed to convey historical instances of domination and oppression (evidenced by the silencing of teachers) and the political actions taken by individuals to express opinions and overcome domination and control (evidenced by the finding and gaining of teacher voice). For example, the work of Gitlin (1990) attempts to develop teacher voice as a political form of protest to enable school change. He proposes and begins to explore the use of educative research based on the work of Carr and Kemmis (1986). Educative research fosters a form that "gives a say to practitioners" and "exposes some of the myths surrounding [more traditional] scientific research" (p. 447).

Gitlin began his first attempt with a group of twenty of his students in the cooperative master's program at the University of Utah. He focused the theme of his course on an educative research project in which teachers were instructed to write a school history to identify school structures, read critical education theory literature such as Eisner's (1979) *The Education Imagination* and Apple's (1986) *Teachers and Text,* write personal school histories to explore the self, and pose any question they wanted to pursue through a dialogical model. Although Gitlin made great strides toward giving teachers voice in educational research, he reports that

> . . . teachers really didn't have a choice. I had used my privileged position to structure the experience and in so doing, lost an opportunity to challenge the dominant relationship between researcher and practitioner. (p. 450)

He concluded that even for teachers who did begin to find their voices, there was "no structure in place at the school level that would allow their voices to be heard" (p. 465).

The work of Miller (1990) carried these ideas one step further. Miller attempted to create a space in which the voices of teachers could be heard. In the role of university professor, Miller invited five educators to work together by developing a collaborative teacher-researcher project. Through her collaborative work with these teachers, Miller reported that the teachers and she were able to "share the constantly emerging and changing nature of [their] voices" (p. 7).

Miller (1990) shared the stories of this collaboration in *Creating Spaces and Finding Voices: Teachers Collaborating for Empowerment*. Although collaborative research became "the space" for these teachers and a university professor to find their voices, this collaborative group realized that "teachers' voices, in all their similarities and differences, still are not heard in the clamor of educational reform and in agendas for research on teachers' knowledge" (p. xi). Perhaps creating spaces and finding voices must occur in the context of teacher-initiated change and school reform, for only then can a school structure be created and sustained to allow the teacher voice to be heard.

METHODS/DATA SOURCE

This current study of school and teacher change was initiated by teachers. After an inservice workshop in summer 1990, four elementary-school teachers approached me and asked for assistance in the process of making changes in their practices. Since teachers were the initiators for this study, the research focused on their concerns and continually involved them in the research design process, data collection, and interpretation of data. Termed "action research" by Carr and Kemmis (1986), this approach to educational research attempts to alter the traditional relationship between the researcher and those studied so that the relationship is no longer alienating and teacher-silencing (Gitlin, 1990). Instead, teachers become researchers themselves, and the university researcher's role is "to facilitate the development of teachers' reflective capacities" (Elliot, 1988, p. 164).

The methods employed in the collaborative research project were interpretive (Erickson, 1986); that is, they involved the collection and interpretation of qualitative data through observation, ethnographic interviewing, document analysis, and dialogue journals. Journal writing served as teachers' written conversations and university researchers' reflections. Following Schön's (1988) theories of reflective coaching, the dialogue journals enabled me to enter into a collaborative process with the teachers creating a "hall of mirrors" to illustrate the process of reflection. Through our writings, the teachers and I became "researchers in and on practice whose work depended on [our] collaboration with each other" (Schön, 1988, p. 26).

Following in the tradition of symbolic interactionism (Jacob, 1987), a constructivist epistemology (Bruner, 1986) was embodied into my collection and interpretation of data and generation of assertions. Initial research questions, formed as I accepted the invitation extended by these teachers and their principal, were: (a) What changes do these practitioners choose to make?; (b) How do teachers make sense of the change process?; and (c) What is the nature of school and community culture with respect to educational change? Like Belenky, Clinchy, Goldberger, and Tarule (1986), who studied women's experiences and problems as learners and knowers, I had not anticipated that "voice was more than an academic shorthand for a person's point of view" (p.18). As our collaborative research project progressed, it became apparent that teacher change and school change were intricately intertwined with the development of a sense of teacher voice.

Therefore, consistent with the development of teacher voice, I have chosen to present the supporting data for my interpretations as stories of these teachers' experiences of change. Although I have attempted to preserve each of these teachers' voices through inclusion of transcribed tape recordings of our conversations and excerpts from our dialogue journals, these stories are still embedded within my story of the emerging nature of our work together. Subsequently, these teachers' stories are told through my narration and therefore are embedded in my own culture, language, gender, beliefs, and life history as a white middle-class woman, former elementary-school teacher, and current university researcher interested in constructivism as a way of knowing and critical pedagogy as a way of understanding power and control issues in education.

The following assertion was one of a number of assertions generated from this study of teacher and school culture change (Dana, 1991; Dana & Pitts, 1993). The assertion is the result of our yearlong collaborative inquiry and constitutes a grounded theory (Glaser & Strauss, 1967).

Assertion: Traditionally, a culture of seclusion and isolation has served to contain teachers' voices within the four walls of their classrooms. Teachers yearn for professional opportunities for their voices to be heard beyond their four walls.

Southside: A Culture of Isolation and Seclusion

During the first phase of this study, I was concerned with learning the salient features of the school culture and beginning our collective inquiry by asking the teachers during the initial interview such questions as: (a) What is most important to you?; (b) What is your definition of change?; (c) What changes do you want to make?; and (d) What is your vision of school change? After three months of formal and informal interviews and participant observation in classrooms at "Southside Elementary School," one dominant theme emerged. Every teacher I interviewed during the first three months (totaling twelve) spoke of a feeling of isolation, a loss of connectedness with their peers due to the growing size of Southside in recent years, and the desire to, in the words of one teacher, "see beyond the four walls of my classroom" (interview transcript, October 12, 1990).

In contrast to a desire to connect with others and engage in dialogue with peers, norms of seclusion and separation were embedded in the culture of Southside. These norms became evident through an analysis of field notes collected during my participant-observation sessions, which occurred three to five times weekly and lasted three to six hours. Seclusion was suggested by the physical layout of Southside (map constructed in field notes, September 25, 1990). Each classroom was four walls unto itself. In all but the classrooms in the newer kindergarten and first-grade wing and some third-grade classrooms, there were no adjoining doors to neighboring classrooms. Some classrooms were even separated from the main building, being housed in portable temporary buildings. Throughout my field notes taken during the first three months of participant observation, I noted that with few exceptions, classroom doors remained closed at all times.

Seclusion was felt at other school locations as well:

> The faculty lounge was a minute space, four walls constructed of cinder blocks painted stark white, measuring roughly only 8 foot square. Small windows allowed some light into the space, but as they were located just below the ceiling, allowed no one to see out (field notes, September 25, 1990).

Often, I would spend hours "hanging out" in the faculty lounge, talking with and observing teachers. On frequent occasions, there were not enough chairs for faculty members at lunch or on break. Therefore, the one space designated for classroom teachers to come together was too small and uninviting. Consequently, I noted that this space was used infrequently by faculty members, often just during their twenty-minute lunch period, which was always scheduled with the same grade level.

Following this lunchtime grouping tradition, teachers were isolated from faculty members who taught on grade levels other than their own. I observed that each grade level group not only ate lunch together, but was housed in its own wing, and attended special area classes as a group at approximately the same times each day. Teachers were grouped into teams by grade level, and grade level meetings often took place when children were at a special area class, or before or after school.

Even when teachers did have an opportunity to converse with peers who taught other grades, most remained close to their grade level cohorts. In October I attended my first faculty meeting, noting that "it appeared to me that for the most part, grade-level groups sat together" (field notes, October 4, 1990). The norm that at faculty meetings everyone was to be seated at a table with others from the same grade level was confirmed in my subsequent attendance at each faculty meeting. Few teachers ventured beyond the invisible boundaries that separated each grade. There appeared to be a degree of comfort found in remaining close to those who taught the same level; yet, teachers, in their interviews with me, voiced dissatisfaction with this comfort. Their vision was to delegitimize the norm of seclusion and separation and legitimize a new norm of collegiality.

Their vision was articulated and clarified on January 8, 1991, when the teachers and I met. The meeting was also attended by the principal, who had expressed interest in our work and joined in our collaborative effort to make classroom and school changes. I began the meeting by sharing the data (expanded field notes and interview transcriptions) I had collected in the first phase of the study:

> I thought I'd start with what I thought is the most interesting because it came out with every single person that I talked to. It is the idea of, and this is in one teacher's words, "seeing beyond the four walls of my classroom. . . . " I guess, I called it when I started marking the data, I called it collegiality. . . . What I want to do is just start with that, and throw it out and see if this is something that you feel; is this something that you want to look at? (meeting transcription, January 9, 1991).

The dialogue that followed this question indicated that these teachers' feelings of isolation and separation had been silently building for years. The question created a space, perhaps for the first time, where teachers could explore the possibilities of a more collegial culture, a culture that encouraged and supported school and classroom improvement. As they discussed possibilities, they voiced hopes and dreams of improvements that would occur within the four walls of Southside. One possibility included reconceptualizing the faculty meetings. The following quotes, excerpted from that meeting, highlight the possibilities discussed:[1]

---

1. I continued to collaborate with these teachers during the writing of their stories. Throughout this study and my writing, the teachers read transcripts, field notes, and narrative accounts, often offering feedback and suggestions. Yet, these teachers chose to remain anonymous for the purposes of this research report; therefore pseudonyms have been used in the telling of each of their stories.

Pam: . . . Also sharing. I mean if we could have one person share one idea at every faculty meeting. Stand up. This is what I saw that I liked, at another school, at another classroom. This is working really great for me. I mean if somebody has a great discipline system and it's working, then it should be shared.

Helen: You could share whatever. You could share something you were doing or something that was happening.

Nancy: Along with faculty meetings, here's an idea that I was thinking about. Maybe we could have a faculty meeting . . . basically the way we teach kids, you know, cooperative learning. . . . You have groups where you are mixed up in grade levels and the idea is that you take two to five minutes to share an idea that you use with your classroom.

Helen: We could have cooperative learning groups in the faculty.

Sally: We could pick a subject for the day. You know . . . to give people ideas.

Peg: You know, the topics, generally could change all along. We could have, "Come in with something that you normally teach you think is going to be boring with the kids, and you found something that works that is exciting. Come in with something exciting." You know, it doesn't have to be reading or math.

Principal: You know, that works not only for you all but it works for speech, it works for Chapter I, it works for physical education. And we have to keep that in mind too.

Helen: I think that the faculty meeting would be a good way to introduce it to the whole group.

Peg: When we call the faculty meeting, we will need a set of instructions for the faculty. You come with an idea from your classroom. . . . I think the really important factor there is getting all grade levels represented in the group and not one grade level in a group. We could have groups of maybe three or four. . . . We don't have to go into how [the faculty] is going to be divided up, but I think it should be explained to them that we are going to have groups.

Sally: Heterogeneous.

Peg: Heterogeneous meaning that you will not be all with third grade.

Pat: Could we rotate groups?

Peg: Oh, I think we should. Maybe every two or three times.

Nancy: Do we have a date we want to shoot for, for one of these meetings, or do we want to meet again?

Pat: We need to tell the faculty.

Principal: Next time we could meet together would be the 24th. Two weeks from Thursday. . . . I would love to be able to devote fifteen minutes at the beginning to some idea sharing and keep the meeting short enough that we could do that and still deal with whatever business to get out at a decent time, but to be able to start with some idea sharing on that day.

Sally: I would like for Ted [the principal] not to do it because this will not be a test. I don't want any teacher to think that they are going to get observed or evaluated.

Peg: Yeah. (General agreement from teachers.)

Sally: Like to introduce it this Thursday; I would like some teacher to do it.

Peg: I will. Yeah, I'll do that.

At this time, I no longer could discern the audiotape of our meeting as a chorus of spontaneous voices broke into separate conversations. In some conversations, the teachers already began to share ideas and materials with each other. Another conversation produced the logistics of that next faculty meeting at which the ideas that were voiced would be reported to the faculty by Peg and Sally. From the excitement expressed through the teachers' dialogues, it appeared that the groundwork for building a culture of collegiality and caring was in place. From this meeting forward, the teachers' action research focused on reconceptualizing faculty meetings to allow for cross-grade-level small group discussion of professional issues. Through small group and large group discussions at faculty meetings, evidence of a changing culture emerged. The change was best summarized by one teacher's comment at the end of the year, "We became more of a team this year than we've ever been" (group meeting transcript, May 30, 1990).[2]

This change was most welcomed by Pam and Kit, two of the newest faculty members at Southside. Their story describes the socialization of teachers into a culture of isolation and seclusion, a culture that silences teachers' voices, and prevents visions of educational change from being implemented.

Socialization into Isolation: Pam and Kit's Story.

Pam and Kit were relatively new to Southside, having taught four years in intermediate grades and two years in primary grades, respectively. Their stories

---

2.   A full account (including supporting data) of the story of reconceptualizing faculty meetings to allow for discussion of professional issues and the subsequent change in culture can be found in Dana, 1993 and Dana, Pitts, Hickey, and Rinehart, 1992.

evidence the socialization of teachers into a culture of isolation and silence reported by researchers such as Lortie (1975), Britzman (1991), and Kincheloe (1991). Kincheloe states:

> Teacher education has failed to connect teacher education coursework with the teaching workplace in any more than an obvious, technical way. Devoid of theoretical and analytical frames, young teachers fall easy prey to an unceremonialized initiation into alienation and disillusionment of the . . . teaching workplace (p. 15).

Pam reflects on her preservice teacher education:

> I heard in college that teachers won't share. If you have a good day you don't tell anybody. . . . I was told to be careful when you come in, you know, not to toot your own horn (Pam, interview transcript, December 19, 1990).

Pam's socialization into the culture continued during her first year of teaching at Southside:

> I feel a lot of teachers are not open to having their door open for other teachers. I mean, that was the hardest thing for me my first year. When [the principal] was coming in here, there was no problem. But as soon as my peer teacher would walk in here to observe me, I mean, I would be a wreck. And I think it's because they're a teacher . . . that was intimidating. . . . It's funny how people will not share. And if it's good things it sounds like you are bragging and you've got your act together, which to me, we need to hear more good things (Pam, interview transcript, December 19, 1990).

Kit's socialization into the culture of Southside and the culture of teaching was similar to Pam's. Kit tells the story of her first year of teaching, during which she was shunned by her grade level cohorts for sharing ideas and having enthusiasm for teaching:

> Teachers are just so isolated. . . . For one thing, I wasn't accepted at first . . . [Other teachers on the grade level] thought I was going to outdo them . . . [The principal] spoke very highly of me and they didn't like that at all. . . . He told them that I could teach them so much. No one who's been teaching for fifteen years wants to hear that this little bop is going to come in here and teach them anything. . . . They didn't want to

have anything to do with me. . . . Excluded me, being nasty to me. . . . So, I just kept to myself. And I was up for [a first year teacher award] and not a single one of them wrote a letter for me. . . . They thought I was bragging (Kit, interview transcript, January 22, 1991).

Kit had not only been socialized into a culture of isolation, but into the "grade level" normative structure as well. Kit reflects on her vision for the school:

I think we need to be more of a unit instead of grade levels. That really bothers me . . . grade levels' sticking together. Who cares? You know? Who says that we need to be segregated, and that's the way I see it. Why can't you discuss things with another grade level? Why can't you sit with whoever you want to?. . . . We have to be more open, more willing to discuss things. . . . I don't think you should hide everything (Kit, interview transcript, January 22, 1991).

Kit's questioning of the existing culture challenged the norm that defined her role at Southside. Her questions led to behaviors that were inconsistent with the norm of isolation and grade-level segregation that she encountered as a first-year teacher. For example, she spoke of grade-level seatings at faculty meetings:

I didn't do that. And they did not like that, and they thought that I was so wrong, because I didn't sit with them, and I thought, I can sit where I want to sit (Kit, interview transcript, January 22, 1991).

The result for Kit was frustration, anger, and alienation from her grade level peers. She chose to teach a different grade level the following year. Yet, Kit's frustrations carried into her second year of teaching on a different grade level. After a reading of her January 22 interview transcript of her reflections on her first year of teaching, Kit wrote in her journal:

I finished reading the transcript. . . . It was funny to read my words. . . . Right now I don't feel like I'm doing a very good job. . . . Throughout the transcript I said "frustrated." I really didn't realize how frustrated I was until I read my own words. Maybe some of those negative vibes are still alive from last year. . . . I can't figure out what I'm doing wrong. I feel like it is all my fault, but I know it really can't be. Why am I doubting myself? Is it the lack of support from my peers? Is it the system? Or am I just not a "good" teacher? (Gosh, I'm digging deep into my thoughts.) (Kit, journal entry, February 5, 1991).

I responded in Kit's journal:

> I'm not sure why you are doubting yourself. . . . There are many questions that I've been wondering about. Probably the best questions are the ones you posed at the end of your last journal entry—Have you thought about these any more or come any closer to finding an answer?
>
> - Why am I doubting myself?
> - Is it a lack of support from peers?
> - Is it the system?
> - Or am I just not a good teacher?
>
> You mentioned you were digging deep into your thoughts—I think that's what is so powerful! It's through "digging deep" and "questioning" that we grow, although "growing" can sometimes be a painful process (Kit's journal, response transcript, February 12, 1991).

That same day, Kit responded to her original questions:

> Why am I doubting myself? I don't know exactly. . . . Maybe why I'm doubting myself is the fact that I'm unable to teach how I feel comfortable and this "old way" (. . . *No* talking or communication with others, book work only, nothing exciting, boring stuff. YUCK!!) is stifling my creativity.
>
> Is it a lack of support from peers? Well, unconsciously it could be . . . I'm lonely and tired of this portable [building]!
>
> Is it the system? *Yes!* I'm tired of being treated like I'm worth nothing. I'm not the only one.
>
> Am I not a good teacher? I really and truly believe that I'm a super teacher. Yes I feel that I am an outstanding teacher who is frustrated with many things that are affecting my creativity (Kit, journal entry, February 12, 1991).

For Kit, the culture of isolation continued to cause frustration, resulting in her doubting her non-traditional classroom teaching techniques. In a culture of isolation, it is difficult to change classrooms practices that deviate from the norm (in Kit's words, "the old way of teaching"). In essence, the culture of isolation stifles new classroom practices. Therefore, a prerequisite to creating and sustaining new classroom practices becomes changing the culture to one of collegiality, in which peers form partnerships with one another that enable them to look within the four walls of their school for innovative ideas and improvement. A culture in which teachers voice their ideas, value the knowledge created through dialogue with their peers, and act on that knowledge by voicing support for one another can foster changes in both school-wide and classroom practices. As evidenced by Kit's story, a culture of isolation can defeat attempts at educational change.

IMPLICATIONS AND CONCLUSIONS

The ongoing research at Southside Elementary has identified a school culture dominated by seclusion, separation, and isolation. As evidenced by the stories of Pam and Kit, this school culture is embedded in a larger "culture of teaching" that socializes new teachers to conform with norms of isolation and seclusion. Together, Southside's culture and culture of teaching are in direct conflict with the need expressed by female teachers to "connect" with their peers.

Belenky and her co-authors (1986) categorize women's perspectives on knowing into five major epistemological classifications: "(1) *Silence,* a position in which women experience themselves as mindless and voiceless and subject to the whims of external authority; (2) *received knowledge,* a perspective from which women conceive of themselves as capable of receiving, even reproducing, knowledge from the all-knowing external authorities but not capable of creating knowledge on their own; (3) *subjective knowledge,* a perspective from which truth and knowledge are conceived of as personal, private, and subjectively known or intuited; (4) *procedural knowledge,* a position in which women are invested in learning and applying objective procedures for obtaining and communicating knowledge; and (5) *constructed knowledge,* a position in which women view all knowledge as contextual, experience themselves as creators of knowledge, and value both subjective and objective strategies for knowing" (p. 15).

From the epistemological perspective of Belenky and her co-authors (1986), the culture of isolation and separation found at Southside fosters not only teacher silence, but received and procedural ways of knowing. Such a culture of schooling is reflective of the Western tradition, valuing attributes associated with the masculine: autonomy and independence. Of little or no value become "the development of interdependence, intimacy, nurturance, and contextual thought" (Belenky, et al., 1986, p. 7). Yet, these attributes are valued by women and essential to "overcoming epistemic dualisms conditioned by procedural knowledge and assuming the power to construct knowledge" (Helle, 1991, p. 54).

Therefore, from a critical theorist perspective, women have been prevented from becoming constructed knowers. The culture of isolation has served to perpetuate the patriarchal nature of schooling; it keeps women, who compose the majority of the elementary education teaching force, from becoming empowered and having a voice in educational reform movements and change efforts. It may be that not until a school culture becomes collegial will teachers begin to build meaningful partnerships with one another, and become empowered to create and sustain educational change in their classrooms. Teacher educators, both at universities and in the public schools, can change the culture of teaching by creating opportunities for preservice and inservice teachers to engage in collaborative work and dialogue with one another.

REFERENCES

Apple, M. W. (1986). *Teachers and text: A political economy of class and gender relations in education*. New York: Routledge and Kegan Paul.

Bacharach, S. B. (Ed.). (1990). *Education reform: Making sense of it all*. Needham Heights, MA: Allyn and Bacon.

Barth, R. S. (1990). *Improving schools from within: Teachers, parents, and principals can make a difference*. San Francisco: Jossey-Bass.

Belenky, M. F., Clinchy, B. M., Goldberger, N. R., & Tarule, J. M. (1986). *Women's ways of knowing: The development of self, voice and mind*. New York: Basic Books, Inc., Publishers.

Blumer, H. (1969). *Symbolic interactionism*. Englewood Cliffs, NJ: Prentice-Hall.

Britzman, D. (1991). *Practice makes practice: A critical study of learning to teach*. Albany, NY: SUNY Press.

Bruner, J. (1986). *Actual minds, possible worlds*. Cambridge, MA: Harvard University Press.

Carnegie Commission. (1986). *Task force on teaching as a profession, a nation prepared: Teachers for the 21st century*. New York: Carnegie Forum on Education and the Economy.

Carr, W. & Kemmis, S. (1988). *Becoming critical: Education, knowledge and action research*. New York: Doubleday.

Culver, C. M. & Hoban, G. J. (Eds.). (1973). *The power of change: Issues for the innovative educator*. New York: McGraw-Hill.

Dana, N. F. (1991). Four walls with a future: Changing educational practices through collaborative action research. Unpublished doctoral dissertation, The Florida State University, Tallahassee, FL.

Dana, N. F. (1993, April). Teachers for change: An elementary school program for enhancing school climate. Paper presented at the annual meeting of the American Educational Research Association, Atlanta, GA.

Dana, N. F. & Pitts, J. H. (in press). The use of metaphor and reflective coaching in the exploration of principal thinking: A case study of principal change. *Educational Administration Quarterly, 29* (3), 323–328.

Dana, N. F., Pitts, J. H., Rinehart, B., & Hickey, E. (1992, Feb.). Creating a culture for change: The university researcher, principal, and teacher family. Paper presented at the Association of Teacher Educators 1992 Conference, Orlando, FL.

Deal, T. E. (1984). Educational change: Revival tent, tinkertoys, jungle, or carnival? *Teachers College Record, 86*(1), 124–137.

Eisner, E. (1979). *The educational imagination.* New York: Macmillan.

Elliot, J. (1988). Educational research and outsider-insider relations. *Qualitative Studies In Education, 1*(2), 155–166.

Erickson, F. (1986). Qualitative methods in research on teaching. In M. Wittrock (Ed.), *Handbook of research on teaching.* (3rd ed., pp. 3–36). New York: Macmillan.

Fullan, M. (1991). *The new meaning of educational change.* New York: Teachers College Press.

Goodlad, J. I. (1975). *The dynamics of educational change: Toward responsive schools.* New York: McGraw-Hill Book Company.

Gilligan, C. (1982). *In a different voice: Psychological theory and women's development.* Cambridge: Harvard University Press.

Gitlin, A. D. (1990). Educative research, voice, and school change. *Harvard Educational Review, 60*(4), 443–466.

Glaser, B. G., & Strauss, A. L. (1967). *The discovery of grounded theory: Strategies for qualitative research.* New York: Aldine Publishing Co.

Helle, A. P. (1991). Reading women's autobiographies: A map of reconstructed knowing. In C. Witherell & N. Noddings (Eds.). *Stories lives tell: Narrative and dialogue in education* (pp. 48–66). New York: Teachers College Press.

The Holmes Group. (1986). *Tomorrow's teachers: A report of the Holmes group.* East Lansing, MI: The Holmes Group.

Jacob, E. (1987). Qualitative research traditions: A review. *Review of Educational Research. 57*(1), 1–50.

Kincheloe, J. L. (1991). *Teachers as researchers: Qualitative inquiry as a path to empowerment.* New York: The Falmer Press.

Kohlberg, L. (1984). *The psychology of moral development.* New York: Harper & Row.

Lakoff, G. & Johnson, M. (1980). *Metaphors we live by.* Chicago: The University of Chicago Press.

Lortie, D. (1975). *Schoolteacher: A sociological study.* Chicago: University of Chicago Press.

Marshall, H. H. (Ed.). (1990). Metaphors we learn by [Special issue]. *Theory Into Practice, 29*(2).

Miller, J. L. (1990). *Creating spaces and finding voices: Teachers collaborating for empowerment.* Albany, New York: State University of New York Press.

McDonald, J. P. (1989). When outsiders try to change schools from the inside. *Phi Delta Kappan, 71*(3), 206–212.

Richardson, V. (1990). Significant and worthwhile change in teaching practice. *Educational Researcher, 19*(7), 10–18.

Schön, D. (1988). Coaching reflective teaching. In P. P. Grimmett & G P. Erickson (Eds.), *Reflection in teacher education*. New York: Teachers College Press.

Scott, K. (1987). Missing developmental perspectives in moral education. *Theory and Research in Social Education, 15*(4), 257–273.

CHAPTER 2

School/University Partners in Research: The Potential and the Problems

ALLISON WHITE
Centennial High School
Champaign School District

GLORIA RAINER
Martin Luther King Elementary School
Urbana School District

RENEE CLIFT

SHERYL BENSON
University of Illinois at Urbana-Champaign

ALLISON WHITE is the English and fine arts department chair at Centennial High School in Champaign, Illinois, where she has taught for fifteen years. She is a member of the Illinois State Board of Education's Language Arts Assessment committee, Writing Assessment Validation Team, and Teacher Education Accreditation Committee. She also serves as a cooperating teacher and school-based coordinator for the Secondary Collaborative Project.

GLORIA RAINER is a teacher at Martin Luther King Elementary School in Urbana, Illinois. King's population is multi-national, as well as economically, racially, and ethnically diverse. Ms. Rainer has served on numerous state and district committees. She has also served as a cooperating teacher and a clinical instructor in the Elementary Year-Long Project.

Note: Author names are listed in reverse alphabetical order to denote equal contributions to this chapter.

RENEE T. CLIFT is an Associate Professor of Curriculum and Instruction at the University of Illinois at Urbana-Champaign where she teaches a course in methods of teaching English, as well as graduate courses in research on teaching and teacher education. She is the coeditor of *Encouraging Reflective Practice: An analysis of issues and exemplars,* and author of articles appearing in the *Journal of Teacher Education* and the *American Educational Research Journal.*

SHERYL BENSON is the Director of Clinical Experiences for the Department of Curriculum and Instruction at the University of Illinois at Urbana-Champaign. In addition, she serves as the Co-Director of the Year-Long Project. Her research interests include the influences of cooperating teachers on learning to teach and collaborative teacher education programs.

ABSTRACT

Two classroom teachers from the Urbana and Champaign schools and two professors from the University of Illinois at Urbana-Champaign discuss the potential and problems in school/university research partnerships. A brief history and development of two collaborative teacher education programs, one at the secondary level and one at the elementary level, are described to define the context of the developing understanding of the role of research in collaborative teacher education. To hear the different voices, each of the four participants responded to three vignettes that present collaborative teacher education research issues. Each vignette deals with a different research methodology and different groups of participants. Three major issues were identified from the discussion of the vignettes. The first issue was that not all four participants agreed on the interpretation or course of action for each vignette and bring different value systems to the discussion. Second, there is a need to incorporate different voices heard in the development and implementation of teacher education programs. Third, ongoing research and development implies changing traditional practices and learning new roles. The participants agreed the bridge between university-based instruction and public school instruction can be strengthened through collaborative research.

Preservice teacher education has served as a well-traveled, albeit architecturally controversial, bridge between university-based instruction and public school instruction. A certain discomfort and uneasiness among those who travel the bridge daily and those who remain firmly entrenched on either side have been well documented by researchers, teachers, and prospective teachers (Bush, 1977; Lanier & Little, 1986). Nevertheless, public schools and universities both acknowledge that they represent two communities that share a common purpose. Participants in both institutions are concerned with curriculum content, instructional strategies, and learning environments. All are committed to designing educational experiences that enable students to develop socially, emotionally, and intellectually. Within the past two decades, we have seen many teacher educators advocate closer collaboration among all participants who are concerned with teaching and learning (Clift, Veal, Johnson, & Holland, 1990; Goodlad, 1990). The four of us represent a larger set of colleagues in the Champaign-Urbana area who have begun to struggle with the meaning of such collaborative work.

Throughout the past five years we have worked together to develop, implement, and evaluate two pilot programs in collaborative teacher education based at the University of Illinois at Urbana-Champaign. The professional relationships we have developed have been tested and strengthened as we have collected and analyzed data through program evaluation and action research designs. Some of these data confirmed our optimism that we were making progress and that program outcomes are beneficial for prospective teachers and experienced educators. These encouraging data were causes for celebration. Other data, crucial to the ongoing redesign of our programs, identified areas that were not as positive. Nonetheless, at times we construed these events as causes for celebration too, since we were learning what not to do.

In sharing these data, however, we have begun to realize that many participants do not view the outcomes of research as helpful. This has led us to wonder whether we have failed to understand fully the complexity of establishing collaborative programs that include strong research components. It is our experience in working as partners that the ethical, ideological, and pedagogical issues separating universities and public schools will be difficult to broach and even more difficult to resolve. Sharing successes is easy; sharing negative information can be politically, personally, and professionally troubling. Our specific purpose in this chapter is to discuss our developing understanding of the role of research in collaborative teacher education.

Oftentimes chapters such as this are written by university-based educators whose job descriptions include responsibility for scholarly writing. Recently, a number of teachers and university faculty have expressed a growing discomfort with the absence of teacher voice from discussions of teacher education curriculum and research on teaching and learning (Hunsaker & Johnston, 1992; Cochran-Smith & Lytle, 1993). Our experiences and our conversations over the past few years lead us to agree that writing about collaboration benefits from the collaborative construction of text. We believe it is important to raise the issues of the role of research in collaborative teacher education programs together across the teacher education role groups we represent.

In this chapter we briefly describe the structure of two current programs to set the context for our discussions. We then present three hypothetical vignettes that capture a subset of the research issues we have faced or expect to face in the near future. Because we have come to realize that all parties do not have a common viewpoint on data collection, analysis, and dissemination, we break into separate voices to respond to each of the vignettes. Our voices unite again in the final section of the chapter as we summarize the challenge facing all participants in collaborative teacher education who are interested in assessing the anticipated benefits and the unintended side effects of research.

TWO EVOLVING PROGRAM STRUCTURES

The University of Illinois at Urbana-Champaign College of Education faculty and public school personnel in Urbana, Champaign, Chicago area suburbs and other nearby districts have long worked together in varied cooperative relationships for teacher education. Many times, the work reflected the interests of one or a small group of university faculty members; often the work was initiated by requests from the school districts. Although many people were excited by and committed to cooperation and collaboration for teacher development, the structure of university-based teacher education remained a loose collection of required courses.

The relationships among faculties in all institutions were often pleasant, but expectations for prospective teachers varied widely, and there was little communication among university-based teacher educators or field-based teacher educators. There was virtually no systematic communication across institutions. Sometimes, there was strong tension among participants, even though everyone professed a common concern for improvements in teaching. Against this background, the University of Illinois entered the Holmes Group (1986) and began to envision a revision of the teacher preparation curriculum.

The Year-Long Project for Elementary Teachers

In summer 1987, faculty and administrators from the College of Education and teachers and administrators from the Urbana Public Schools resolved to bridge the gap between theory and practice in teacher preparation and to establish a stronger trust between the university and the public schools. In practice this came to mean that classroom teachers, university faculty members, and university students collaboratively design curriculum and teach prospective teachers in what we call the Year-Long Project (YLP). The program began in fall 1989 and was expanded to include the Champaign School District in fall 1991.

Each prospective teacher works with three different public-school placements, participating in the school year from beginning to end. Simultaneously, they participate in instructional blocks co-taught by university faculty, graduate students, and Champaign and Urbana teachers. Thus, classroom teachers may serve as cooperating teachers for as many as three university students during the school year and have an opportunity to teach on an instructional team.

To maintain trust between the university and public schools, time for joint decision making and planning is crucial. The YLP Advisory Committee, comprised of teachers, YLP students, university faculty, and program administrators, makes decisions concerning general policy, procedures, schedules, and student assignments. The committee has created program agendas for four cooperating teacher inservice meetings, responded to suggestions for changes resulting from program evaluations, and acted on requests for grant participation and research studies.

To build a common understanding of teaching and learning is also an important program component. Three instructional teams (Curriculum and Instruction, Language and Literacy, Science and Social Studies), comprising university professors, graduate students, and classroom teachers, have developed a curriculum that combines curriculum theory and practice with classroom experiences. Planning for these courses occurs during the summer, supported by university funds. Course presentations, reading of students' assignments, and evaluation are the responsibility of all instructional team members. Involvement in school reality shapes, to a great extent, the content and pedagogy of all class sessions.

Each year, all of the program components are evaluated. The program-evaluation data indicate that teachers who participate in the YLP do so because of the professional challenge, the additional help in the classroom, and the opportunity to be informed about current trends in education. Other reasons include: the opportunity to reflect on their own teaching as a result of the program structure that encourages ongoing communication with other cooperating teachers; the continuous conferences and question-answer sessions with students; and the collaborative evaluation of the university students' work. The program contains features that teachers helped to design and, therefore, perceive as important and philosophically compatible with their own belief system.

In addition, several doctoral students and faculty members have investigated participants' perceptions of immediate and short-term effects of the program on classroom teaching. These data have indicated areas of program success and have identified program shortcomings. Content and delivery are revised each year based, in part, on these data. One indication of the growing success of the YLP is that student requests to participate increase each year. Thus, we face the challenge of staffing an expanded program within the limitations of public school placements and university faculty lines. We also face a decision of whether the YLP model should become our only program for elementary-school teacher preparation. Research on teaching and learning within the YLP, along with program evaluation data, will have a strong effect on any decisions about the future of elementary teacher preparation.

The Secondary Collaborative Project

Informal discussions between a faculty member and a Champaign senior high school principal quickly led to school-level meetings with senior high school department chairs to reform the current university program for prospective secondary teachers in fall 1988. Early brainstorming sessions produced the concept of a program including middle school and senior high school teaching experiences, because secondary-education majors become state certified from grades six through twelve. At this point, the middle school principal and a middle school teacher from a school adjacent to the senior high school joined the planning discussions.

To meet the challenge of converting compatible philosophies into an operational program, we had to acknowledge the existing instructional and administrative structures of all three schools, as well as the political and fiscal realities. One such reality was the autonomy with which the faculty in each of the three institutions was accustomed to operating. Consequently, the design team began to educate our respective faculties to an understanding of the shared needs and benefits of a collaborative program through the professional acknowledgment that each sector has an essential role to play in educating student teachers.

Currently, the Secondary Collaborative Project (SCP) is a semester-long student teaching experience in which teacher candidates join a team of teachers at the middle school for eight weeks and work with two senior high school teachers simultaneously for another eight weeks. In both placements, the teacher candidates teach only four classes because they are simultaneously taking a content-specific methods course taught on the public school campus by a university professor. In addition, the role of "supervisor" has been virtually eliminated because of the university-supported release time for building coordinators. Teachers are released part-time from their classroom responsibilities to coordinate and support the student teachers' development. The coordinators act as liaisons between the student teachers, cooperating teachers, university professors, and school administrators. One concern about broadening the school-based support for student teachers was that they might feel burdened by attempting to meet the expectations of numerous taskmasters. Program-evaluation data indicate students' appreciation for the opportunity to consider and reflect upon multiple perspectives as they attempt to determine their personal teaching identities.

As with the elementary program, we have worked to develop a structure for collaborative decision making. Initially, decisions for the SCP were made by the original design team; however, that was expanded to include an advisory council comprising representatives of the student teachers: each grade level at the middle school, each of the four participating academic disciplines at the high school—the school coordinators, the methods instructors, and the university student-teaching coordinator. A school representative and a university representative co-chair the council, and all members initiate discussion of issues and concerns that often become program policy recommendations.

Through the recommendations of the advisory meetings, students' self-analyses, program-evaluation data, and several action-research studies, we have continued to refine our program. Indicators of success include an increased student demand for admission and a request from the Urbana secondary schools to participate. In spring 1993 the SCP expanded to include Urbana schools, thus enabling us to double admissions. To accommodate the expansion, university faculty and school faculty have been meeting monthly to discuss nationwide issues and trends in collaborative teacher education, while maintaining a sharp focus on how we might continue to improve. We remain aware, however, that we are still accountable to financial and political forces that may be affected by our program evaluations and by our faculties' ongoing research.

In the Year-Long Project and the Secondary Collaborative Project we have moved far beyond a model in which schools are asked to look to the university for expert knowledge on teacher education program policy, with teachers as the consumers of that knowledge. The classroom teachers share their unique expertise with university faculty as they work side by side to help shape and guide prospective teachers. As a local administrator who was involved in the original design of the Year-Long Project stated, "Finally, there is a really professional relationship between the classroom teacher and the student teacher, and between the classroom teacher and the professor."

As we continue to develop these professional relationships, we find that one issue continues to surface in our discussions: the role of inquiry within all of our programs in teacher education. Is research on teacher education an integral part of the design, development, and revision of our teacher education programs? We have wrestled with this question since we began our initial discussions. In addition to the program evaluation data mentioned above, reports of participants' perspectives were built into the design of both collaborative projects; several doctoral students and professors have collected data on the experiences of program participants and one student has completed case studies of three program graduates. The respective advisory committees cleared all of the research efforts, but all program participants have not been pleased with all of the research findings. As a result of these studies and of anticipated research endeavors, the four of us have begun to consider the promise and the problems involved when participants in collaborative endeavors study themselves and one another. In the next section we share some of the issues that we, as individuals, have identified as important to any discussion of research conducted within collaborative teacher education programs.

ISSUES IN THE STUDY AND PRACTICE OF COLLABORATIVE TEACHER EDUCATION

Following are three vignettes that are, for the present, hypothetical scenarios. Each represents a different research methodology, includes different groups of participants, and raises issues that are simultaneously useful and problematic. In universities whose mission is primarily research and development, it is quite possible that in the near future a professor, graduate student, or practitioner collaborator may design a research project similar to one described below. After each vignette, we discuss the possible contributions of such research to teacher education programs, our colleagues and ourselves. We also raise our concerns about consequences of such research that may inadvertently harm participants, program, or both.

Vignette #1: Program Entry Characteristics of Aspiring Elementary Teachers

Professor J. is interested in teachers' developing knowledge of concepts in physics. She has received a rather large grant to conduct a longitudinal study of elementary teachers' knowledge upon program entry, and the changes in knowledge that do and do not occur as they work in science methods courses and in elementary school classrooms. She administers a preliminary knowledge survey to her sample of seventy-eight students. In response to questions about basic concepts, she discovers that over half of the students have conceptions that differ from scientifically acceptable explanations. She also discovers that many of the students have made computational errors in working through some of the problems in her survey. Professor J. is not a science methods instructor. She is a member of a different department from the one primarily responsible for preservice teacher education. How should Professor J. proceed?

Allison - Secondary Collaborative Project Coordinator

Preparing student teachers to address the needs of a complex, challenging, and changing student population must override issues of professional power and autonomy. Traditional patterns of hierarchical blame laying must be discarded in place of collaborative efforts to best equip student teachers for the realities of the public school classroom. Public school teachers often express concerns about university students who seemingly lack basic skills and knowledge. One explanation may be that accountability for acquisition of these remains unassigned. If the student enters college lacking fundamental necessities, the college science professor may be aware only that the student is struggling with higher-level concepts and may not feel it appropriate to remediate the student, even if deficiencies are uncovered. The methods instructor's role is not normally defined as one who should emphasize basics; the expectation understandably exists that the student teacher will arrive in methods courses having mastered those. Finally, the cooperating teacher will experience a high degree of frustration if a student teacher arrives in the classroom with discipline-specific deficiencies and will intervene to protect the interests of the schoolchildren. Unless greater articulation occurs in the goals and objectives of colleges of education, colleges of arts and sciences, and the public schools, the situation described in this vignette may continue, not only in the preparation of elementary-school teachers, but in the education of secondary teachers as well. Reaching consensus on solutions requires abandonment of personal and institutional needs for autocratic modes of operation. This is difficult, but necessary, to accomplish. Professor J., if she has the courage, should share her survey results and initiate constructive dialogue among her colleagues and the public schools.

Gloria - Year-Long Project Cooperating Teacher

As a classroom teacher, I would applaud Professor J.'s interest in conducting such research and in responding to quiet suspicions that there are some students who are at the door of their professional semester and who lack basic knowledge. This is a puzzling and frustrating phenomenon which often causes cooperating teachers to question university courses, program designs and even the admission standards applied to these students. Secondly, I would be interested in learning more about the qualitative and quantitative benefits which accrue to the students at incremental stages of the methods coursework and classroom participation. That is, *what* do they learn and *where?* I would encourage her to invite the science methods instructors as well as a small group of public school classroom teachers to identify together those physical science units typically taught in the K-6 curriculum, along with the accompanying basic scientific concepts. Within an intensive "science lab" setting the methods instructors and classroom teachers would introduce to the education students the science processes and a variety of activities and projects which demonstrate a scientific concept. The university students would also receive guidance in conducting personal research in the development of a science unit. It is imperative that we all share responsibility for providing necessary assistance to the students. To do the work together discourages the assigning of blame to other parties than our own, and through the shared investment we provide a unified effort by which the possibility of complete student preparation is greatly increased.

Sheryl – Program Administrator

As the program administrator, I would recommend that Professor J. share this information with all members of the elementary education faculty. The findings of her survey present vital data for consideration by both teacher education and science education faculty. Together we need to interpret the findings and review what implications might result. Some of the questions I would raise during our discussions would include some the following issues. Is there an established body of facts or certain processes that are essential for beginning teachers? Do the questions on the survey correlate to content that is currently being included in elementary schools' science curriculum? Do elementary education candidates need a prerequisite course of basic skills before taking her class? Is there too much covered in the one course? Is one teaching strategies for process learning or only teaching isolated facts? Were the appropriate questions asked on the survey? I would hope through our joint efforts that we could improve the preparation of appropriate science knowledge, science concepts, and science teaching strategies for elementary teachers.

Renee – Methods Instructor and Researcher

As I read through studies of teacher knowledge, I am often struck by the relative ease of measuring what people don't know as opposed to the difficulty of helping them construct knowledge. Clearly Professor J. has identified what may be a gap in prospective teachers' knowledge. She now has several options, one of which may threaten the validity of her research: participation in an intervention. She has a choice between devising ways to help these students think through what they do and do not know about physical science, and then helping them reconstruct their knowledge, or she can continue to study the efforts of those directly charged with doing so. As someone who advocates action research in both teaching and teacher education, I would hope that she would choose the former. But there are many valid reasons for remaining apart from the action. One reason is that members of the teacher education department may not welcome her help. A second is that she may not have time to engage in both program design and research (a common complaint of many researchers). A third reason is that the research tradition in which she works may oppose the intermingling of intervention and inquiry. There are others as well. My point here is that we who are committed to both research and teacher education must engage in serious study of how our professional and institutional relationships can work to benefit teachers' learning as well as academic vita.

Vignette # 2: A Survey of Participants' Perceptions of an Experimental Program in Teacher Education

> *B. is a doctoral candidate at a nationally recognized state university. She and her major professor, Dr. Z, have been collecting survey data concerning participants' views of their experimental teacher education program. B. intends to use much the data in her doctoral dissertation. Results of the faculty survey indicate competing and contradictory perceptions of the value of university faculty involvement with, and commitment to, teacher education. Results of the student survey indicate strong satisfaction with fieldwork and equally strong dissatisfaction with coursework. Results of the teacher survey indicate a strong commitment to working with novice teachers. The dean asks for access to the analysis to help determine continuation of the experimental program. What is Dr. Z's responsibility here?*

Allison – Secondary Collaborative Project Coordinator

As a public school teacher committed to teacher education who has invested three years of personal and professional time and energy to development of a collaborative teacher education program, it becomes difficult to accept that university faculty within the College of Education might question the value of their involvement with the preparation of future teachers. I fail to understand the purpose of a College of Education if it is not just that. Do faculty members understand that research, even research conducted "on" schools instead of "with" schools, loses meaning unless transference to the classroom occurs? Certainly, the researcher and the university might benefit from publications and conference presentations resulting from research, but those interests seem rather shallow given the enormous potential implications for changes in education based upon research conducted in and with public schools. Dr. Z must serve as advocate for university commitment to, and involvement with, teacher education. She, and other teacher education advocates within the college, must convince the dean to assert the leadership necessary to continued development of mutually beneficial relationships with the public schools.

Gloria - Year-Long Project Cooperating Teacher

It is not unexpected to me to learn that some university professors might not value or wish involvement with teacher education. In so many universities, decisions concerning promotion and tenure are based on research activities. Service to local school districts and/or the time-intensive involvement in teacher education programs are generally not valued as highly as participation in more traditional research. One wonders whether the university administration might change its policy and priorities, if it came about that work done with teacher preparation acquired greater status? Ultimately, given such altered priorities, might not more university professors be enthusiastic participants? As a classroom teacher, I would hope that any college of education would assume as a primary responsibility that of preparing teachers. Data can and should be used as a compelling basis for change and modification. I would hope that data analysis could be used publicly as such an impetus for improving a program, without fear that it might signal the program's death knell.

Sheryl - Program Administrator

As the program administrator, I would support the dean's request to have access to Dr. Z's and doctoral candidate's survey data. Since this information is to be used in a doctoral dissertation, it is public knowledge. In a conference, I would remind the dean that this should not be the only information used to make the decision on the continuation of the experimental program. I would want to know the faculty's and classroom teachers' evaluations of the program. Their input would provide other insights to provide a more balanced picture of the program. My goal as program administrator is continually to review programs and make changes based on relevant evaluations from all participants. I would probe for further explanations of why the students were so dissatisfied with coursework. Is there a lack of communication between the course instructors and teachers in the classrooms? Is there a perception that the course is not relevant to actual practice? Why are university faculty members not perceived as demonstrating a strong commitment to teacher education?

Renee – Methods Instructor and Researcher

This brings up the sticky question of who owns data. It is my opinion that the research community has not addressed this with regard to data collected about school-university collaborations. This can present a serious problem for people who are working on doctoral dissertations. Can student B. and her advisor deny a request from a dean? Will the student be more at risk politically if she does or does not comply? Should any evaluation data automatically be available to all parties in the collaboration? And in what form should the data be disseminated? I suggest that the student has the obligation to share her results, but that any request for data prior to analysis be declared out of bounds.

Vignette #3: A Case Study of a Successful Teacher Education Partnership

A group of teachers, graduate students, and professors (all participants in a collaborative program focused on improving teaching and learning in senior high schools) has been meeting monthly to discuss issues of equity in education. The group collectively decides to study its own participants as they conduct their own classes and advise students. The program, which has gained a local reputation for excellence, is much larger than the study group. One of the program directors sends a memo cautioning the group about the political ramifications of negative information being shared with others. What should the group discuss at their next meeting?

Allison – Secondary Collaborative Project Coordinator

Why do researchers conduct research? An underlying premise must be that if we know and understand factors impacting circumstances, we have an opportunity to continually improve. Improvement does not imply failure as a precondition; it merely indicates the possibility to perform even more effectively. This mind-set must be conveyed to and shared by participants in the collaborative program before public sharing of negative information occurs; otherwise, the repercussions might be antagonism and withdrawal of support if participants feel their efforts are devalued and criticized. Not only must participants embrace a mind-set conducive to action research, issues regarding validity and voice must be resolved. What credence should we give to highly emotional reactions to circumstances and people within the student teaching experience? How may we include the diverse voices of students, student teachers, cooperating teachers, site coordinators, and methods instructors without irreparably damaging professional relationships? Should negative information be shared only within the forum of the study group? What benefits might argue for sharing negative information publicly? The study group must collectively address issues of this sort before proceeding; they cannot afford to ignore the political realities and potentially negative ramifications.

Gloria – Year-Long Project Cooperating Teacher

One motivation to participate in such a project would be to engage in personal evaluation and group discussion of ways to improve teaching. When one does this in a "program group" context, one is more vulnerable to openly sharing insights, fears, experiences and hopes. It has been my experience that when a group's ground rules are discussed and agreed upon beforehand, trust increases and discussions are more forthright. The fact that there is a concern about the release of negative information must be communicated with the group, which must also fully discuss the political implications. The group should decide together upon a policy to which they will adhere concerning the sharing of study results, not as an effort to suppress the results but to present the issues in a balanced and fair manner.

Sheryl – Program Administrator

During the next meeting of this group, I would share my reasons why negative information could be harmful. Anytime investigations are conducted, suggestions for changes are offered. Even when concerns are stated as suggestions for improvement, they are often interpreted as negative factors. It is very easy for negative factors to be taken out of context and perceived as much larger problems than in reality. Members of this group should remember that even a small amount of negative information can influence public perceptions of the program. These perceptions may significantly affect funding, recruitment of students, and faculty participation. It is always wise to be careful about how negative information is shared with those other than program participants.

Renee – Methods Instructor and Researcher

It is oftentimes tempting to think of research as a quest for knowledge for its own sake. But research is a social and political activity conducted within social, emotional, and political settings. In a sense, all of these vignettes illustrate the point that thinking through a research project involves much more than defining a set of empirical questions and matching methodology to those questions. It is my opinion that we who are teacher educators and researchers are developing a new form of inquiry that openly acknowledges the value dimensions of research. Groups such as the one in the vignette are in operation; they are pioneers who must not proceed naively. I would recommend that the group design and conduct their study, but that they proceed carefully. I would also recommend that program administrators think about their roles in assisting those who wish to study themselves. We cannot afford to be more concerned with suppressing problems than improving programs for teachers, prospective teachers, or children.

ACROSS THE VIGNETTES

In this final section, we move to a combined discussion of the issues implied by our separate responses. The first issue is also the most obvious: We do not agree on the interpretations of each vignette, nor do we recommend the same courses of action. The two university representatives sometimes disagree, as do the two public school representatives. In other words, we cannot assume that similar employers or teaching assignments imply similar views of research and researchers. Although the four of us might be able to negotiate a consensus, it is important to recognize that we all begin from different vantage points and bring different value systems to the discussion.

Furthermore, many "voices" who will be affected by the research conducted within our collaboration remain unheard. The voices of public school students—the ultimate benefactors or victims of research projects conducted within the schools—and their parents are notably absent. Dissenting faculty members, representatives of colleges of arts and sciences, university and public school administrators, and teacher candidates are also underrepresented. Failure to listen to and air those voices as research is designed and as findings are reported may antagonize those people who were not present throughout the discussions. For collaborative projects to function effectively, some level of harmony and understanding must be maintained. We believe that collaborative program structures must allow for inclusion of the diverse voices as research in and on the program is authorized and monitored. Although we feel that programs of research will ultimately strengthen the collaborative endeavor, we worry that research may inadvertently harm that which researchers are trying to understand.

Our individual responses all presumed a commitment to program continuation, for we are all very proud of our efforts to date. But program commitment is something we cannot take for granted. We believe that commitment must be nurtured and renewed, and at the same time we believe that we cannot define commitment as blinding ourselves to necessary changes and improvements. This means that we must actively work to create an environment in which data-based discussions analyzing teaching and learning are encouraged and supported. We realize that we cannot assume that all of our colleagues share our enthusiasm for such analyses.

Enlisting cooperating teachers and fellow teacher educators who are actively engaged in the preparation of future teachers requires a commitment to ongoing coaching and feedback. This requires time. Classroom teachers, who frequently sponsor extracurricular activities, are already overloaded with large classes composed of students whose needs are increasingly diverse. Consequently, they may question the importance of participating in research or discussions of research. Forcing the issue is likely to decrease their willingness to invest their time, talents and energies in mentoring new teachers. As we think through program design and ongoing research agendas, we must allow for diverse modes of participation.

This introduces our second issue: diversity in program participation. *Diversity* is a word that typically connotes issues of race, ethnicity, and gender in current discussions of educational issues. We would like to suggest that our working conception of diversity be expanded to consider varying perspectives on the roles of the teacher educator and the varying backgrounds that prospective teachers bring to our programs. Collaborative programs heighten our awareness of diversity by magnifying networks of communication and interdependence. No longer are the personalities and philosophies of only teacher candidates, cooperating teachers, classroom students, and university supervisors the primary elements of diversity, although, even factoring those into an equation for success has sometimes proven complex and difficult. Now, other parties also have a vested interest in program design and implementation. Developing strategies that facilitate communication and respect for divergent viewpoints becomes critical. We recognize that we are talking about a political issue as well as an educational issue. When it is impossible to engage in profitable dialogue, we deny ourselves the sharing of experiences, knowledge and passion that might have resulted in true inroads in assisting students in social and intellectual growth.

We are interested in the extent to which data collection and analysis can inform our communication across roles and institutions. At the same time, we are concerned that the voice of researchers (or any single role group) not be accorded supreme status or final authority. Public school teachers have often experienced the dilemma of sorting through research results that may be conflicting, of being urged to embrace research results that have too narrow a focus to be helpful. To the degree that time and resources permit, we would like to see more collaborative research efforts that include participants from schools and universities. We are convinced that through collaboration the university and the public schools can learn from each other as they identify areas of mutual concern and establish priorities for research. It is within such a context of partnership that real changes in professional behavior can occur for public school teachers and university professors.

This brings us to our third and final issue: Collaborative teacher education that incorporates ongoing research and development implies changing traditional practices and learning new roles. Contained within the vignettes are several educational roles: professors, researchers, university administrators, teachers, graduate students, school administrators, and students. In our programs, many of the participants occupy several roles simultaneously. Teachers are also graduate students; professors are also parents; teacher candidates are parents and research assistants. We are finding that our collaboration is moving us toward blurred role distinctions and that our time is diffused among many roles.

In many ways this is exciting, for we are challenging unproductive assumptions and we are learning more and more about one another's worlds. In some other ways this is troubling, for we find ourselves facing situations we have never faced before. We also worry about expecting more and more from teachers, professors, and administrators while providing them with less and less support. For example, writing this chapter has not been equally easy; two of us are full-time teachers and two are professors who travel frequently. Nevertheless, we did not want to take the option of having one or two people do the writing, because we feel committed to sharing insights across institutions and individual experiences. Only one of us has a job description that includes professional writing as a clear expectation. The others were not obligated to write; participation was by choice. We began this chapter by talking about the bridges between public schools and universities; we conclude by suggesting that collaborative research and writing can help in redesigning and improving those bridges—as long as collaboration is viewed as working *with* one another as equal partners toward mutually beneficial goals.

REFERENCES

Bush, R. N. (1977). We know how to train teachers: Why not do so! *Journal of Teacher Education, 28,* 5–9.

Clift, R., Veal, M. L., Johnson, M. & Holland, P. (1990). Restructuring teacher education through collaborative action research. *Journal of Teacher Education, 41* (2), 52–62.

Cochran-Smith, M. & Lytle, S. (1993). *Inside/outside: Teacher research and knowledge.* New York: Teachers College Press.

Goodlad, J. I. (1990). *Teachers for our nation's schools.* San Francisco: Jossey-Bass.

Holmes Group. (1986). *Tomorrow's teachers.* East Lansing, MI: Author.

Hunsaker, L. & Johnston, M. (1992). Teacher under construction: A collaborative case study of teacher change. *American Educational Research Journal, 29,* 350–372.

Lanier, J. E. & Little, J. W. (1986). Research on teacher education. In M. C. Wittrock (Ed.) *Handbook of research on teaching,* (3rd edition, pp. 527–569). New York: Macmillan.

CHAPTER 3

University/School Partnerships: Exploring Tangible and Intangible Costs and Benefits

R. CARL HARRIS
Brigham Young University

MELANIE F. HARRIS
Rees Elementary School

R. CARL HARRIS is the Coordinator of the Partner Schools Network for the Brigham Young University–Public School Partnership. The program was recognized as a 1989 ATE Distinguished Program in Teacher Education. Dr. Harris was named 1990 Teacher of the Year by the Utah Association of Teacher Educators. His research interests are field-based teacher education, university-school collaboration and teaching as thinking.

MELANIE F. HARRIS is an intern coordinator at Rees Elementary School in the Nebo School District, and executive assistant to the director of the BYU-Public School Partnership. Her research interests include school/university collaboration and thematic curriculum development.

ABSTRACT

This study of costs and benefits in twenty-three partner schools of a ten-year-old university-school partnership has sought to explore the inner workings of one genre of partnerships in education. We have undertaken to define tangible and intangible costs and benefits for schools and university educators and their respective institutions. The major tangible variables we studied were time, services, and facilities. The significant intangible variables were pressure, communication, control, educational quality, and empowerment. We discovered that the school's and university's relative investments when given dollar values are 62 percent and 38 percent, respectively, for one year's operation. When computed on a per partner-school basis, the dollar value invested by the university-school partnership is $32,502. Although the school's contribution is valued at 62 percent of the total, the university's share is eight times as great when computed on a per student basis: (school = $68.87, university = $565.32).

OBJECTIVES

No genre of partnerships in education has been more hopefully advocated for simultaneously reinventing teacher education and schooling in the final decade of the twentieth century than professional development or partner schools in university-school partnerships (Carnegie, 1986; Goodlad, 1990; Holmes, 1986; Lieberman, 1989; Yinger & Hendricks, 1990). However, because of the complexity of university-school collaboration and the relative newness of the partner schools model, little is known about their inner workings (Kennedy, 1991). It was the purpose of this study to explore one year's worth of tangible and intangible costs and benefits for twenty-three partner schools supported by a university-school partnership in its tenth year of operation.

PERSPECTIVES

The basic interdependence between universities and schools provided a logical basis for investing in these types of partnerships in education. Theobald (1990) explains how both institutions' unmet needs are satisfied by linking their work:

> Public schools have an unmet need for better teachers. In order to produce these better teachers, universities need access to exemplary school settings in which to place their student teachers and to conduct research on effective practices. This research in turn can be used by the schools to improve the educational experiences provided to elementary and secondary students. These well-prepared elementary and secondary students will eventually meet the universities' unmet need for excellent undergraduate and graduate students. And so on. (p. 2)

One such educational partnership, now beginning its tenth year of collaboration, is the Brigham Young University–Public School Partnership (Harris & Harris, 1992). It is an aggressive experiment in finding and using the common ground between university and school cultures. External evaluators have called this partnership one of the most mature and successful collaborative efforts in the nation (Clark & Wilson, 1990).

The partnership in education has been framed by four shared values: university and school partners share a common goal for educational renewal; university and school educators actively participate in all facets of the partnership; university and school educators promote equity and trust between the partners; and university and school educators balance self-interest and selflessness (Harris & Harris, 1991).

Goodlad, a longtime proponent of site-based, university-school collaboration, proposed the simultaneous renewal of schools and the education of educators through organic or symbiotic collaboration between universities and schools as equal partners (Goodlad, 1984, 1986). The Brigham Young University–Public School Partnership, one of the first university–school partnerships to respond seriously to Goodlad's proposal, is the oldest continuously functioning member of Goodlad's National Network for Educational Renewal. This partnership's longevity permits an investigation to explore the costs and benefits of operating partner schools along tangible and intangible dimensions.

SIGNIFICANCE OF THE STUDY

The places where school and university educators join in a mutually beneficial enterprise are called partner schools (Goodlad, 1990). In partner schools, school and university educators connect in a common effort to reinvent education through the preservice preparation of new teachers, the professional development of practicing teachers, curriculum reform for young learners, and inquiry about the first three processes. Because "Not many true professional development schools exist today . . ."(Kennedy, 1991, p. 664), little information is available about their inner workings, influence, problems, costs, or benefits. Some scholars assert, in fact, that the partner-school model is too new for meaningful study. For example, Arends (1990), writing in the 1990 ASCD Yearbook on connecting the university to the school, was skeptical: "The problems facing schools and colleges of education in universities are incredibly complicated. Even though myriad remedies abound, none are close to being implemented" (p. 134). This study was designed to examine the costs related to a university and several school districts working together to reform the university teacher-preparation program and the schooling in sites where new teachers practice-teach.

The identification of cost-benefit variables allows policy makers to compute costs and benefits in this or any other university-school partnership. Good quality analyses of costs and benefits should lead to better fiscal and program policy making. For educators who are considering the partner-school model as an agent of change, grounded descriptions of costs and benefits will assist them in deciding on their degree of involvement. Basic reform of education must be supported by long-term commitments while eschewing quick-fix projects. Other educators who are well into collaboration at partner-school sites need to monitor their progress continually so that needed adjustments can be made to assure the desired return on investments. Viable accounting of reform work will also guard against the tendency of advocates to overinflate benefits and opponents to overinflate costs.

ORIGINS OF THE PARTNERSHIP

At the same time that *A Nation at Risk* was prepared by the National Commission on Excellence in Education (1983), Goodlad consulted with the dean of the BYU College of Education, which produces about half of the new teachers in the state of Utah, and superintendents from five Utah school districts, which enroll about one-third of the public school students in the state. Out of this meeting the university-school partnership was organized in April 1984 with six equal partners making up the partnership governing board: the superintendents of the five school districts and the College of Education dean (Williams, 1988). Task forces for principal and teacher education were formed, and by spring 1986, four elementary schools had accepted an opportunity to become partner-schools.

"Partner-school" is a designation given a school as it enters into a long-term, collaborative relationship with the university's Department of Elementary Education. The university and the schools agreed, as equal partners, to work for the renewal of schools and improvement of teacher education. Each partner-school was assigned a volunteer member of the university elementary teacher-education faculty, along with approximately eighteen BYU students majoring in elementary education. The school principal, the teachers, and the university coordinator worked on a renewal agenda structured around four partner-school tasks: (1) preservice education for new teachers; (2) inservice education (staff development) for practicing teachers in the school; (3) curriculum development to improve the learning experiences of pupils, and; (4) research and evaluation to foster university and school inquiry (Harris, et al., 1989).

METHOD

Identifying Cost/Benefit Variables

To arrive at the salient intangible variables, we used interpretive research methodologies (Bogdan & Biklen, 1982; Erickson, 1986; Geertz, 1973; Goetz & LeCompte, 1984). Qualitative data were collected from three sources: participant observation of district councils, school councils, linking workshops, partnership conferences, partner-school committee meetings, preservice teacher observations, consensus evaluation of preservice teachers, and academies held in partner-schools for preservice teachers over the course of one year; one formal, thirty-to-sixty minute semistructured interview and many informal interviews with twenty-three principals, twenty-three teacher leaders, nine professors, thirty-two preservice teachers, and thirty-two cooperating teachers; and documents including minutes from all council and committee meetings, articles published by university and school educators, technical reports, preservice teachers' lesson plans and written reflections, theses, dissertations, and research data gathered by university faculty.

Constant comparison (Glaser & Strauss, 1967) was used to combine and categorize the data from observations, interviews, and documents. In this process each idea, action, or situation was compared to previously categorized data and added to all appropriate categories. Categories were then grouped in broader categories. Next, we identified salient topics for costs and benefits attributed to either schools or university. A topic was considered salient if numerous school and university informants said or implied that it was important and written documents validated the same.

A crucial stage in the overall analysis of costs and benefits was differentiating tangible variables, that is, those potentially reducible to quantitative terms such as dollars, hours, and square feet; from intangible variables, i.e., qualities and values that cannot be meaningfully reduced to a monetary figure, such as growth, involvement, empowerment, fulfillment, and learning. For costs and benefits to be associated with partner-schools, they must directly or indirectly result from the partner-school effect. If a professor would have supervised university students at a school site regardless of its partnership status, and if the supervision had been conducted in the same traditional manner predating the partnership, then the cost of the professor's time cannot be attributed to the partner-school effect.

Cost and Benefit Variables

Cost and benefit variables focus on educational units within two unique educational settings: twenty-three elementary schools in four public school districts and the college of education in the largest private, church-related university in the nation. When tangible (potentially reducible to dollars) and intangible (not reducible to dollars) costs and benefits are described for each setting, eight variable categories result (See Figure 1):

1. Tangible school/district costs: time, funds, and facilities.
2. Intangible school/district costs: pressures, communication, and control.
3. Tangible university costs: time, funds, and facilities.
4. Intangible university costs: pressures, communication, and control.
5. Tangible school/district benefits: time, funds, and facilities.
6. Intangible school/district benefits: educational quality, communication, and empowerment.
7. Tangible university benefits: time, funds, and facilities.
8. Intangible university benefits: educational quality, communication, and empowerment.

Tangible Costs Expressed in Dollars

We sought to put a dollar value on all tangible resources related to the operation of twenty-three partner-schools that operated during one full calendar year. An important caveat is in order: No new dollars from university or school sources were used in partner-school operation, and thus none is included in these calculations. Nor do these figures represent any additional funds from external sources. All values represent existing funding and resources in established university and school operations budgets that existed when the analysis was done. Resources have been used in different ways to support collaborative work, but the total resource pool has remained constant.

In this study, *resources* means the significant use of time, services, and facilities directly related to partner-school operation. We count these dollar values as actual costs to the party supplying the resources and potential benefits to both parties. For example, a school provides space for university students and their professor to hold seminars associated with field experience. The cost of the space is borne entirely by the school. The university (students and professors) benefits directly, since scheduling of fieldwork is facilitated by holding seminars in a school instead of on campus miles from the classrooms where university students observe and practice-teach. The benefit to university students increases when examples are given from real practice by cooperating teachers in the school where the seminar is being held. The teachers and principals benefit indirectly because university students can be in the classrooms longer and become active contributors to the school's culture. In some cases, teachers and principals choose to join the seminars with the

COSTS

TANGIBLE

SCHOOL/DISTRICT
Educator Time
-Meetings to plan and coordinate renewal
-Communicating about renewal
-Attending staff development sessions
-Developing renewed curriculum
-Assisting in data gathering
-Observing/reflecting with student teachers
-Writing summative evaluation reports
-Planning with student teachers
-Consulting with university coordinators
-Scheduling & giving demonstration lessons
-Traveling between schools and to campus
-Assisting in presentation of findings
Funding
-Limited job enlargement funds
-Travel expenses to report at conferences
Facility Use
-Use of copy machine, materials, telephones
-Space for academy, seminars, lunch, parking

UNIVERSITY
Educator Time
-Meetings to plan and coordinate renewal★
-Preparing & presenting staff development★★
-Assisting to develop curriculum★★
-Gathering, analyzing, summarizing data
-Observing/reflecting with student teachers
-Assessing student teachers' written work
-Trouble shooting with teachers & principals
-Scheduling & giving model lessons★★
-Preparing & presenting in academy★
-Traveling between schools & campus★,★★
★Also administrators ★★University specialists
Funding
-Honorarium to cooperating teachers
-Assistantship to graduate students
-Salary to adjunct faculty/interns
Facility Use
-Printing, telephone, secretaries, parking, AV equipment, stationery, mail

INTANGIBLE

SCHOOL/DISTRICT
Pressures
-Increased intellectual, emotional, & psychological load on teachers and principals while mentoring student teachers
-Increased complexity of work when engaging in renewal tasks
-Teachers take professor viewpoint & expertise into account for decisions
-Teachers/principals open themselves to critical analysis by professors
Communication
-Increased communication, networking, cooperation, planning, & thoughtfulness working with larger teams of colleagues
Control
-Teachers are not constantly engaged in direct contact with students
-Principals are not constantly engaged in direct contact with administrative tasks
-Pupils & parents exercise flexibility in having novice & other teachers in class
-Administrators share power & information with teachers, principals, & university professors

UNIVERSITY
Pressures
-View theories through the sceptical lens of the practitioner's experience & skill
-Professors open themselves to critical analysis by teacher/principal practitioners
-Conflict over resource priorities/allocations
Communication
-Increased communication load with non-university colleagues
-Professors not constantly engaged in direct contact with university students/faculty
-Professors take teacher/principal viewpoint & expertise into account for decisions
Control
-Professors share governance of teacher education with teachers/principals
-Reward system broadened to include building non-campus infrastructure
-Professional and professorial interests jointly considered
-Application of creative work focused on local more than national audiences
-Administrators share power & information with professors, teachers, & principals

FIGURE 1
Tangible and intangible cost and benefits in school-university collaboration.

BENEFITS

TANGIBLE

SCHOOL/DISTRICT

Educator Time
-University faculty time to collaborate with school/district partners
-Student teachers/interns on request
-Staff development at little or no cost
-Released time for site visits, inservice, curriculum development, & research when student teachers take over classrooms

Funding
-Honorarium to cooperating teachers
-Assistantship to graduate students
-Salary to adjunct faculty/interns
-Assistance with transportation to conferences for reporting research findings

Facility Use
-Printing, telephone, secretaries, parking, AV equipment, stationery, mail
-BYU library card, rooms for conferences

UNIVERSITY

Educator Time
-Teacher & principal time to collaborate with university partners
-District administrator & specialist time to collaborate with university partners
-Presenters in academies, seminars, workshops, campus classes, conferences
-NCATE informants
-Access to full spectrum of curriculum materials
-Assistance in counseling student teachers
-Service on campus advisory councils
-Readily available source of subjects for research projects

Facility Use
-Use of copy machine, materials, telephone
-Space for academy, seminars, lunch, parking

Funding
-Limited job-enlargement funds

INTANGIBLE

SCHOOL/DISTRICT

Educational Quality
-Increased quality of school learning
-An enlivened curriculum that inspires student learning for intrinsic reasons
-Instructional skills and content knowledge updated because of being "on stage"

Communication
-Engagement in cross-school, cross-district dialogue about renewal issues
-A voice in determining how new teachers are prepared
-Parent recognition that their local school is at the forefront & in a growth pattern

Empowerment
-Assistance with systematic data gathering, analysis, and interpretation
-Added incentive to remain current with state of the art teaching/learning strategies
-An opportunity to participate in screening new entrants into the ranks of teaching
-Active participation in and contact with participants in the national reform effort
-Increased status through having practical experience valued

UNIVERSITY

Educational Quality
-Higher quality preparation of new teachers
-Sites where student teachers can observe models of best practice
-The university community can directly influence the quality of public schooling
-The wisdom of practice enriches theory-driven university thinking
-Long-term collaboration fosters constant improvement in teacher education rather than fragmented projects
-Meaningful topics for professors to study, write about, & report

Communication
-Assistance in systematic data gathering, analysis, & interpretation
-Networking opportunities with similar projects nationally & internationally

Empowerment
-Moral support & encouragement from practitioner colleagues
-Enhancement of university's national stature

FIGURE 1

Tangible and intangible cost and benefits in school-university collaboration.

university students. In these cases, the school educators may benefit directly because they pick up ideas for change in curriculum from the seminars, and when implemented, these ideas may benefit the schools' students.

To compute school educators' time, we consider partner-school work of partner-school coordinators (teacher leaders), cooperating teachers, principals, and district administrators. University educators' time computations include the partner-school work of faculty, the department chair, and the executive director of the partnership. Schools and university employ support staff such as secretaries and custodians (see Table 1). These individuals' partner-school work has not been included because in our judgment, their roles have not been appreciably changed by the partnership initiative.

In this analysis, services will include: use of school and university libraries, telephones, and photocopy machines; travel within the partnership; travel beyond the partnership to conferences or study trips to other partnerships; hosting of guest educators who have come to study the partnership; and parking (see Table 2). Several other nominal services that are not included are use of computers, printers, modem, FAX, overhead projectors, VCRs, camcorders, tape recorders, and other such equipment.

The third resource category is facilities. Facilities include classrooms, conference rooms, auditoriums, faculty lounges, commons, and kivas at the partner-schools and university (see Table 3). No dollar value has been given to use of restrooms, hallways, office space, work and faculty preparation rooms, custodial space, and food-serving areas. Again, these latter facilities have received only nominal change in use directly due to partner-school operations.

The purposes for which the facilities were used include: seminars and academies conducted for preservice teachers; inservice and professional development workshops for partner-school teachers; district councils at which school and university representatives from each partner-school coordinate reform work within each district; strategic planning for school, district, and partnership initiatives; linking workshops that brought teachers and professors together from all partner-schools in the partnership to define problems and solutions; and partner-school committee meetings to facilitate continuous, cross-district, cross-school communication and collaborative effort.

RESULTS

Tangible Costs

Time The major tangible cost variable to school and university partners is time. The upper left-hand quadrant of Figure 1 lists a variety of ways in

TABLE 1
Twelve months of time use for 23 partner schools in the BYU–Public School Partnership

Purpose	School Educators' Hours (Est. Teach. $17/hr*, Prin./Admin. $23/hr**)					University Educators' Hours (Est. Associate Prof. $23/hr***)					School + University
	Coord n=23	Coop T n=250	Prin n=23	Dist n=4	Total n=300	Coord n=9	Chair n=1	Ex Dir n=1	Method n=4	Total n=15	Total Hours n=315
Dist Council n=7 @ 2 hrs	322	N/A	322	56	700	126	N/A	N/A	N/A	126	826
Sch Council n=7 @ 1 hr	161	1750	161	N/A	2072	63	N/A	N/A	N/A	63	2135
Linking Wkshp/Conf n=2 @ 6 hrs	276	3000	276	48	3600	108	6	6	48	168	3768
Part Sch Com n=2 @ 2 hrs	92	N/A	92	16	200	36	4	4	N/A	44	244
Observations n=8 @ .5 hr	1200	1000	900	N/A	3100	9000	N/A	N/A	16	9016	12116
Consensus Eval n=4 @ 1 hr	92	1000	92	N/A	1184	36	N/A	N/A	N/A	36	1220
Academies n=2 @ 4 hrs	184	2000	92	N/A	2276	150	N/A	N/A	N/A	150	2426
Inservice n=4 @ 3 hrs	276	3000	138	N/A	3414	108	N/A	N/A	48	156	3570
Curriculum n=7 @ 2 hrs	138	3500	69	32	3739	126	N/A	N/A	56	182	3921
Research n=7 @ 2 hrs	230	3500	115	16	3861	252	N/A	N/A	56	308	4169
Travel varied	184	250	184	20	638	864	2	2	16	884	1522
	8 hrs/	1 hr/	8 hrs/	5 hrs/		96 hrs/	2 hrs/	2 hrs/	5 hrs/		
Total Hours	3155	19000	2441	188	24784	10869	12	12	240	11133	35917
Total $	53635	323000	56143	4324	437102	249987	276	276	5520	256059	693161
Hrs/Partner Sch	137	826	106	8	1077	473	0.52	0.52	10	484	1561
$/Partner Sch	2329	14042	2438	184	18993	10879	12	12	230	11132	30125

*Teach.–$25,614; 185 days @ 8 hrs/day.
**Prin./Admin.–$41,910; 229 days @ 8 hrs/day.
1990–91 Report, Utah State Office of Education, Salt Lake City, UT

***$37,573; 40 weeks @ 40 hrs/week
Faculty Survey 1990–91, Office of Institutional
Research, Oklahoma State Univ., Stillwater, OK

TABLE 2
Twelve months of services for 23 partner schools in the BYU–Public School Partnership

School Service	$	University Service	$	School + University $
LIBRARY/MEDIA CENTER n = 25 @ $4	1000	**LIBRARY/MEDIA CENTER** n = 198 card @ $5	990	1990
TELEPHONE n = 23 @ $10/mo x 9 mo	2070	**TELEPHONE** n = 9 @ $10/mo x 9	810	2880
PHOTOCOPY n = 23 @ .03/pp x 20 pp/wk x 32	442	**PHOTOCOPY** n = 9 @ .03/pp x 500 pp/mo x 9 mo	1215	1657
TRAVEL IN PARTNERSHIP n = 23 @ .29/mi x 8 veh x 100 mi	5336	**TRAVEL IN PARTNERSHIP** n = 9 @ .29/mi x 2930 mi	7620	12,956
TRAVEL TO CONFERENCES n = 20 @ $200	4000	**TRAVEL TO CONFERENCES** n = 9 profs @ $500 n = 20 teachers @ $100	6500	10,500
HOSTING n = 5 study teams @ $50	250	**HOSTING** n = 5 study teams @ $300	1500	1750
PARKING n = 100 cars @ $2/day x 30 days	6000	**PARKING** n = 230 @ $2/day x 2 days	920	6920
TOTAL $s	19,098		19,555	38,653
$/PARTNER SCH	830		850	1680

TABLE 3
Twelve months of facilities use for 23 partner schools in the BYU–Public School Partnership

Purpose	School Facilities				University Facilities				School + University			
	Freq.	Rms.	$/Rm.	Total $	Freq.	Rms.	$/Rm.	Total $	Freq.	Rms.	$/Rm.	Total $
Seminars	210	210	25	5250	N/A	N/A	N/A	N/A	210	210	25	5250
Academies	35	35	25	875	N/A	N/A	N/A	N/A	35	35	25	875
Inservice	48	48	25	1200	43	57	79	4490	91	105	54	5690
Dist Councils	32	32	50	1600	7	10	57	565	39	42	52	2165
Strategic Planning	N/A	N/A	N/A	N/A	9	12	54	645	9	12	54	645
Linking Wkshp	N/A	N/A	N/A	N/A	2	9	76	685	2	9	76	685
Part Sch Com	N/A	N/A	N/A	N/A	2	9	76	685	2	9	76	685
Total $	325	325	28	8925	63	97	73	7070	388	422	38	15,995
$/Partner Sch	14	N/A	N/A	389	2.7	N/A	N/A	308	17	N/A	N/A	697

which time is used to renew schooling and teacher preparation. Teachers and principals spend time in formal talk with university professors and one another in regularly scheduled partner-school council meetings at the school, district, and partnership level. These meetings focus on reforming teacher preparation and schooling. Reform dialogue includes issues such as what revisions are needed in the way student teachers gather evidence of learning; how to create portfolios of pupils' work; and what research shows about making reflection in and on practice. Time logs kept by school and university educators showed that on average about twelve hours a month are spent in formal dialogue.

Even more time consuming is the continuing informal dialogue. Because the university professors spend over half of their university load time in the schools, they frequently meet teachers and principals in the halls, faculty lounges, preparation rooms, and classrooms. Interchanges include small talk about family, sports, hobbies, politics, and general scuttlebutt. However, informal dialogue is not limited to small talk. Topics may include questions from the university supervisor to a principal about a student teacher who is having trouble controlling an active group of fifth-grade boys, or a teacher asking a professor to look at some writing the teacher is preparing for presentation at a regional conference. Time logs kept by university professors show on average sixteen hours per month for informal dialogue, whereas school educators show on average ten hours per month of talking informally. Time spent talking about reform is time not spent preparing lessons, directly teaching students, gathering data, or writing articles for publication.

This study specifically included time used by school and university educators for eleven partner-school related activities: (1) district partner-school councils; (2) partner-school councils; (3) linking workshops; (4) cross-district partner-schools committee; (5) observations and mentoring of preservice teachers; (6) consensus evaluation of preservice teachers; (7) academies conducted in partner-schools for preservice teachers; (8) inservice and professional development activities for cooperating teachers; (9) curriculum renewal and development to enhance the daily learning experiences of pupils; (10) research on questions jointly and separately derived by school and university educators to study preservice, inservice, and curriculum processes; and (11) travel between schools and the university. The data reveal that $18,993 worth of time is provided by school educators and $11,132 worth of time is provided by university educators for each of the twenty-three partner-schools within one year for a total of $30,125 per partner-school (see Table 1).

Services Those funds previously used to send school and university educators to regional and national conferences to report their independent research or projects now support presentations related to collaboration and reform of education. Wages previously paid to part-time, retired principals or teachers for intermittent supervision of student teachers are now paid to master teachers who have become clinical faculty and partner-school coordinators. School supplies and telephones that used to be for the exclusive use of school staff now accommodate university students and professors. University vans transport professors and school educators to state, regional, and national conferences at no cost to the individuals.

The school and university costs of seven services were studied: library and instructional media center use for checking out books, kits, videotapes, and films; telephone calls; making photocopies; travel within the partnership; travel beyond the partnership to attend conferences; hosting visitors who come to study the partnership; and parking privileges. We found that schools provided services valued at $830 per partner-school, the university provided services valued at $850 per partner-school, and together they provided services valued at $1,680 per partner-school (see Table 2).

Facilities Parking lots, preparation rooms, restrooms, faculty lounges, and instructional space in schools, at district offices, and on the university campus have more people using them as a result of the partner-schools' efforts. Teachers and district staff go to the campus to make presentations, deliver or receive staff development, conduct strategic planning, plan networking meetings, conduct committee work, and attend or assist in instructing graduate programs. Professors and university students go to the schools and district offices for seminars, observations, case studies, demonstration teaching, data gathering, inservice videotaping, hosting outside guests, practice teaching, and curriculum reform. Since the formation of the partnership, the schools and the district have not charged the university for using facilities. The reverse is also true. The university conference center normally charges substantial fees for use of its conference rooms, auditoriums, and media equipment but has waived charges for partner-school educators. All custodial, maintenance, and utility costs continue but are absorbed by the respective institutions.

The dollar value of facilities resulted in schools providing $389 worth per partner-school and the university providing $308 worth per partner-school. Jointly they provided $697 worth per partner-school (see Table 3).

Summary When dollar values for time, services, and facilities were calculated, we found that the school provided $20,212 in value per partner-school, the university $12,290 in value per partner-school, and together they provided $32,502 in value per partner-school. When computed on a per student basis, the schools provided $68.87 in value, the university $565.32 in value (see Table 4).

TABLE 4
Twelve months of tangible costs/benefits for 23 partner schools in the BYU–Public School Partnership

Tangible Cost/Benefit	Schools	University	School + University
TIME, TOTAL $	436,839	25,6036	692,875
$/PARTNER SCH.	18993	11132	30125
SERVICES, TOTAL $	19,098	19,555	38,653
$/PARTNER SCH.	830	850	1680
FACILITIES, TOTAL $	8925	7070	15,995
$/PARTNER SCH.	389	308	697
TOTAL $	464,862	282,661	747,523
$/PARTNER SCH.	20,212	12,290	32,502
$/STUDENT	68.87	565.32	103.11
	n= 6750*	n= 500**	n= 7250

* 27/CLASS, 250 CLASSES

** INCLUDES EARLY FIELD, PRACTICUM, STUDENT TEACHING, INTERNS, EARLY CHILDHOOD, SPECIAL EDUCATION

Intangible Costs

Pressure The heaviest intangible cost for the teachers and principals is including the renewal of teacher preparation along with their primary responsibility of promoting learning in youth. This means they must take into consideration the values, mission, and culture of university faculty. Similarly, the heaviest cost to university faculty is to assist in renewing staff and curriculum development that influences the quality of pupil learning along with their primary responsibility of preparing new teachers and conducting research on the partner-school effect. University faculty now have to deal with the stereotypes, perceptions, and needs of practitioners in a new way. Teachers, principals, and district staff now have to consider the opinions and biases of professors. Each partner's world has become more complex and less predictable because another partner's values and culture are being addressed.

Communication A costly intangible variable has been the exposure of each institution's inner workings, assumptions, and culture to the full view of the other. Professors attend school faculty meetings and find out, for the first time, the politics of allocating career-ladder and job-enlargements funds. Teachers attend national conferences and meet, for the first time, the plethora of ideas with which professors are bombarded. Professors who have not taught young learners for years come under the direct scrutiny of seasoned teachers when they teach demonstration lessons. Teachers who have never attempted a systematic analysis of another teacher's instruction reveal their ineptitude before an experienced university observer. Loss of mystique has been an intangible cost. Collaborators committed for the long term can maintain few secrets from one another. They must communicate candidly with one another perhaps, for the first time.

Control School and university educators must share or give up some of their power, expertise, decision making, and turf with people they may have heretofore misunderstood—or worse, not respected. It is widely known that professors have often viewed practitioners as bolstering utilitarian and vocational perspectives on teaching that ultimately perpetuate existing practice (Cochran-Smith, 1991; Goodman, 1986). When professors want to disparage practitioners' professional attitude, they may be heard to criticize the "make and take" approach to professional development. On the other hand, school-based practitioners frequently perceive professors as out of touch with reality, lost in a world of theorizing, and burdened with inflated views of their own worth (Goodlad, 1990). They resent and resist professors who have traditionally condescended, with their "superior" scholarly knowledge, to work with school practitioners. These unproductive and untenable positions must be given up. No group of professionals has a monopoly on insight, problem-solving skills, or knowledge.

Tangible Benefits

Time In the domain of tangible benefits, costs for one partner are usually benefits for the other. A professor's time spent showing teachers how to implement a literature-based reading program is a cost to the professor but a benefit to the faculty. It may benefit the professors also, since their preservice university students may practice-teach under cooperating teachers who received the additional training. School faculty time spent showing university students how a literature-based reading program is operated in actual classrooms is a cost to the teachers, but a benefit to the professors who have their university students apply the ideal practices in the field (see Table 1).

Services University specialists do not normally charge for workshops and school specialists do not charge for presentations in on-campus courses or serving as informants on NCATE panels. As previously noted, school personnel have ridden without charge in university vans to regional and national conferences. University professors have been joined by school collaborators in making conference presentations. Teachers have helped formulate questions for inquiry and opened their classroom doors to joint school-university data gathering. Job enlargement funds have been used by schools to pay teachers for some of the extra time they spend in partner-school work such as supervising university preservice teachers and serving on committees (see Table 2).

Facilities Other important tangible benefits for school and university educators include free use of facilities, information-processing equipment, and telephones. The college of education has provided university library cards and helped teachers learn to make computer-based ERIC searches. Annual partnership conferences to which all partner-schools, task forces, and committees send representatives are held on campus at the BYU Conference Center at no cost to schools or districts. On a few occasions, when the conference center was booked, the annual conference was held at a district high school at minimal cost to the partnership. When a principal takes a whole faculty to the university conference center for a strategic planning retreat, the university shoulders the full cost of maintenance, utilities, and overhead. The principal and the faculty use the facility free of charge and accomplish uninterrupted planning (see Table 3).

Intangible Benefits

Educational Quality Better education for youth and adult learners is the supreme intangible benefit variable. Student learning in schools should be enhanced and the ability of new teachers to teach should be increased. According to their respective mission statements, neither the public schools nor the university has any reason to exist if their primary clients are not served.

By the same token, the collaborative renewal work involving partner-schools and the broader partnership has no validity unless it improves schooling and teacher preparation.

To determine improvements in quality teacher preparation, we are gathering data in several ways: university professors are comparing practice-teaching outcomes in partner vs. non-partner-schools (Harris & Harris, 1993); principals and cooperating teachers are contrasting the program in which new teachers participate and their resulting level of preparedness to their own teacher-education experiences before the partnership; recent graduates are being surveyed for their evaluations of how well partner-school-based teacher education prepared them for teaching; teacher educators from other university-school partnerships who have visited and studied this project are providing unsolicited feedback; the recently completed NCATE team assessment which identified the partner-schools project as one of seven college strengths, is being analyzed (NCATE, 1991); and survey data that measure the perceptions of cooperating teachers on multiple occasions over a six-year period are being interpreted (Harris, Baird, & Harris, 1993).

For evidence that supports the improved quality of learning in the schools, we are examining the following types of data: a partner-school teacher's masters thesis (Roberts et al., 1992) revealed that students' higher cognitive processes in a partner-school were significantly superior to that of students in a non-partner control school; parents report (Harris, et al.,1987) that their children come home with stories about being impressed with units on the environment, water cycle, seed germination, the Persian Gulf, etc. that their BYU student teacher presented. Other parents have commented on their children's enthusiasm for writing in comic book formats, going through distinctive stages of the writing process and having their final product published and housed in the school library. Others have voiced delight at new levels of musical, artistic, and kinetic skills they have observed as their children participated in school programs heavily aided by student teachers; all partner-school principals assert that many of their teachers are more consistent in applying best classroom practices since being influenced by partner-school involvement. These same principals often extend their reasoning to conclude that if they find increased teacher skill they will also find increased learning by those teachers' students; student teachers report in their written reflections, which are verified by field faculty records from direct observations, that cooperating teachers are giving their student teachers the freedom and even encouragement to implement the writing process, conceptual math, hands-on science, productive thinking, and cooperative learning patterns. If these methods are more effective in facilitating learning than having students fill out worksheets in passive, quiet isolation, then we have good reason to believe the quality of learning has been enhanced.

Communication Benefits beyond improved new teachers are apparent. The partnership in general, and partner-schools specifically, brought national recognition to the university (e.g. Goodlad, 1987; 1991). For example, third-party evaluators (Clark & Wilson, 1990) from the National Network for Educational Renewal (NNER) report: "The creation of 'partner-schools' (frequently referred to as professional development centers) is one of the most strongly advocated reforms in teacher preparation. Our visits to other universities and our conversations with teacher education specialists throughout the nation cause us to believe that it is a reform about which there is more talk than action. In the BYU partnership we observed a number of such partner-schools functioning in a more sophisticated fashion than many of the experts are able to describe in their imagining about what such institutions should be like."

School educators are also experiencing the intangible benefit of increased communication with the larger educational community. One school team ventured to establish a cross-grade, cross-aged organization for grouping students and employed an integrated, thematic structure to bring students in contact with the curriculum (Harris & Harris, 1992). In every way, this school's program breaks long-cherished traditions. Because of its partner-school status, the school sought and gained opportunity to present at a regional conference. In response to that presentation, numerous university and school educators from within and beyond the state have made site visits, made extended telephone conference calls, and sent letters of support to the district's central administration. The supportive communication has energized the team's spirits and gained greater encouragement from the district administration.

Empowerment Other intangible benefits are apparently accruing to school educators. They include increased ownership, empowerment, involvement, and satisfaction with their chosen work. Lofgreen's (1988) study verified that teacher efficacy had more support and strength in the ambience of a partner-school than in a control non-partner school. Johnson (1990) documents the isolation teachers experience and their search for collaboration with other educators. School educators at all levels report, and university people concur (Harris & Harris, 1991), that the partner-schools network within and among the four participating districts has made significant progress in solving the problem of teacher isolation.

IMPLICATIONS FOR TEACHER EDUCATION AND SCHOOLING

The application of normative economic principles to partnerships in education may provide the analytical and conceptual tools we need to determine net effect.

One strategy is to discover a "Pareto improvement." Vilfredo Pareto, an Italian economist, developed this concept of efficiency: Any change in resource allocation is considered a Pareto improvement if at least one person is better off from the change and no one is worse off (Musgrave & Musgrave, 1984; Tresch, 1981). In the case where there are "winners" and "losers," a Pareto improvement can still be realized if the winners can compensate the losers for their losses (Theobald, 1990). In this view, change that leads to Pareto improvement is more efficient and thus desirable. Judgements can be based on either of two questions: First, did some people benefit while no one was worse off? Second, were losers compensated by winners? The best scenario, of course, would be to find that all parties are better off and see themselves as winners. For this or any other partnership in education that includes schools and universities, what does the cost-benefits analysis reveal about winners and losers?

The Pareto improvement question takes on greater relevance when extended by a social justice dimension as developed by Rawls (1971). It measures the worth of change by the impact on the "primary goods" received by the least-advantaged individual or group. Primary goods are those that everyone finds important regardless of lifestyle (Strike, 1988). Worded differently, the social justice question is, "Does the water reach the end of the row?"

If we assume that students and teachers/professors are the least-advantaged individuals or groups in the two professional cultures, what does this cost-benefit study reveal about Pareto improvement and social justice for these groups? Guided by the Pareto improvement standard, university students and school students appear to be clear winners; schoolteachers and professors seem to be both winners and losers. No group seems to experience a neutral effect.

University Students

The intangible benefits to university students include: access to cooperating teachers who are high-quality models; frequent feedback from teacher/principal/professor teams; evaluation based on expectations aligned between the schools and university; and initiation into the professional culture by supportive, well-informed, growth-oriented practitioners (Baird, 1992). Tangible benefits to university students are manifest in the time-use study (see Table 1). Of the eleven ways in which school and university educators use their time, three—observations, consensus evaluation, and academies—focus on preparing preservice teachers for 44 percent of all time used.

School Students

Intangible benefits to school students result when young, talented, well-traveled, idealistic preservice teachers bring fresh enthusiasm and lesson material into their classrooms and learning experiences (see Figure 1). Practicing teachers frequently comment about the new thinking stimulated by a novice teacher fresh out of university courses. Practicing teachers use discretionary time, created when their student teacher is solo teaching, to develop new units, prepare new materials, or seek stimulation from in-service and site visits (Harris & Harris, 1993). With new energy and ideas, practicing teachers can then upgrade their curriculum to the further benefit of their students (Anderson, 1992). The tangible indicators suggest less emphasis in partner-schools on curriculum development that directly impacts school student activity than on university student work. Our study revealed that only 11 percent of school and university educators' time was directed at curriculum, compared with 44 percent at preservice preparation activity (see Table 1).

Teachers and Professors

Teachers and professors both win and lose. As intangibles, teachers and professors increased their ability and willingness to network and communicate, which has created an atmosphere of mutual respect. New thinking about how to reinvent teacher education and schooling has resulted as frequent interaction and serious dialogue have taken place over several years. School and university educators see their respective student groups benefiting from partner-schools work. They take satisfaction from seeing the progress and knowing that their professional efficacy and initiative have had much to do with the progress (see Figure 1). However, networking and communication have added pressure and taken time.

As tangibles, district councils, school councils, linking workshops, and partner-schools committee meetings, not to mention increased telephone calls and mailings, have accounted for 20 percent of all partner-school-related time use (see Table 1). This was 7,003 hours used by the 315 school and university educators that went for other activities before the partnership. Professors are still plagued with the challenge of balancing the labor-intensive work of mentoring preservice teachers along with the time consumed in driving from campus to the various partner-school sites. Only 11 percent of partner-school time is used in research pursuits. Field-based university faculty continue to fall short in the university expectations for scholarship, for example, gathering, analyzing, and writing up data. They face the challenge of integrating their teaching, research, and service within the partner-school model.

CONCLUSION

This study of costs and benefits in twenty-three partner-schools of a ten-year old university-school partnership has sought to explore the inner workings of one genre of partnerships in education. We have undertaken to define tangible and intangible costs and benefits for school and university educators and their respective institutions. The major tangible variables we studied were time, services, and facilities. The significant intangible variables were pressure, communication, control, educational quality, and empowerment. We discovered that the school's and university's relative investments when given dollar values are 62 percent and 38 percent, respectively, for one year's operation. When computed on a per partner-school basis, the dollar value invested by the university-school partnership is $32,502. Although the school's contribution is valued at 62 percent of the total, the university's share is eight times as great when computed on a per student basis (school = $68.87, university = $565.32).

Nearly all school and university participants agree that the work of reinventing teacher preparation and schooling has been an added load in tangible and intangible terms. However, most school and university educators agree that the benefits to their respective student groups and their own professional growth have compensated for the extra effort. Several new partner-schools have joined the partnership since this study was completed and the partnership has survived transitions through three department chairs, four college deans, two university central administrations, and new superintendents in all five participating school districts. These facts suggest that we "walk our talk." What is our work for the future? We must foster the forces that have resulted in wins for individuals and groups and address the patterns that have caused losses.

REFERENCES

Anderson, K. J. (1992). The partner-school effect in curriculum and instruction reform. Unpublished master's thesis, Brigham Young University, Provo, UT.

Arends, R. I. (1990). Connecting the university to the school. In Bruce Joyce (Ed.), *Changing school culture through staff development, 1990 ASCD Yearbook*. Alexandria, VA: Association for Supervision and Curriculum Development.

Baird, J. E. (1992). Survey of graduates from the Department of Elementary Education at Brigham Young University, 1991–92. Unpublished technical report. Department of Elementary Education, Brigham Young University, Provo, UT.

Bogdan, R. C., & Billen, S. K. (1982). *Qualitative research for education: An introduction to theory and methods*. Boston: Allyn & Bacon.

Carnegie Forum on Education and the Economy (1986). *A nation prepared: Teachers for the 21st century*. Report of the Task Force on Teaching as a Profession. NY: Carnegie Forum.

Clark, D. & Wilson, C. (1990). Interim report. Memorandum dated 22 May, 1990 to Joe Bishop, Executive Director of the BYU–Public School Partnership from Dick Clark and Carol Wilson, The National Network for Educational Renewal, 574 West Sixth Avenue, Denver, CO 80204.

Cochran-Smith, M. (1991). Reinventing student teaching. *Journal of Teacher Education, 42*(2), 104–118.

Erickson, F. (1986). Qualitative methods in research on teaching. In M.C. Wittrock (Ed.), *Handbook of research on teaching* (3rd ed., pp. 119–161). New York: Macmillan.

Geertz, C. (1973). Thick description: Toward an interpretive theory of culture. In C. Geertz (Ed.), *The interpretation of cultures* (pp. 3–30). New York: Basic.

Glaser, B. G., & Strauss, A. L. (1967). *The discovery of grounded theory: Strategies of qualitative research.* New York: Adline de Gruyter.

Goetz, J. P., & LeCompte, M. D. (1984). *Ethnography and qualitative design in educational research.* Orlando, FL: Academic Press.

Goodlad, J. I. (1984). *A place called school: Prospects for the future.* New York: McGraw-Hill.

Goodlad, J. I. (1986). Linking schools and universities: Symbiotic partnerships. Occasional Paper No. 1, Center for Educational Renewal. Seattle: College of Education, University of Washington.

Goodlad, J. I. (1987). Schools and universities can-and-must work together. *Principal, 24*(3), 9–14.

Goodlad, J. I. (1990). *Teachers for our nation's schools.* San Francisco: Jossey-Bass.

Goodlad, J. I. (1991). Why we need a complete redesign of teacher education. *Educational Leadership, 49*(3), 4–10.

Goodman, J. (1986). Making early field experience meaningful: A critical approach. *Journal of Education for Teachers, 12*(2), 109-125.

Harris, M. F., & Harris, R. C. (1992). Glasser comes to a rural school. *Educational Leadership, 50*(3), 18–21.

Harris, R. C., & Harris, M. F. (in press). Renewing teacher education and public schooling via university/school collaboration: A decade-long case study. *Contemporary Education.*

Harris, R. C., & Harris, M. F. (1993). Partner schools: Places to solve teacher preparation problems. *Action in Teacher Education, 14*(4), 1–8.

Harris, R. C., Baird, J. E., & Harris, M. F. (1993). Partner school effect on educational reform: A six-year longitudinal study. Paper presented at the annual meeting of the American Educational Research Association, April 12-16, Atlanta, GA.

Harris, R. C., & Harris, M. F. (1991). Symbiosis on trial in educational renewal. *Researcher, 7*(2), 15–27.

Harris, R. C., & Harris, M. F. (1992). Preparing teachers for literacy education: University-school collaboration. *Journal of Reading, 35*(7), 572–579.

Harris, R. C., Andersen, D., Argyle, S., Baird, J., Bloom, L., McDougal, B., & Billings, T. (1989). Teacher education in partner-schools: School/university collaboration in preservice, curriculum development, inservice, and research. The 1989 ATE Distinguished Program in Teacher Education Finalist presentation. 69th Annual Meeting of the Association of Teacher Educators, February 18–22, St. Louis.

Harris, R. C., May, D., & Argyle, S. (1987). Parent response to gifted programming. Unpublished raw data.

Holmes Group, (1986). *Tomorrow's teachers.* East Lansing, MI.: Holmes Group, Inc.

Johnson, S. M. (1990). *Teachers at work: Achieving success in our schools.* New York: Basic Books.

Kennedy, M. M. (1991). Policy issues in teacher education. *Phi Delta Kappan, 72*(9), 659-665.

Lieberman, A., ed., (1989). *Building professional cultures in schools.* New York: Teachers College Press.

Lofgreen, K. B. (1988). Teacher efficacy in a partner-school. Unpublished doctoral dissertation. Brigham Young University, Provo, UT.

Musgrave, R. A., & Musgrave, P. B. (1984). *Public finance in theory and practice* (fourth ed.). New York: McGraw-Hill.

NCATE (1991). *Brigham Young University, College of Education Institutional Report.* National Council for Accreditation of Teacher Education. Provo, UT.: Brigham Young University.

National Commission on Excellence in Education. (1983). *A Nation at Risk: The imperative for educational reform.* Washington, DC: U.S. Government Printing Office.

Rawls, J. (1971). *A theory of justice.* Cambridge, MA: Harvard University Press.

Roberts, C., Ingram, C., & Harris, R. C. (1992). The effects of special versus regular classroom programming on higher cognitive processes of intermediate elementary aged gifted and average ability students. *Journal of the Education of the Gifted, 15*(4), 332-343.

Strike, K. (1988). The ethics of resource allocation in education: Questions of democracy and justice. In D. H. Monk, & J. Underwoods (Eds.), *Microlevel school finance: Issues and implications for policy* (pp. 143–180). Cambridge, MA: Ballinger.

Theobald, N. D. (1990). Financing and governance of professional development or partner-schools. Occasional Paper No. 10. Center for Educational Renewal, University of Washington, Seattle, WA.

Tresch, R. W. (1981). *Public finance: A normative theory.* Plano, TX: Business Publications.

Williams, D. D. (1988). The Brigham Young University-Public School Partnership. In K. A. Sirotnik & J. I. Goodlad (Eds.) *School-University Partnerships in Action,* New York: Teachers College Press.

Yinger, R. J., & Hendricks, M. S. (1990). An overview of reform in Holmes Group institutions. *Journal of Teacher Education, 41*(2), 21-26.

Contexts: Implications and Reflections

D. JOHN MCINTYRE
Southern Illinois University

Research is meaningful to the practitioner when it comes alive, when it goes beyond numbers and statistical analysis and touches professional and personal lives. The three articles in this division bring life to the data by making the connections between the theoretical literature supporting partnerships/collaboration and the practice of partnerships/collaboration. The foreword to this division highlighted the characteristics and features of successful collaborative efforts. These articles address these characteristics using real examples and real people to tell their story. Although each of the authors utilized a different approach to the topic, several common strands are shared by each article. The major strands to be discussed in this section are: (1) the importance of voice to successful collaboration; (2) the transformation of roles; (3) the commitment of all partners; and (4) the potential for change through collaboration.

IMPORTANCE OF VOICE TO SUCCESSFUL COLLABORATION

The use of voice as a metaphor emerged through feminist literature in the '80s and has since been adopted to aid in understanding the context of schooling. Educators, such as Miller (1990), Britzman (1991), and Richert (1992), employed the metaphor of voice to indicate the "use of language to explain, describe, question, explore or challenge" (Richert, 1992, p. 189). Unfortunately, the teacher's voice has often been missing in many attempts to reform schooling and teacher education. Too often, change has been mandated from the district office or from the state legislature without any consideration of classroom professionals.

The emergence of teacher voice is a relatively new phenomenon. The rigid structure and hierarchy of schools and the educational community's reward system tend to isolate teachers from participating in any change effort or sharing their voices with each other. The inability to collaborate within a school creates a ceiling on how much teachers can learn from each other (Fullan & Hargreaves, 1991).

Fullan (1993) states that the ability to collaborate on a small and large scale has become essential in today's society. The theme of the works in this section supports the notion that collaboration is essential in today's schools, also. Dana's article, "Building Partnerships to Effect Educational Change: School Culture and the Finding of Teacher Voice," used an ethnographic approach to focus on the lack of teacher voice in efforts for educational change. Using the methods of collaborative action research, she collected and interpreted data through participant observation, interviewing, document analysis, and dialogue journals.

Dana's findings regarding collaboration at the school level support much that has been written elsewhere about this subject. Simply, the culture of the school silences teachers' voices. She found a school, much like others, where the physical context promoted seclusion and isolation. Each classroom was isolated from the others by four walls; each grade level was also isolated from the others. In addition, she discovered that when teachers did have an opportunity to interact, they elected to remain with others within their own grade level. This reinforces Iannacconne's (1964) thesis about school primary groups and how they form. However, Dana also found that although the teachers were comfortable with this compartmentalization, they were, at the same time, dissatisfied with this comfort.

Perhaps the most powerful element of Dana's article, as with most ethnographic studies, is the incorporation of the words or "voices" of Pam and Kit, two first-year teachers. In their own words, these two beginning teachers bring meaning and life to the research findings by describing the isolation, frustration, and anger experienced by novices. Kit's story is especially noteworthy because it describes the reactions of grade-level peers to a beginning teacher who questions the norm and existing school culture. In short, a teacher who challenges the norm tends to be greeted with alienation and growing isolation.

The article by White, Rainier, Clift and Benson, *School/University Partners in Research: The potential and the Problems,* also addresses the issue of teacher voice. Taking a different approach than Dana, the authors present four hypothetical vignettes that could confront partners in a collaborative research effort. At the conclusion of each vignette, two teachers, the university's program administrator and a university methods instructor discuss the contribution of the research to teacher education and raise concerns about potential consequences to the participants and the partnership.

This article shares the voices of professionals who bring varying perspectives to each situation. This is important to the notion of sharing voices in a partnership. In this instance, the partners (within and between roles) do not always agree. In a venture that lacks focus or a common set of goals, this disagreement could wreak havoc on the partnership. However, it is clear that all participants share a commitment to the collaborative project and that the voices, although they sometimes disagree, are still heard by others. It is when the voices are stifled or discarded, as with Dana's subjects, that discontent and dismembering of the partnership can occur.

White et al. also discuss the voices that are not heard within some partnerships. These are the voices that are affected by research within a partnership and include the students, their parents, university students, and others. The authors assert that failure to listen to these voices, as research is designed and findings reported, may antagonize these people. They believe that collaborative programs must include this diverse range of voices as research in and on the program is authorized, conducted, and monitored. This inclusion of all voices involved in the collaborative effort must extend beyond the research efforts and include all aspects of the partnerships. The key to any successful partnership is open, honest communication. This can happen only when all the voices are sought, listened to, and respected.

Utilizing the metaphor of voice to study and better understand the context of schooling is in its infancy in teacher education. However, it has the potential to be a powerful tool to educate prospective and experienced teachers about their environment and their relationship to it. Perhaps Richert (1992) states it best:

> Beyond affecting their ability to work effectively, however, is the issue of voice and living powerfully. Preparing teachers to exercise their voices prepares them to act with agency in their own lives. It is with an eye towards empowerment of that magnitude that I believe we must examine our work in teacher education. For it is towards the teacher who lives and works with agency that we will look for leadership and hope in the coming years of school change (p. 197).

Transformation of Roles

A second strand that emerges from the articles in this division is the transformation of roles that occurs within a collaborative partnership. These are the roles that we assume often evolve from the goals and functions peculiar to any particular institution. It has already been stated that the organizational values of schools and universities differ and, because of this difference, participants from these institutions have assumed certain expected roles that can bring them into conflict with their partners.

White et al. address this issue in Chapter 2. Their assessment of the University of Illinois' collaborative efforts with surrounding school districts highlights the notion that collaboration often leads to blurred role distinctions. Professors become classroom teachers. Classroom teachers become researchers. Professors become more concerned with the learning skills of K-12 pupils. Classroom teachers become more concerned with the preparation of teachers.

Harris and Harris' article, *University/School Partnerships: Exploring Tangible and Intangible Costs and Benefits,* also addresses the issue of redefining roles. The elementary schools working with Brigham Young University as partner schools developed task forces including the school principal, cooperating teachers, and university coordinator to collaborate on issues regarding preservice teacher education, staff development, curriculum development, and research and evaluation. Their data indicate that the professionals working in the partner schools spend many hours in roles that are nontraditional for their job assignment. For example, professors spend many hours working in the school with teachers dealing with issues relevant to the elementary classroom. Although this might be expected of any professional in the field of education, it belies the image of the professor working on a college campus isolated from the real world.

This integration of roles can lead to a reconceptualization of the traditional school classroom and of the traditional teacher-education program. Whether these efforts lead to varying versions of professional development schools or not, the merging of the classroom teacher's and the professor's roles will force us to rethink how we approach the organization—both structurally and fiscally—of schools and teacher-education programs, how we define and assess the responsibilities of the professionals within each institution, and—for teacher educators—how we define our profession.

Although White et al. bring this issue to the reader's attention, it would have been interesting to have more information concerning these "blurred role distinctions." Future research regarding collaborative efforts might examine the transformation of roles within these partnerships. How do the participants perceive this transformation? Do participants from the different institutions perceive the transformation equally? Is there a relationship between commitment and transformation? How do the administrators of the various institutions perceive this transformation? The answers to these research questions would contribute to a better understanding of collaborative efforts and might quicken the transformation of our profession.

Commitment of All Partners

The third common strand among the three articles is the commitment of all partners necessary for a collaborative effort to meet its goals. The responses to the vignettes included in the White et al. article indicate that the authors are committed to this collaborative effort. In several cases, respondents reiterate their commitment to teacher education and the collaborative effort of the university and the school districts. Their responses reveal a sense of what is good for the partnership and what is good for the individuals within the partnership.

Commitment can also be measured by the resources devoted to the collaborative effort. White et al. discuss the commitment of time for those individuals involved in the partnership. University faculty have the opportunity to teach on an instructional team, serve on an advisory committee, conduct action research, and present papers at professional meetings as well as teach regular classes on campus. The article does not address the university's reward system and how it rewards the effort a university faculty expends to further the partnership.

Classroom teachers have the opportunity to serve as a cooperating teacher to as many as three university students during a school year, teach on an instructional team, serve on an advisory commitee, conduct research, present papers at professional meetings, etc. Time devoted to the partnership is in addition to teaching pupils within their classrooms. The article does not indicate what compensation, if any, is afforded to the classroom teacher for the time committed to the partnership. The university reward system and the compensation of teachers are important factors to consider. If no reward exists for the effort, other than internal and professional satisfaction, commitment may lessen.

Harris and Harris deal with the issue of resource commitment in a unique approach: examining the contributions of the school and university partners in actual dollars. Their data indicate that on a per partner-school basis, the dollar value invested by the university-school partnership is $32,502. A true partnership should require sharing resources on an equal basis. The Brigham Young–Partner School Program is a good example of collaboration of resources. For example: the schools use university meeting space at no cost; university vans transport teachers to state and regional conferences; university faculty use school classrooms for instruction; university faculty use school phones, copying machines, etc.

Harris and Harris' study can serve as a model for other reseachers interested in actual cost commitment to a collaborative teacher-education partnership. The authors provide a framework for estimating costs and benefits for the university and participating schools in terms of tangible variables: time, services, and facilities; and in terms of intangible variables: pressure, communication, control, educational quality, and empowerment. Figure 1, in particular, is extremely useful for highlighting the costs and benefits of school-university partnerships. In this day of limited budgets, the Harris and Harris study provides a starting point for moving a discussion of potential costs from rhetoric to facts.

THE POTENTIAL FOR CHANGE THROUGH COLLABORATION

The potential for change through collaboration is the final common strand that is woven through these three chapters. Fullan (1993) implies that teacher education programs must begin to reconceptualize the moral purpose of teaching as a change theme. He believes that the new standard for the future is that every teacher must strive to become effective at managing change. However, the three articles and the related literature illustrate that teachers cannot become change agents if the current school culture of seclusion and isolation remains the dominant theme. Dana asserts that during her project, it became obvious that teacher change and school change were intricately intertwined with the development of an acknowledgement of teacher voice. If collaboration can encourage change by empowering teachers and teacher educators, by transforming traditional education roles and by renewing educators' commitment, then teachers and teacher educators are more likely to view themselves as change agents. If this occurs, then K–12 students and teacher-education students will benefit.

White et al. discuss the political ramifications of true collaborative efforts by raising the issue that school-university partnerships bring together institutions that often have divergent points of view. The diversity enriches the partnership but also introduces its true strength and fragility. Different parties now have a vested interest in program goals, design, implementation, and assessment. The authors highlight the need for developing strategies that facilitate communication and respect for divergent points of view. However, White et al. point out that it is this dialogue between partners—sometimes with different frames of reference—that facilitates "the sharing of experiences, knowledge, and passion" that eventually leads to encouraging the social and intellectual growth of students. In other words, it is the diversity of viewpoints shared in an environment of respect, trust, and commitment that brings about change in a collaborative schools-university endeavor.

Both Dana and White et al. incorporate research as a focus of their chapters. Dana describes a collaborative action-research project that focused on reconceptualizing the faculty meetings at an elementary school to encourage cross-level small group discussion of professional issues. She discovered that through small and large group discussions at faculty meetings, a changing school culture began to emerge. What began as a collaborative research project in an elementary school resulted in the beginning of change in the traditional school milieu.

White et al. encourage more collaborative school research efforts that include professionals from schools and universities. These collaborative efforts heighten the opportunity to transform traditional educator roles as teachers begin to assume the role of researcher. Hattrup and Bickel (1993) describe the initial difficulty of bridging the gap between teacher and researcher that is encountered when initiating a collaborative research project. Teachers live in a world that is tightly constrained by a schedule and have little time for reflective thought on classroom activities. Researchers, on the other hand, operate in highly flexible environments and can devote time to peer interaction and self-reflection. What emerged, however, was a new understanding and transforming of each other's roles and, for the teachers, a new sense of empowerment that was lacking before the collaborative effort. Oja and Pine (1987) also discuss the implementation of collaborative action-research groups as a vehicle for contributing to educational theory and practice and improving the relationship between schools and university.

SUMMARY

The chapters reviewed in this section reveal that true collaborative efforts between schools and universities are the foundation for reform and change in schooling and in teacher education. If the goal is the improvement of learning for all students, then both institutions must commit their resources toward this endeavor in a partnership committed to changing existing practices. These papers indicate that collaboration is a complex endeavor that requires commitment of staff, resources, and funding. Most of all, it requires a commitment of the soul! We must work together so that every beginning teacher is fully prepared for the first day in the classroom, so that every child has an equal opportunity to learn and so that the stories of Pam and Kit become obsolete.

REFERENCES

Britzman, D. (1991). *Practice makes practice: A critical study of learning to teach.* Albany, NY: State University of New York Press.

Fullan, M. (1993). Why teachers must become change agents. *Educational Leadership, 50*(6), 12–17.

Fullan, M. & Hargreaves, A. (1991). *What's worth fighting for in schools?* Toronto: Ontario Public School Teachers' Federation; Andover, MA: The Network; Buckingham, UK: Open University Press; Melbourne, Australia: Australian Council of Educational Administration.

Hattrup, R. & Bickel. (1993). Teacher-researcher collaboration: Reliving the tensions. *Educational Leadership, 50*(6), 38–40.

Iannacconne, L. (1964). An approach to the informal organization of the school. In D. E. Griffiths, ed., *Behavioral Science and Educational Administration, The Sixty-Third Yearbook of the National Society for the Study of Education, Part II.* Chicago, IL: University of Chicago Press.

Miller, J. (1990). *Creating spaces and finding voices: Teachers collaborating for empowerment.* Albany, NY: State University of New York Press.

Oja, S. & Pine, G. (1987). Collaborative action research. *Peabody Journal of Education, 64*(1), 96–113.

Richert, A. (1992). Voice and power in teaching and learning to teach. In L. Valli, ed. *Reflective teacher education: Cases and critiques* (pp. 187–197). Albany, NY: State University of New York Press.

Partnerships in the Laboratory and Clinical Preparation of Teachers

---

Teacher Preparation: Overview and Framework

KENNETH R. HOWEY
The Ohio State University

KEN HOWEY is Professor of Teacher Education and former Director of the Center for Collaborative Studies in Teacher Education at The Ohio State University. He is the primary investigator in the ongoing Research About Teacher Education (RATE) Study, now in its ninth year. He has written more than 100 publications concerned with the education of teachers at all phases of their careers.

THE PROBLEM

Our problem in teacher education is not only preparing teachers better but preparing teachers who can and will teach *all* children well. How we prepare these teachers, especially in laboratory and clinical settings during initial teacher preparation and into the first years of teaching, is the subject of this introduction to the following three chapters.

Why teachers for *all* children? The days of "Dick and Jane," the two-child nuclear family nestled cozily in a comfortable home framed by a white picket fence, are as distant a reality for millions of youngsters in this country as are their academic success and social development in school. The percentage of youngsters who tragically live in conditions characterized by deprivation in the United States is *increasing* not decreasing. The large number of youngsters failing and dropping out of school is simply unacceptable. And how is this unacceptable situation being combatted? The annual Research About Teacher Education Study (1991) clearly shows graduating teachers are mostly white, monolingual, and unfamiliar with these conditions. Studies further reveal that our prospective teachers neither believe that they are prepared to teach youngsters in such settings nor do they desire to do so (Howey, 1989). Their view, usually from a distance, of youngsters tangled in a web of poverty is captured by the comments of a preservice teacher in the Holm and Johnson chapter (1984): "I don't want to teach in those classrooms because there would be: . . . a lack of respect of authority . . . they wouldn't do what you want them to do . . . they wouldn't be able to concentrate because they wouldn't be eating right . . . they could fall behind."

This viewpoint clearly signals major changes that need to be made in terms of teacher education. This prospective teacher reveals much both about her beliefs about inner-city youngsters and how they learn (or, from her perspective, don't learn) and her beliefs about teaching. Beliefs guide action and this novice teacher holds stereotypical beliefs very limiting to her ability, as a teacher, to help others.

HOW DOES ONE LEARN TO TEACH?

One of the major factors differentiating more experienced from less experienced, preservice, or beginning teachers is the nature of their beliefs about schools, teaching, and learning (Livingston and Borko, 1989). It is essential that from the outset of their preparation, the beliefs of prospective teachers are examined and confronted and not in a sterile, one time, manner but rather as an ongoing supportive and educative activity that serves as the cornerstone of learning to teach. Beliefs about learners and learning and corresponding decisions about teaching need to be made explicit, publicly shared and defended, and with more than personal opinion.

The image of teaching that this novice conveys is that of an authoritarian, teacher-directed classroom with youngsters in highly competitive situations wherein some fall further and further behind in a curriculum in which content is "covered" and time for learning is held constant. Her views of constraints to student success contradict the inherent potential for most everyone to succeed academically with appropriate instruction. A contemporary conception of teaching—which views learning as active, largely self-directed, and responsive to and for group norms that enable learning from one another for everyone's academic and social success—appears foreign to this student.

Similarly foreign is a conception that *learning to teach* itself is a highly *intellectual* activity, data based, and continually oriented to moral considerations. One simply cannot infer the essence of quality teaching by observing others teach—although certain habits of civility or lack thereof are likely incorporated in this way. Nor does one learn to instruct primarily by the opportunities for repeating specific teaching methods—unless one embraces a basically technical and narrow view of teaching. Rather the cornerstone of learning to teach is acquiring the abilities and disposition to critically analyze teaching/learning episodes to make public the tacit thinking and feeling of both teachers and students. One learns to teach through sustained, structured discourse on the "whys" and "so whats" of teaching and learning, as well as the "hows" of this complicated endeavor.

First, the novice teacher needs to observe and *hear* the veteran teachers (and professors) explain and justify their teaching as they interact with students. Then, over time, as these prospective teachers examine and publicly defend their own teaching, they will draw on richer and more defensible sources to explain, justify, and guide their teaching. Surely teaching should *not* be a basically unexamined activity concentrated largely upon the dispensation of knowledge. Similarly, learning to teach, whether in well-conceived laboratory and clinical settings or in school-based contexts, need *not* be and should *not* be receiving episodic feedback about overt teacher "performance" and whether it coincides with "conventional wisdom" or teaching tactics that are "research" based. Nonetheless, normative practice in the "supervision" of preservice and beginning teachers tends to focus on teachers' observable behaviors. Supervisory "conferences" do not tend to focus on teachers' beliefs, assumptions, and intentionalities and certainly not on the reasoning and perceptions of the primary participants in these endeavors—the pupils themselves. Given the distance between where we are and where we have to go in clinical preparation, the following three chapters in this text provide clues to a bolder, more contemporary, and more *potent* form of clinical preparation for teachers.

But first allow me to return to the major point here, unless major changes are made in how we prepare teachers to deal effectively with complexity and plurality in schools, a problem of major proportions in this society will continue. Redressing this problem is obviously not simple and surely it involves more than placing prospective teachers too quickly and too extendedly in elementary and secondary schools under dubious supervision.

Such practices tend to deter rather than attract high-quality preservice teachers to teaching. Considerably improved and quite different preparation is needed for novice teachers to succeed in difficult-to-teach-in settings and this preparation involves a more thoughtful developmental sequence of laboratory and clinical preparation as one would expect in *professional* training.

PRESERVICE TEACHER PREPARATION AT PRESENT

Preservice teachers graduating from present programs of teacher preparation prefer to teach in the suburban and smaller communities from which they most often matriculate. Much of their reluctance to teach at-risk youngsters, I believe, can be traced to the abbreviated nature of their teacher preparation, especially contrasted with other professional training. Frankly, these novices typically have not been able to develop a repertoire of teaching abilities and understandings, tested and personally defended, that allows them to take on the multiple challenges of urban classrooms.

At this time, the "clinical" preparation of teachers can be characterized as anemic. It is typically compressed into 10 to 15 weeks of "student teaching," 400–500 total hours with wide variations in quality control and the school context in which it is pursued. One need not compare this to other *professional* training to underscore the inadequacies of such practice as Gideonese (1986) underscores:

> Let us look at a real apprenticeship program. I would guess it will come as a surprise to many (as it did to me) that electricians in apprenticeship programs in Cincinnati spend more hours (660 as compared to 510) in class instruction than University of Cincinnati secondary education students do in the didactic portion of their secondary professional training program, which is half again as extensive as the average program nationally. Furthermore, the apprentice electricians spend a full 8000 clinical hours under the direct supervision of journeymen electricians, nearly 27 times the equivalent clinical experience in student teaching! Moreover, no journeyman may ever assume responsibility for more than a single apprentice. The ratio never exceeds 1:1! Such analytical comparisons may not be wholly fair. But they are certainly provocative! (p. 194)

Is it any wonder then that many teachers leave the classroom within three years, especially when assigned to more demanding assignments? *Laboratory* preparation to lay the foundation for acquiring a range of teaching skills is largely non-existent in current teacher preparation. No one would expect a physician to begin her or his diagnostic training while working with patients. No one would dream of boarding a plane where the pilot was in her first week of "practice" flying. No one would expect an attorney "to practice" in a courtroom. Yet, beginning teachers are largely left to learn to teach in classrooms after a very abbreviated apprenticeship or "student" teaching which too often incorporates few of the practices that recent research reveals are needed to learn to teach well. Thus, learning to teach reduces itself to trial and error for many teachers.

Complex teacher reasoning demands more complex teacher preparation as it embraces many abilities. For example, learning to teach calls for the *continuing diagnosis* of a wide range of problems, not only academic but social and often highly emotional as well. Learning to teach also calls for the deep understanding of powerful concepts from multiple disciplines as a *prerequisite* to representing these concepts in multiple ways for others. Initially at least, learning to teach calls not so much for interactive teaching skills as diagnostic abilities—the ability to critically examine the nature of teaching and learning, especially that of accomplished teachers and their learners; a precondition for gaining insights into the complexities and subtleties of teaching before instructing others. This inquiry into their own practices is for understanding and developing increasingly defensible reasons for their conduct as teachers. This ability is referred to as teacher pedagogical reasoning. Learning to become a highly skilled teacher demands opportunities to inquire, reflect, analyze, and practice in *laboratory* and *clinical* settings initially: in settings conducive to analysis and teacher *preparation*.

In spite of this need schools and colleges of education everywhere are characterized by conventional classrooms, lecture, and discussion, followed by uneven and abbreviated apprenticeships in schools. When one examines the limited fiscal support for teacher preparation across the country, especially laboratory and clinical preparation vis-a-vis those provided in other professions, many problems in elementary and secondary schools can be attributed to the truism "that you get what you pay for," at least in terms of how teachers are prepared.

One can argue with some persuasion that teacher education, and much of elementary and secondary teaching for that matter, missed much of the 20th century in terms of employing technologies that can enable learning. When prospective teachers are asked about what they believe teaching to be, they typically view it in terms of *how* they have been taught during more than 12 years. The beliefs of the teacher quoted at the outset are somewhat understandable, if not defensible. This is to say that teaching today remains primarily talking, with the chalkboard and the textbook serving as pervasive teaching aides (Howey, 1988).

AN ALTERED ROLE FOR PRESERVICE TEACHER EDUCATION

From this perspective, teacher educators such as myself have a responsibility to exemplify a broader and more powerful range of instructional activities and teaching approaches in the preparation of teachers on our *campuses* than witnessed currently. I submit that the seeds for the disposition to continuously inquire into one's instructional practice and to support that practice with principled reasoning—with decisions that are data-based, theoretically grounded, and morally oriented—need to be nurtured in pedagogical laboratories and teaching clinics and through the utilization of instructional cases in a campus setting if these practices are eventually to become habits in the more complex, frenetic classroom.

For example, our prospective teachers should view dozens of hours of video representing both principles that guide the teaching profession and the pervasive problems encountered. They should examine teaching and learning episodes from the vantage point of and with the concomitant conceptual lenses provided by the psycholinguist, political scientist, social psychologist, cognitive scientist, and cultural anthropologist as well as the classroom teacher, student, and parent. These multiple perspectives brought to bear on video representations of teaching and learning in a laboratory setting lead to informed *professional* judgment. Taking on critical, multiple perspectives of teaching and learning demonstrates applied research and vividly illustrates the scholarly bases for separating these judgments from conventional wisdom. What a physician sees, and *why,* is vastly different than what the layperson observes, even in cursory examinations. Similarly, what a teacher sees and *why* should be very different than what the layperson observes in teaching/learning episodes.

Again, preservice teachers should be able to engage in these preparatory activities in which complex phenomena can be represented from multiple perspectives, through several media, and at a time and in a manner conducive to learning. They should be able to inquire critically in a setting and at a pace that fosters such activity. At present, critical examination of instructional practice is neither fostered well in the lecture hall nor the teacher's workplace. This is hardly to say that preparation in the workplace is not critical; of course it is. The position here is that we need to be much better prepared as teachers prior to activities for learning on the job.

I would further argue that until we can send larger numbers of teachers into the workplace better *disposed* and *able* to undertake critical examination of their practice, we won't substantially change the character and culture of that workplace.

THE INTERSECTION WITH SCHOOL REFORM

It is both arrogant and irresponsible for those of us in teacher education to call for major alterations in teaching and learning without altering many of our instructional practices. We cannot with any credibility exhort changes in schools from the distance of the lecture hall or the printed page. Enlightened and contemporary views of teaching and learning to teach over time *intersect* in a major way with school reform; thus we have a major obligation as well to school reform. Let's look at a couple of examples. We have underestimated the challenge of preparing teachers well. Thus, it appears that preservice preparation increasingly will extend into the first years of teaching and in the context of K–12 schools. The preservice preparation of teachers as now constructed simply is less potent than many assume it to be, especially in terms of the ability of graduating teachers to teach in schools with diverse student populations or with youngsters whose home environment is characterized by poverty (Research About Teacher Education Studies [RATE], 1989). It is increasingly clear that teachers learn a very considerable amount about teaching in the first one to four years of teaching, especially if prepared for how to continue learning. Until now we have considerably underestimated this critical period in terms of the education of teachers and hence have done little planning for it. In the decade ahead, however, this period of time will—or at least should—become a focus in teacher education or learning to teach. This period of time also represents the time and distance between the concept of initial teacher *licensure*—likely deferred in the future—and the concept of advanced teacher *certification,* especially as the latter concept is being aggressively advanced by the National Board for Professional Teaching Standards.

As a second example of our responsibility to elementary and secondary schools, we could cite a convergence of studies underscoring that much of the *continuing* professional development of teachers throughout their careers should be deeply embedded in a school context wherein teaching and learning are characterized by experimentation, systematic inquiry, and the intellectual discourse. Teachers in such a school culture could then indeed be described as part of a "learning community."

With the need to extend initial preparation more systematically and more fully into early years of teaching and to embed much of continuing professional development for all teachers more naturally into ongoing school activities, it is difficult to uncouple conditions needed for learning to teach from school restructuring for better teaching and learning. In this regard and, in summary, this protracted teacher preparation into the early years of teaching is indeed the *shared* responsibility of campus-based teacher educators with those in K-12 schools. As the following chapters address the clinical preparation of preservice and beginning teachers, I would ask the reader to bear in mind the caveats put forward here and the relationships drawn.

THREE RESEARCH REPORTS

What follows is a set of three chapters that address partnerships in clinical settings. The first study focuses on the readiness of preservice teachers to shape cultural partnerships with and between the children in their classrooms.

The second study uses data provided by preservice student teachers to develop a typology of five cooperating teacher-student teacher relationships. The third chapter reports survey data from a longitudinal study of traditional and nontraditional students beginning their first year of teaching.

REFERENCES

Gideonese, H. D. (1986). Guiding images for teaching and teacher education. In T. J. Lasley (Ed.). The dynamics of changes in teacher education (pp. 187–198). Washington, D.C.: American Association for Colleges for Teacher Education.

Holm, G. & Johnson, L. N. (1994). Shaping cultural partnerships: The readiness of preservice teachers to teach in culturally diverse classrooms. In M. O'Hair & S. Odell (Eds.). Partnerships in education. Fort Worth: Harcourt Brace & Company.

Howey, K. R. (1989). Research about teacher preparation. *Journal of Teacher Education,* 40, pp. 23–27.

Howey, K. R. (1988). Why teacher leadership? *Journal of Teacher Education,* 39, pp. 28–31.

Livingston, C. & Borko, H. (1989). Expert-novice differences in teaching: A cognitive analysis and implications for teacher education. *Journal of Teacher Education,* 40, pp. 36–42.

RATE III (1989). Teaching teachers: Facts and figures. Washington, D.C.: American Association of Colleges for Teacher Education.

RATE V (1991). Teaching teachers: Facts and figures. Washington, D.C.: American Association of Colleges for Teacher Education.

CHAPTER 4

Shaping Cultural Partnerships: The Readiness of Preservice Teachers to Teach in Culturally Diverse Classrooms

GUNILLA HOLM
LYNN NATIONS JOHNSON
Western Michigan University

DR. HOLM is a sociologist of education. She teaches courses on the social context of schooling, ethnographic research methods, and multicultural education. Her current research focuses on at-risk students, popular culture, and girlhood.

DR. NATIONS JOHNSON is formally prepared in curriculum development and the study of schooling. She teaches courses on social studies methods, multicultural education, dialogic teaching, and middle school education. Her current research focuses on dialogic teaching and the development of multicultural perspective.

ABSTRACT

This chapter reports the results of a study conducted to identify the readiness of preservice teachers to shape cultural partnerships with and between the children in their classrooms. Twelve preservice teachers were interviewed about their life experiences as children, as students in the university, and as preservice teachers. The interviews focused specifically on the cultural experiences each person had had and what they identified as necessary in their multicultural preparation. The interviews were audiotaped, transcribed, and coded for patterns of response to the interview themes. Three of the most prominent results of the study revealed: 1) that the preservice teachers each had a keen desire to become multiculturalists; 2) that the preservice teachers were seriously underprepared to shape cultural partnerships; 3) that the preservice teachers identified two kinds of experience that they valued as critical components in their multicultural preparation but found deficient in their program of study: carefully guided participation with model teachers who have particular facility in their work with diverse student populations, and multicultural course work that is tied to participation experiences.

SHAPING CULTURAL PARTNERSHIPS: THE READINESS OF PRESERVICE TEACHERS TO TEACH IN CULTURALLY DIVERSE CLASSROOMS

Multicultural education is a controversial subject. Because it is in the process of definition, the field is in flux, as different interest groups vie for recognition and equitable representation. Multicultural education is currently in great demand throughout most regions of the nation and has brought hope and focus to those serving culturally diverse populations. The interest and concern of teachers, parents, and politicians regarding multicultural education is well warranted, considering the current and projected demographic complexity of the United States.

The demographic trends in education clearly show that the majority of teachers will be required to teach an increasingly heterogeneous student population. Conversely, the teacher pool is becoming increasingly homogeneous (Grant & Secada, 1990). "In 1986 while only 10.4 percent of public school teachers were Black, Hispanic, Asian-American/Pacific Islander, or American Indian/Alaskan Natives, 89.6 percent of our public school students came from these backgrounds" (Paine, 1990, p. 2). Additionally, as large numbers of teachers approach retirement, the proportion of women who are entering and graduating from teacher education programs is becoming larger, resulting in an even more feminized teacher corps (Center for Education Statistics, 1987).

At present our nation's population is more than 80 percent white, of European descent, with 12 percent African-American, 6.4 percent Hispanic, and 1.6 percent Asian (Nieto, 1992). By the year 2000, students from microcultural backgrounds will constitute between 30 and 40 percent of the school population (Hodgkinson, 1985). By the year 2050, demographers anticipate that the white population will decrease to approximately 60 percent, the black community will increase slightly, the Asian population will increase tenfold, and the number of Hispanics will triple. "By the last quarter of the next century, those who are now referred to as 'minority' are expected to be the majority" (Nieto, 1992, p. 6). In a related vein, between 20 percent and 25 percent (depending on their age) of this nation's children live in poverty (Reed & Sautter, 1990). This percentage is even higher among children from microcultural groups. And educationally speaking, a high percentage of these students are at risk of dropping out (Gage, 1990).

In response to these demographic data, the field of multicultural education has expanded rapidly. Researchers have identified and examined critical issues that are important to the future of our diverse students. In particular, research has shown that when teachers have effectively utilized their knowledge about the diverse cultural backgrounds of their students, the teachers' expectations of their students have changed, and the students' academic achievement has increased (Moll & Diaz, 1987; Trueba, 1989; Vogt, Jordan, & Tharp, 1987).

In this chapter, this effective use of one's cultural knowledge is referred to as *shaping cultural partnerships*. The meaning of the word *partnership* has particularly strong cultural application. A partnership is a condition in which "one . . . has a share or part with another or others; one . . . is associated with another or others in the enjoyment or possession of anything" and one is "a partaker, sharer" (Oxford English Dictionary, 1991, p. 278). Therefore, when teachers thoughtfully shape cultural partnerships, students and teachers share their cultures and are associated with one another in the enjoyment and possession of their shared knowledge and experience. They become both partakers and sharers of culture. Cultural partnerships are relationships that grow from, and are nourished by, the integration of two crucial cultural elements: people's knowledge of one another's cultural background with pluralism in both belief and practice. Conversely, cultural partnerships are weakened and eventually succumb in the absence of pluralism and/or in the presence of cultural ignorance and bigotry.

The role of teachers in promoting cultural partnerships in schools is pivotal. The fertile environment in which cultural partnerships grow and mature is one in which a teacher:

1. Has knowledge of the diverse cultures s/he serves
2. Is committed to pluralism in belief and practice
3. Thoughtfully shapes a classroom environment that:
    A. Fosters respect, trust, confidence
    B. Cultivates critical thought
    C. Affirms diversity
    D. Encourages solidarity

E.   Provides avenues for constructive criticism and conflict resolution within, across, and between cultures (Nieto, 1992).

This kind of environment allows young people to flourish in their development and to become thoughtful, contributing members of their primary cultures and of the larger society.

Cultural partnerships with and between children are particularly fragile, given the nascent character of youth. At the same time, this nascency allows for rapid growth and development of cultural partnerships. Long-term sustenance for the maturing of these cultural partnerships then becomes a critical factor, that is, a cultural partnership will not mature should the environment become hostile. The role of the teacher in promoting a classroom environment that sustains the maturation of cultural partnerships is pivotal as well, recognizing: 1) that what has been learned can be unlearned when necessary social and cognitive nourishment is withdrawn or withheld; and 2) that the social reverberations that occur when cultural partnerships disintegrate are far-reaching.

OBJECTIVES

The study described herein was conducted with a focus on this pivotal role of the teacher as cultural caretaker. The researchers examined how prepared preservice teachers are to shape cultural partnerships with and between their students. In particular, we focused our attention on their life experiences with regard to cultural diversity and how their life experiences molded their current views and promoted their preparation, or lack thereof, to shape cultural partnerships. The examination has proceeded in light of an explicit university commitment to cultural diversity.

THE CULTURAL BELIEFS AND LEARNING OF PRESERVICE TEACHERS

Educational and multicultural researchers have identified crucial cultural belief and learning patterns among preservice teachers.[1] Five of these patterns were central in shaping the objectives of this study:

---

1   It is important to recall that the cultural background of the teacher population in the United States is becoming increasingly homogeneous, that is white, of European descent. Approximately 89.6 percent of our teacher population fits this description, while only 10.4 percent does not. (See page 84.) The preservice teacher population in the university where the data for this research were collected followed the same pattern. (See pages 87–88.)

1. Preservice teachers show a resistance to recognizing and rejecting their stereotyped cultural beliefs; especially resistant to change are perceptions regarding African Americans (Baker, 1973).
2. Preservice teachers tend to avoid issues related to cultural diversity; instead, they individualize differences and focus on problems with skill-related needs rather than issues of race/ethnicity, class, and gender (Grant & Koskela, 1986).
3. Preservice teachers tend to lean on their earlier experiences as schoolchildren in dealing with cultural issues, even though in most cases their experiences were in all white classrooms (McDiarmid & Price, 1993).
4. Preservice teachers often consider categorical differences, such as ethnic and racial dissimilarities, as problematic and as a "potential barrier to learning" (Irvine, 1985).
5. Few preservice teachers consider cultural diversity as a positive aspect in the classroom.

These five patterns provide clear cause for concern. Not only are cultural ambivalence and ignorance common among preservice teachers, but their ability and/or willingness to confront their cultural misconceptions is nil. Adding to this already problematic picture are the related patterns that researchers have found in the higher education system:

1. Preservice teachers rarely have opportunities to expose and explore their own beliefs and attitudes in their teacher education courses or field experiences (McDiarmid & Price, 1993).
2. Multicultural education is included in field experiences only when it is promoted by someone in charge (Grant & Koskela, 1986).
3. Preservice teachers are frequently exposed to increasing amounts of information, which in itself does not affect them seriously (McDiarmid, 1989). In fact, what is learned at the university engages students at an intellectual level but does not enable them to transfer the information to their subsequent classroom practice (Davidman, 1990; Grant & Koskela, 1986).

Given these current realities, a close examination of the cultural beliefs and concerns of the preservice teachers participating in this study was undertaken. The rationale framing the research purports that if teacher education seeks to eliminate cultural inequality in the schools, we must understand the societal forces that have shaped the current cultural beliefs of preservice teachers; how preservice teachers view those beliefs within the context of multicultural education; and what they identify as necessary in reforming their cultural beliefs and practices as they prepare to shape cultural partnerships in their classrooms.

DESCRIPTION OF THE UNIVERSITY, THE EDUCATION PROGRAM, AND THE STUDENTS

The study was conducted in a large midwestern state university with a seven percent minority population. The teacher education program has an even smaller minority population of five percent. As of the 1991–92 academic year, 52 percent of the undergraduate population was female and 48 percent was male. According to the university mission statement in 1990, the university is committed to cultural diversity. One of the educational goals, according to the university's undergraduate catalog, is to help structure student learning so that students can appreciate and understand the significance and ramifications of our diverse cultural and ethnic heritage. However, these consequences are not specified.

The university committee on cultural diversity and access focuses almost exclusively on race and marginally on ethnicity and gender in its report on cultural diversity. As stated in this report, the university has increased minority enrollment in the '80s and has instituted a variety of programs ranging from orientation sessions on multicultural awareness to scholarships for minorities. Social class was not considered as part of cultural diversity in this report, although there is evidence that schools do not adequately prepare the impoverished for college (Kozol, 1991; Rose, 1990).

The teacher education program at the university follows the NCATE standards and requirements. According to NCATE (1990, p. 62) cultural diversity is defined as referring "to the cultural backgrounds of students and school personnel, including their ethnicity, race, religion, class and sex. In the NCATE review, particular attention to race and sex is expected." No explanation is given as to why attention to social class is not expected. Following the NCATE guidelines, the teacher education program asserts that the study of culturally diverse and exceptional populations is infused throughout the curriculum. Through a wide variety of observations and participation in schools as part of the teacher education program, students are also given pedagogical knowledge about how to teach culturally diverse students. According to these documents, preservice students should have at least some exposure to multiculturalism during their undergraduate studies.

The education program at the university provides some formal coursework that includes multicultural education and related topics. For those enrolled in the elementary education program, a required course has been designed that includes the study of culture and multicultural education. For those enrolled in secondary education, there is not a required course that focuses on multicultural education; however, the study of schools in society and related social and cultural issues are the primary focus of a course required for all education students. In addition, all education students are required to take a course in women's studies, an effort to focus on gender as culture and sexism. There are a number of elective courses available on campus that focus on subjects such as race/ethnicity, class, and gender, but these are courses that education students would need to take beyond their regular course requirements. There are no required or elective multicultural education courses directly linked to a field experience.

THE RESEARCH POPULATION AND METHODS

The study centers on in-depth interviews with a sample of preservice teachers. An announcement soliciting volunteers for interviews about cultural diversity and multicultural education was distributed through the university preservice teacher coordinators. Twelve preservice teachers volunteered to participate and were interviewed during their student teaching semester, either winter or fall 1990. The sample consisted of eight preservice teachers of white, European descent and four preservice teachers of African-American descent. During these two semesters there were no preservice teachers from Asian, Hispanic, or Native American backgrounds. Three of the participants were male, nine were female.[2] Eleven participants were from middle-class backgrounds, one was from a working-class background. Half of the interviewees were traditional students (ages twenty-one to twenty-five) and the other half were nontraditional students (ages twenty-five and up). They grew up in a variety of settings ranging from rural to city neighborhoods.

The participants in this study were doing their student teaching in diverse settings: in elementary schools, middle schools, and high schools; in urban and suburban areas; in predominantly white classrooms, and in classrooms with a 6:4 majority to minority population ratio. The diversity of this population in terms of cultural background, that is, gender, age, race, and geographic root, as well as the variety of school settings in which they were teaching, provided a potentially rich diversity of perspective.

Each interview lasted approximately one and one-half hours. Interview themes included: the life experiences of the preservice teachers as they related

---

2   It is important to recall the increased feminization of the teacher work force when examining this 3:9 male:female ratio. (See page 84.) It is also important to note that the ratio of males to females enrolled in this department of education as preservice teachers is 2:9.

to their own cultural diversity as children and as students at the university; how they experienced cultural diversity during their student teaching; and what they identified as necessary in their multicultural preparation. The interviews were audiotaped and then transcribed. The transcriptions were then coded according to these same interview themes described above.

RESULTS: CULTURAL DIVERSITY EXPERIENCES DURING CHILDHOOD

This group of preservice teachers experienced very little cultural diversity while growing up. All twelve grew up in white neighborhoods. Some of the white interviewees knew overt racism in their homes and communities, but for most it was a more subtle atmosphere of racial and social class prejudice. Several spoke of it as covert discrimination found in unspoken attitudes, the ways in which people grouped themselves during social events, and in their other day-to-day living experiences. Three of the white interviewees spoke of the effects of growing up in homes that were racially bigoted. They were haunted by concerns about racism and stereotyping. They raised these concerns in the context of their student-teaching experience, not wanting to be perceived as bigoted, yet feeling the internal tendency toward prejudice. One preservice teacher who had grown up in a home that was racially bigoted and attended schools that were primarily white described the experience in this way:

> It's so easy to stereotype when I get frustrated: 'The students don't understand me; that is their problem.' I prepared myself for a challenge. But in reality it's been more of a challenge than I thought it would be. And just in terms of being put in an environment that is multiracial, I try so hard at times just to be open-minded and to be teachable in the area of race, and yet sometimes I find myself going back to that habitual thinking.

Another interviewee described the powerful role the home environment played in counteracting what might have become a seedbed of racism. The interviewee is white; the neighborhood he grew up in is white, with the exception of two black families. The school he attended was desegregated by court order when he was in the first grade. The experiences this interviewee had as a child in the school were positive until one day he was victimized:

> Well, I guess fourth and fifth grade is when I started to experience racial problems and animosity and conflict between blacks and whites. First it

wasn't something that happened to me personally. I would see it happening to my friends, where during lunch in the gym there was a separate wrestling room and the black kids would open the door and literally kidnap a white kid and throw him in there, beat him up, and then let him out again. And I don't know why, but there never seemed to be any adults around who knew about this game that was being played. That happened to me a couple of times where I happened unluckily to be by the door when it was opened and I was thrown in there . . . my parents went out of their way to be open-minded—we always had black friends around, my parents were both professors and we had black students who lived with us on a number of occasions because they couldn't afford dorms and didn't have the money . . . so I knew there were good black people. So I didn't make generalizations and I just feel fortunate because I think I had exposure that a lot of kids didn't. That's why I didn't form generalizations.

The role of youth experiences in home, school, and neighborhood was seen, then, as a primary factor in the formation of cultural beliefs and understanding.

RESULTS: FORMAL EDUCATION EXPERIENCES WITH CULTURAL DIVERSITY

Most of the interviewees attended racially segregated schools. There were few minority students in those schools, with the exception of three interviewees, who went to court-ordered desegregated schools for a few years. The black preservice teachers had all gone to schools that were mostly white.

None of the interviewees recalled any multicultural curricula from their youth. Their multicultural education took place in the university, in classes and through other kinds of experiences they shared with students from diverse cultures, with professors on campus, and in school settings to which they had been assigned. One interviewee spoke of African literature as a helpful multicultural course. A black interviewee spoke positively of a course that focused specifically on the black population in the U.S.:

I didn't really find out about Malcolm X until I actually came to the university. I was a sophomore when I found out about him. I was like, where are these black leaders coming from? I never heard of them . . . he [the professor] made sure that you knew, before you left that class, some of the other black leaders, other than Martin Luther King.

Two other courses were mentioned that were helpful in preparing curriculum and shaping cultural partnerships with children in the classrooms. The two courses were designed to focus on multicultural education and children's literature; these were seen as particularly helpful during the student teaching experience and for future classrooms.

In general, the interviewees state that the university should do more to prepare them to teach diverse populations. Several saw a great need for more practical experiences with diverse populations of children:

> . . . one of the things that really bothered me was, here people are getting ready to graduate; they are in their final semester; they haven't been in a classroom with black people. Quite honestly, I think the university needs to take a step back and reevaluate their student teaching and participation programs. I don't care whether you're white, black, or purple, participation should require that everybody spend time in a school system, here in town, that is predominantly black.

Multicultural education is highly prized by these preservice teachers. For the most part, they value the coursework they have had; they also think that more coursework should be offered that is multiculturally oriented. In particular, they see a great need for more practicum experiences in culturally diverse settings under the guidance of exemplary teacher role models.

RESULTS: PRESERVICE TEACHER PERCEPTIONS OF CULTURAL DIVERSITY

Most preservice teachers had some minority students in their classrooms and schools during their student teaching. Black students were perceived by most as a discipline problem, but they avoided casting blame on them. Instead, the problem was seen as being in the troubled family of the students. Their families and communities were seen as having serious problems and the students were seen as victims of circumstance. These troubled families and communities were seen as unsupportive, creating poor student attitudes, and exposing students to crime and drugs. Because of these circumstances, the student teachers believed the children were angry and alienated and carried a sense of hopelessness and failure with them:

> This guy is really angry, racially. I get to see that in his writing: 'White people should be slaves for a while, cause we had to be slaves. If you come from a background like that, it's tough to maintain your good behavior

and stuff like that in school.' It's a cycle. Their parents grew up with no money and all the problems that go with that. The kids don't make it through school sometimes; that's why it's hard to get out once you are in the ghetto. It will be family after family in the ghetto.

The preservice teachers were ambivalent about teaching minority students because of the perceived discipline problems. Perceived features of the black culture, such as loud music, rap music, and loud talking, were also difficult for some preservice teachers to understand:

My problem is Blacks are loud when they get in a group. Sometimes I'll be standing there in the cafeteria and thinking, yeah, that's true, and then I say to myself, well you know, that's a cultural thing, it's no big deal.

Students were willing to acknowledge their cultural intolerance, but were not prepared to resolve the conflicts they experienced. As a result, the potential for shaping cultural partnerships was significantly nullified.

A Narrow Conception of Cultural Diversity

Cultural diversity for these interviewees means having black students in class. Social class, gender, ethnicity, language, and religion are not considered forms of diversity. As seen in the preservice teachers' perceptions of minority students, the reference is to black students. Racism, or race in general, is not seen as an issue in the schools, with the exception of three interviewees. But half of the interviewees saw the students in their schools segregating themselves along racial lines. Sometimes interviewees saw students segregating themselves by subject, for example considering advanced math and science to be white subjects. One interviewee viewed the peer pressure on black students to participate in sports and ignore academics in order to not "act white" as a serious problem. Another interviewee pointed out that students in sports and band are the only ones who are integrated. Surprisingly, no one acknowledged any signs of segregation in the classrooms, although it was acknowledged that there is tracking according to race, with many more minority students being enrolled in the lower-level classes.

Gender As Culture

Gender was never mentioned as part of diversity. When asked specifically about gender, no one perceived any problems. The typical response to questions about gender was "everybody is just a person," even though in the computer lab to which this comment referred, there were no girls. Any problems with re-gard to gender, such as an absence of girls in certain classes, are neutralized by separating them from the teacher's and administration's actions and making them totally dependent on the students.

Language Diversity As Culture

Interestingly, language was not spontaneously mentioned as part of diversity. Language diversity was primarily perceived as referring to black English. Most students thought that standard English should be taught in the class-room because it is necessary to bring students "up to grade level." Students agreed, though, that black English should not be denigrated. Some even ar-gued that it should not be corrected in the classroom, but that students should be advised that black English is "situation bound": that it might be appropri-ate to speak black English with friends, in the hallways, and at home, but not in class.

All Minority Groups Are Seen As the Same

Preservice teachers' ignorance of diversity shows clearly in questions about Hispanics. They do not mention Hispanics spontaneously other than listing them as students in their classrooms. No differences, with one exception, are perceived to exist between blacks and Hispanics: All minority groups are seen as the same. Not even the language difference was mentioned. As one inter-viewee said, "Differences? Not enough to make a comment about it." How-ever, they contradicted this line of reasoning as they shared their perception that Asian and Native American students are different enough to require spe-cial preparation by teachers.

Social Class As Culture

Most interviewees avoided the issue of socioeconomic status by saying that it is difficult to tell what kind of socioeconomic background the students come from. They looked for indicators of socioeconomic background in the cloth-ing students wore, but they found none. They were more willing to ac-knowledge social class differences in the school as a whole than in their classrooms. Supposedly the wealthy and the impoverished students are treated equally in school; still, one student admitted, the wealthy students do not fail. Indirectly, many interviewees perceived the low socioeconomic status of stu-dents as a problem by indicating that family background causes academic problems and that poor students tend to have many more family problems.

Social class was indirectly identified by many as more important than race, but social class was seen as less tangible and more difficult to pinpoint.

Social class conflict between teachers and students was perceived by three students. As one interviewee asserted about a supervising teacher:

> . . . She comes from a very upper-class family . . . She has tons of money right now, and I just think she's one of those stuffy white people. I really think she is . . . I think she has a hard time relating to children. I think she has a hard time communicating and relating to a lot of people that aren't on her status level.

The supervising teacher being discussed was teaching in a school with a high proportion of impoverished and minority students.

RESULTS: PRESERVICE TEACHER PERCEPTIONS OF THE STUDENT TEACHING EXPERIENCE

Only three of the preservice teachers were teaching in schools with a culturally diverse teacher corps. Some preservice teachers considered this a problem for two reasons: 1) They believed that it is difficult for white teachers to deal with minority students; and 2) the absence of minority teachers means an absence of role models for minority students. Because of the homogeneous teacher corps, the black preservice teachers saw themselves as role models both for black and white students.

For those who had a preconception of an ideal school, the culturally diverse classroom was seen as the most desirable. One preservice teacher, who had been raised in a wealthy suburban setting, stated that she had expected a wealthy white school for her student teaching. She ended up in a culturally diverse classroom, and then found this much more interesting and challenging than she anticipated a suburban setting would have been. Another preservice teacher explained that she wanted to teach in a culturally diverse classroom, but not in a wealthy neighborhood because the parents would be too demanding. On the other hand, she did not want to teach in an inner-city school because she feared:

> . . . a lack of respect of authority . . . they wouldn't do what you want them to do. They wouldn't be able to really concentrate because they wouldn't be eating right. They would probably miss a lot of school. They would just fall behind. Lack of motivation, possibly drugs.

Hence, some of our preservice teachers want a suburban middle-class type of diversity. This is again related to their narrow conception of cultural diversity and shows how little they understand their own stereotypes.

A number of other themes emerged from the interviews, reflecting student thinking about multicultural issues. The interviewees are divided on whether minority students have different learning styles. Five students think that minority students have different learning styles, but of those five, only two think that minority students should be treated differently. Five students also think that impoverished and wealthy students have different learning styles. Most tended to support some multicultural education. However, a couple of students avoided the issue by arguing that their teaching and subject matter (such as biology) were neutral. The preservice teachers planned to incorporate multicultural material into their teaching. Several said that there is a need for a cultural awareness group or course, and that awareness is as far as one can go in teaching. Many also mentioned mixed seating and group work as solutions to dealing with culturally diverse classrooms. Few students knew how they would prepare themselves for culturally diverse classrooms after the student teaching experience. Experience was seen as the key to further preparation for those who don't feel totally prepared. As one preservice teacher said, "You just need to have had experience working with all different kinds of people."

CONCLUSIONS

All the preservice teachers in this study think very much alike and have similar life experiences independent of their race, social class, or gender. Even the black preservice teachers do not feel competent to teach the wide range of black students because of their limited exposure to black culture in their largely white, suburban neighborhoods and schools.

Research has pointed to a pattern in which preservice teachers are saturated with information in their courses, only to ignore it when they enter their field settings. Present interviews suggest that our preservice teachers have not been exposed to an abundance of multicultural information. On the contrary, the interviewees thought they needed more coursework and experiences in this area; they have found themselves to be underprepared despite the official commitment by the university and the teacher education program. They acknowledged the value of studying diverse cultures and multicultural education, but they came back repeatedly to practical experience and the great value they placed on exemplary teacher role models. At the same time, these were precisely the elements they found to be consistently wanting.

Despite these perceived inadequacies, the preservice teachers had no plans to further their formal education in this field. They simply planned to develop their understanding through trial-and-error behavior with culturally diverse students. Even the interviewees who sensed that culturally diverse students may have different needs and styles of behavior expressed no intention to modify their style of communication. This hardly seems to be the necessary disposition for shaping cultural partnerships. When trial and error is the approach, trust is not developed. When all students are seen as the same, although in reality they are different, confidence in teacher judgment wanes. Two elements essential in developing cultural partnerships between people—trust and confidence—are then absent, and the potential for shaping cultural partnerships is disrupted.

Despite their disinterest in seeking specialized assistance to improve their cultural expertise, these preservice teachers share a stated desire to become multiculturalists. Their overriding question regarding multiculturalism is "How does one teach a culturally diverse student population?" Preservice teacher willingness to teach from a multicultural perspective is undercut by a narrow conception of cultural diversity. Their thinking corresponds with the college policy of defining diversity primarily in terms of race; yet despite their tendency to focus on race, these preservice teachers refuse to deal with this element of diversity in any depth. By blaming the problems that arise on family background and ignoring race problems in their own classrooms, they can carry on in ways that they find comfortable.

Overall, the interviewees want a problem-free type of cultural diversity in their classrooms. They would appreciate a variety of minority students from a middle-class background who are interested in what the teacher has to say and who are encouraged and supported by their parents. It is important to note that the interviewees made no mention of wanting to develop an interest in what their students have to say, what they have experienced, and what they need. Shaping a cultural partnership requires this kind of interest; it is a mutual effort on the part of teacher and student, with the majority of the responsibility resting squarely on the shoulders of the teacher.

Given U.S. demographic trends and the under-preparation and naivete that we find among preservice teachers, it is imperative that greater efforts be made to prepare preservice teachers for the diverse educational settings they will enter. It is also clear from this study that official policy statements at the university level are not enough to accomplish the needed change at the grassroots.

The lack of preparation at the grassroots, and the preservice teacher identification of fruitful multicultural learning experiences, point to at least three areas in teacher education that need our attention. First, we must provide more multicultural education role models for preservice teachers, master teachers who are adept in shaping cultural partnerships and who actively demonstrate this ability in their day-to-day interaction with students. Second, we must provide more quality multicultural coursework linked to carefully guided and monitored practicum experiences with these master-teacher role models. This would provide the integrated conceptual/clinical framework upon which the thoughtful shaping of cultural partnerships should be built. Third, we must actively assess the cultural results of our printed programs through an ongoing dialogue with, and observation of, preservice and professional teachers, the cultural caretakers of our youth.

REFERENCES

Baker, G. (1973). Multicultural training for student teachers. *Journal of Teacher Education, 24,* 306–307.

Center for Education Statistics (1987). *Digest of education statistics.* Washington, DC: U.S. Government Printing Office.

Davidman, P. T. (1990). Multicultural teacher education and supervision: A new approach to professional development. *Teacher Education Quarterly, 17,* 37–52.

Gage, N. L. (1990). Dealing with the dropout problem. *Phi Delta Kappan, 72,* 280–285.

Grant, C.A., & Koskela, Ruth A. (1986). Education that is multicultural and the relationship between preservice campus learning and field experiences. *Journal of Educational Research, 79,* 197–204.

Grant, C. A., & Secada, W. G. (1990). Preparing teachers for diversity. In W. R. Houston (Ed.), *Handbook of research on teacher education* (pp. 403–422). Association of Teacher Education. New York: Macmillan Publishing Company.

Hodgkinson, H. L. (1985). *All one system: Demographics of education—kindergarten through graduate school.* Washington, DC: Institute for Educational Leadership.

Irvine, J. J. (1985). Teacher communication patterns as related to the race and sex of the student. *Journal of Educational Research, 78,* 338–345.

Kozol, J. (1991). *Savage inequalities: Children in America's schools.* New York: Crown Publishers.

McDiarmid, G.W. (1989, April). Tilting at webs of belief: Early field experience as an occasion for breaking with experience. Paper presented at the annual meeting of the American Educational Research Association, San Francisco, CA.

McDiarmid, G.W., & Price, J. (1993). Preparing teachers for diversity: A study of student teachers in a multicultural program. In M. J. O'Hair and S. Odell (Eds.), *Diversity and teaching: Teacher education yearbook I* (pp. 31–57). Fort Worth: Harcourt Brace Jovanovich College Publishers.

Moll, L., & Diaz, S. (1987). Change as the goal of educational research. *Anthropology and Education Quarterly, 18,* 300–311.

NCATE, (1990). *Standards, procedures, and policies for the accreditation of professional education units.* Washington, DC.

Nieto, S. (1992). *Affirming diversity: The sociopolicital context of multicultural education.* New York: Longman Publishing Group.

The Oxford English dictionary, 2nd Edition (1991). Oxford: Clarendon Press.

Paine, L. (1990). *Orientation Towards Diversity: What do prospective teachers bring?* Lansing, MI: Michigan State University, National Center for Research on Teacher Education.

Reed, S., & R. C. Sautter (1990). Children of poverty: Kappan special report. *Phi Delta Kappan, 71* (10), K1–K12.

Rose, M. (1989). *Lives on the boundary.* New York: Penguin Books.

Trueba, H. T. (1989). Rethinking dropouts: Culture and literacy for minority student empowerment. In H. T. Trueba, G. Spindler & L. Spindler (Eds.). *What do anthropologists have to say about dropouts?* (pp. 27–42). New York: The Falmer Press.

Vogt, L. A., Jordan, C. & R. G. Tharp (1987). Explaining school failure, producing school successes: Two cases. *Anthropology and Education Quarterly, 18,* 276–286.

CHAPTER 5

A Typology of Cooperating Teacher–Student Teacher Relationships: Perceptions of Student Teachers

REBECCA S. BOWERS
Old Dominion University

REBECCA S. BOWERS is Assistant Professor of Science and Math Education in the Darden College of Education at Old Dominion University. Her research interests are in the areas of preservice teacher preparation and development, curriculum and instructional integration, multicultural education preparation, and implications for preservice teacher preparation in science and math education.

ABSTRACT

A select group of student teachers provided data from which a typology of five cooperating teacher–student teacher relationships was developed. The relationship types include apprenticeship, basic mentorship, professional partnership, lack-of-support, and rigidity. Each relationship type is examined to determine its effectiveness in the student teacher's field experience and preparation for the first year of teaching. Questions are raised about the effectiveness of the apprenticeship, lack-of-support, and rigidity types for preservice teacher preparation. Discussion suggests that the most effective approach in the student teaching field experience may include two factors: (a) a combination of the basic mentorship and professional partnership arrangement that includes a *helper, supervisee, partner sequence* in the cooperating teacher-student teacher relationship; and (b) a cooperating teacher inservice that focuses on crucial behaviors of cooperating teachers that affect student teachers.

Abundant documentation has confirmed the influence of cooperating teachers with student teachers' overall classroom performance, especially in their translating theory into instructional practice. Research findings show, for example, that the cooperating teacher serves as a "socializing influence," especially when the cooperating teacher demonstrates "more flexible, adaptable views" of teaching (Bunting, 1988). Moreover, when assigned to cooperating teachers who are trained in supervisory skills, student teachers more actively involve themselves with children and receive more feedback from their cooperating teachers than do student teachers who are placed with untrained cooperating teachers (McIntyre & Killan, 1987).

The purpose of this study was to examine student teaching, paying particular attention to the cooperating teacher's role in facilitating the student teacher's development from student to teacher. Specifically, student teachers' perceptions of their relationship with their cooperating teachers and the degree to which student teachers perceived a partnership with their cooperating teachers were examined. From the student teachers' descriptions of their interactions and perceived relationships with their cooperating teachers, a developmental typology of supervision for cooperating teachers was defined.

Efforts in the direction of codifying effective behaviors of cooperating teachers have been described in Kuehl's (1976) taxonomy and Copas's (1984) research, both of which focused on the cooperating teacher as the pivotal person in connecting university coursework with field experience. What follows is a brief overview of Khuel's taxonomy and Copas's research, which provide the theoretical framework for this study.

Kuehl (1976) developed a taxonomy delineating the forty-three crucial tasks a supervising teacher must demonstrate to facilitate the successful classroom performance of a student teacher. Through a survey, Kuehl asked teacher educators and student teachers to identify the most important tasks of cooperating teachers. Based on the responses of 786 school personnel and student teachers, Kuehl classified data into five groups according to the position classification of the respondents, who included supervising teachers (early childhood, elementary, middle school, secondary/postsecondary, and special education), student teachers, principals, superintendents, and college/university supervisors. Based on the analysis of data from the five response groups, Kuehl found consistency in the degree of importance that school personnel and student teachers placed on cooperating teachers' crucial tasks. His taxonomy of crucial tasks for the supervising teacher included such responsibilities as: guiding the orientation of the student teacher to the classroom; helping the student teacher develop his or her own teaching style;

helping the student teacher to become knowledgeable about each student; and helping the student teacher develop instructional strategies along with curriculum development, classroom management, and discipline strategies.

Copas (1984) called attention to the important part that cooperating teachers play in the development of student teachers' understanding of teaching. Cooperating teachers are seen by student teachers as embodying what it *means* to be a teacher. In her study with 476 student teachers from thirty-one higher education institutions, Copas asked student teachers to describe their perceptions of effective and ineffective behaviors and practices modeled by their cooperating teachers. From a list of 1,490 behaviors extracted from the student teachers' data, Copas identified fourteen "critical requirements" that affect student teachers. She subdivided these fourteen behaviors into six categories. The effective cooperating teacher, according to Copas, is one who is perceived to have provided the help, guidance, and support needed by the student teacher in each of the crucial areas listed in Table 1. Copas asserted that a vital part of cooperating teachers' training should be learning these crucial behaviors, because student teachers need and are receptive to role models who embody "demonstrated competencies in teaching" (p. 53).

Although a limited amount of research has provided information on how experienced teachers assess their student teaching retrospectively, little attention has focused on what happens in the lives of student teachers during their student teaching. This study focused on the student teachers' relationship with their cooperating teachers from the student teachers' point of view. Attention was given to the degree to which student teachers believed that their cooperating teachers were providing the help, guidance, and support needed to facilitate their student-teaching field experience.

METHOD

This study was designed as an inquiry into the developmental and socialization processes through which five student teachers progressed during their fourteen weeks of student teaching. (Each student teacher was assigned to two seven-week school placements.) Data gathering consisted of three methods: (a) nine questionnaires and one essay; (b) classroom observations followed by open-ended interviews with each student teacher; and (c) seminars with the five student teachers. Taken together, these three data-gathering methods constituted a methodological triangulation to increase the internal validity of the findings. Data derived from the seminars and the classroom observations and follow-up interviews were compared with questionnaire responses to determine consistency between the student teachers' written descriptions of their experiences and perceptions, and their oral

TABLE 1:

Degree Cooperating Teachers Demonstrated Copas' (1984) Critical Requirements For Cooperating Teachers That Affect Student Teachers.

CRITICAL REQUIREMENTS FOR COOPERATING TEACHERS	STUDENT TEACHER									
	A		B		C		D		E	
	COOPERATING TEACHER									
	1	*2*	*1*	*2*	*1*	*2*	*1*	*2*	*1*	*2*
ORIENTING BEHAVIORS										
1. Provided the student teacher with information basic to adjustment to the class and school.	5	1	4	5	3	4	5	5	1	5
2. Helped the student teacher locate resource materials, people, and supplementary materials.	5	2	5	5	3	3	5	5	1	5
INDUCTING BEHAVIORS										
3. Provided opportunities for the student teacher to study children and their learning processes.	5	1	3	4	3	4	5	5	2	5
4. Structured responsibilities that gradually inducted the student teacher into full-time teaching	5	3	4	5	2	4	5	5	1	5
GUIDING BEHAVIORS										
5. Helped the student teacher develop skills in planning and evaluating learning experiences.	5	1	4	4	1	3	5	5	2	5
6. Worked with the student teacher in developing skills of presentation.	5	1	4	4	1	5	5	5	1	5
7. Assisted the student teacher in developing skills of discipline and control throughout the student teaching experience.	4	2	3	5	2	4	5	5	1	5
REFLECTING BEHAVIORS										
8. Observed the student teacher and provided feedback on the effectiveness of performance.	5	5	5	3	2	5	5	5	1	5

9. Informed the student teacher of errors in a manner that protected the student teacher from embarrassment.	5	3	5	4	2	3	5	5	1	5
COOPERATING BEHAVIORS										
10. Interrupted the student teacher's lesson at appropriate times and in an appropriate manner.	0	1	0	3	0	0	0	0	0	0
11. Accepted the student teacher as a co-worker of equal status in guiding the learning process.	4	1	2	4	1	4	5	5	0	5
12. Provided for interaction with the student teacher through conferences.	5	1	2	5	4	5	4	4	1	5
SUPPORTING BEHAVIORS										
13. Encouraged the student teacher to explore and develop unique teaching behaviors.	4	1	2	3	2	3	5	5	1	5
14. Demonstrated sensitivity to the emotional needs of the student teacher in personal relationships.	5	1	5	5	3	5	5	5	1	5
Rating Total	62	24	48	59	29	52	64	64	14	65
Cooperating Teacher–Student Teacher Relationship	PP	R	M	A	L	A	PP	PP	L	PP

RATING SCALE

5	Exceptional
4	Exceeds Expectations
3	Meets Expectations
2	Below Expectations
1	Poor
0	No Demonstration

COOPERATING TEACHER/STUDENT TEACHER RELATIONSHIP TYPOLOGIES

PP	Professional Partnership
M	Mentorship
A	Apprenticeship
L	Lack of Support
R	Rigidity

renditions of their experiences. In addition, comparisons were made among the three data sources to determine consistency between the student teachers' descriptions and perceptions of events and those of the researcher. The rate of consistency ranged from 90 percent to 95 percent.

Rationale for Research Method Chosen

Interpretative inquiry, a method of qualitative research, is a phenomenological approach based on four propositions: (a) the definition of a situation is socially constructed through the perceptions of an individual or a group experiencing a similar phenomenon; (b) the research purpose is to understand the events and phenomenon through the perceptions of the participants; (c) the research presentation design is to reveal to the reader the participants' experience of a specific phenomenon; and (d) the researcher becomes immersed in the totality of the research (Firestone, 1987).

Burgess (1984) identified ten characteristics of field research that correspond to the salient features of this interpretative inquiry method. The findings of a study are contextualized within a social, cultural, and historical framework. The research begins with a small number of questions to orient the study, and additional questions arise during the course of the research. This study, for example, was begun with a small number of questions derived from a much earlier study of first-year teachers in an inner-city school setting (Eddy, 1969), along with my own pilot study designed to generate a body of questions inquiring into the developmental and socialization processes of the student teacher/cooperating teacher relationship. The researcher must participate in the social situation under study, such as making classroom observations with follow-up interviews and conducting seminars with the student teachers. The researcher analyzes the questionnaire responses, observation and interview notes, and seminar contributions of each participant to secure each participant's report of the people, events, and settings under investigation. Unstructured interviews and essays complement the structured components of the inquiry. Personal documents and structured components, as in the case of the nine questionnaires, give depth and background to the study. Varying methods of data gathering may be used and integrated to provide reliability and validity, as in the triangulation previously described. Data-gathering consistency was maintained by using equal numbers of questionnaires and classroom visits and follow-up interviews. In addition, each student teacher completed an essay about her student-teaching experiences and attended the six seminars. The researcher disturbs the process under study as little as possible, in this case by not taking on the role of supervisor. Dissemination of research reports is accomplished by following ethical procedures of maintaining confidentiality for the student teachers, their cooperating teachers, and the schools and school systems in which the events occurred.

Procedure

The researcher observed each student teacher four times in each school. The first two observations were designed to meet the school principal and cooperating teacher, to become familiar with the classroom setting and the students, and to talk with the student teacher about initial perceptions of the student-teaching assignment. The second two visits were designed to observe and record incidents of the student teacher's classroom methods and interactions between the cooperating teacher and student teacher both in the classroom and during post-teaching conferences between the student teacher and cooperating teachers. In addition, each student teacher was interviewed using an open-ended questioning format. Each student teacher completed nine questionnaires and one essay. Each questionnaire included two questions about whether the student teacher believed that teaching and management styles had become like those of the cooperating teacher and why or why not; two questions about how free the student teacher felt to "experiment" with varying teaching styles or to teach in her or his "own way;" four questions about lessons the student teacher had taught and why they had gone well or poorly; four questions about interaction with the children in the classroom and how the cooperating teacher provided or failed to provide input; and two questions about the student teacher's perception of the student-teaching experience and any changed attitudes toward teaching that resulted.

The six seminars with the student teachers were designed to discuss specific concerns that they identified. The seminar topics included: initial perceptions of and adjustments to student teaching and the assigned school; classroom management and discipline and assistance provided by the cooperating teacher; and lesson planning, teaching, and assistance provided by the cooperating teacher. Notes were tape-recorded and transcribed after each seminar. The student teachers' statements during the seminars were classified according to the type and degree of support the cooperating teacher provided the student teacher. The seminar data were compared with my classroom observations and the student teachers' responses to my follow-up interview questions.

DATA SOURCE

Two types of qualitative data analyses defined by Burgess (1984) were used in this study. *Descriptive accounts* emphasize detailed descriptions or statements the participants made in the setting or during interviews. *Analytical descriptions* are based on the participants' descriptions or statements, which are the raw data of the study. The data are analyzed for similarities and differences and categorized accordingly. From the categorization, a conceptual scheme emerges.

The questionnaire responses, essays, classroom observations, interview notes, and seminar notes were also compared with Copas's (1984) fourteen "critical requirements of cooperating teachers that affect student teachers" to determine on a Likert-type scale the degree to which each cooperating teacher demonstrated critical requirement behaviors. The ratings were determined on a basis of range of percentage over time of incidents reported in questionnaire items, essays, follow-up interview responses, and seminar notes. Table 1 indicates the results of the comparison with Copas's "critical requirements." The rating scale translates to the following range of percentage of incidents: five equals 100 percent to 81 percent; four equals 80 percent to 61 percent; three equals 60 percent to 41 percent; two equals 40 percent to 21 percent; one equals 20 percent to 1 percent; and zero equals "no incident reported."

RESULTS AND CONCLUSIONS

Data collected from the questionnaires and essays, classroom observations, follow-up interviews, and seminar notes provided descriptions of the interactions between the student teachers and their cooperating teachers. The descriptors were grouped according to the degree and type of support the cooperating teachers provided for the student teachers. The degree and types of support over time, which are identified in this study, resulted in five clusters: (a) support was superior; the cooperating teacher treated the student teacher as an equal partner; (b) support exceeded expectations; the cooperating teacher served as a guide to and encouraged the student teacher; (c) support met expectations; the cooperating teacher required the student teacher to serve as an observer and assistant in the classroom; (d) support was below expectations; the cooperating teacher required the student teacher to model only his or her teaching and classroom management style; and (e) support was poor; the cooperating teacher interacted infrequently with the student teacher.

The following example illustrates the interpretation of the data and the coding of a particular cooperating teacher to a specific type:

Questionnaire Item: Briefly describe ways your cooperating teacher assisted you with a lesson this week.

Week 2: I used Mrs.____'s lesson on directions on a map using a compass. My teacher gave me good do's and don't's when teaching direction. For example, don't say up and down for north and south.

Week 4: Before a lesson on creative writing, my cooperating teacher advised me to have the children write a story before they draw the scene about the story. She has been a tremendous help. We discuss everything together before I follow through with the lesson.

Questionnaire Item: Has your teaching become in any way like that of your cooperating teacher? Why or why not?

Week 6: I find myself saying some of the same expressions and I see myself modeling behaviors in the same way Mrs.____ does. I've watched her teach and, in order for the children to respond to me in somewhat of the same way as they do Mrs.____, I picked up on certain things she does to get the students to listen. But I feel free to teach in my own way. Now, Mrs.____ leaves lesson planning up to me, and she lets me teach in my own way. I might use questioning or hands-on. She doesn't tell me that "this" has to be taught a certain way. We discuss lessons before I teach them. We discuss reasons a lesson was good or ways a lesson might be improved the next time. I make most of the decisions now.

Questionnaire Item: How would you describe your relationship with your cooperating teacher?

Week 7: At first, Mrs.____ wanted me to teach in her style and she observed all my lessons. After a couple of weeks, I started writing my own lesson plans, and she and I would discuss what I was planning to do, what she thought would work or not work. Then she let me teach in my own way. She treats me like I am the teacher, too. She offers me the perfect combination of support and freedom. She advises and encourages me consistently and constructively. She suggests, never insists.

From this student teacher's responses to questionnaire items, the *professional partnership* interaction type emerged and was coded in the following way: (a) During the first weeks, the cooperating teacher provided the lesson plans for the student teacher; the cooperating teacher gave specific directions; (b) During the middle weeks, the cooperating teacher encouraged the student teacher to write her own lesson plans and to make decisions about the classroom; the cooperating teacher and the student teacher discussed the lessons plans before the teaching; (c) During the final weeks, the student teacher developed lesson plans and experimented with her own teaching style; the cooperating teacher treated the student teacher as a co-teacher.

The observation and follow-up interview notes and the seminar notes supported the student teacher's responses to the questionnaires. Other questionnaire items and interview questions were based on Copas's (1984) fourteen "critical requirements of cooperating teachers that affect student teachers" and were used to determine the degree to which the cooperating teacher supported the student teacher. For example, the student teacher was asked to indicate the degree to which the cooperating teacher helped her locate resource materials, people, and supplementary materials. The student teacher indicated that the cooperating teacher was "exceptional" in this requirement. For additional indicators of the degree to which the cooperating teacher supported the student teacher in this example, see Table 1, Student Teacher A, Cooperating Teacher 1.

Data from the other four student teachers were similarly analyzed and coded. A comparison of data from all five student teachers in their interactions with their cooperating teachers produced a typology of five cooperating teacher-student teacher interaction types: a *professional partnership* type (in which the cooperating teacher and student teacher work together as equals or professional peers), a *basic mentorship* type (in which the cooperating teacher serves as a veteran guide, supporting and encouraging the newcomer along the path necessary for mastery in the teaching profession), an *apprenticeship* type (in which a skilled craftsperson invites a novice to learn the craft by observing and assisting the craftsperson), a *lack-of-support* type (in which the key characteristic is indifference on the part of the cooperating teacher), and a *rigidity* type (indicated by a cooperating teacher's unyielding demands for conformity, insisting on inflexible teaching methods and routines). Table 2 provides samples of student teachers' statements, which support the coding of the cooperating teacher-student teacher relationship types in this study.

In this study, four of the cooperating teacher-student teacher relationships were identified as "professional partnerships." Two were designated as "apprenticeships," one was a "basic mentorship," two fell into the "lack-of-support" category, and one fit the "rigidity" classification.

Although no attempt is made in this study to use Copas's "critical requirements" alone to identify the typology categories a particular cooperating teacher-student teacher relationship falls into, the degree to which each cooperating teacher demonstrated these behaviors emphasizes how effective or ineffective the interaction between that cooperating teacher and the student teacher was found to be. The "professional partnership" cooperating teachers demonstrated a high degree of compliance with Copas's critical requirements (62, 64, 64, and 65). The "apprenticeship" cooperating teachers rated 59 and 52 in compliance, and the "basic mentorship" teacher rated 44. On the other hand, the two "lack-of-support" cooperating teachers demonstrated a low degree of compliance with the "critical requirements" (29 and 14). Similarly, the "rigidity" cooperating teacher demonstrated a degree of 24 of a possible 70 in compliance.

We now turn to a more detailed examination of the student teacher-cooperating teacher relationships that emerged in this study, examining each of the five interaction types in turn.

TABLE 2:

Sample Responses from student teachers to questionnaire item, "Describe your relationship with your cooperating teacher."

Relationship Type	Student Teacher's Response: "Describe your relationship with your cooperating teacher."
PROFESSIONAL PARTNERSHIP	At first, we talked at great length about what was going on. Then I was the one who made all of the decisions. I was able to set up the classroom any way I felt was necessary. My cooperating teacher offered good suggestions and constructive criticism, but never overruled my decisions.
BASIC MENTORSHIP	I patterned my teaching after my cooperating teacher because I greatly admired her teaching style. I observed for about a week, and then I took over. I followed her guidelines. I was instructed to give the students three activities a day but the choice of activities was up to me, although she made the final decision about what to be taught.
APPRENTICESHIP	There was no choice for me other than to teach my cooperating teacher's lesson plans and to use her teaching style, because I had to cover what she wanted covered when she wanted it covered. She observed me much of the time and told me what I should have done or not done. I was allowed to try a few things, but other than that I followed her guidelines. I spent a lot of time grading papers and working with groups of students who were behind. I never really worked on my own.
RIGIDITY	My cooperating teacher had the attitude, "Cover the textbook and keep the students under absolute control." She demanded that I absolutely follow "normal routine" and not deviate in the least. I wanted to use an overhead projector, but she would not permit me to. She said the kids would go wild. She told me that I spent too much time explaining the material to the students. She demanded that I use only her lesson plans at first. When I started to write my own lesson plans, I had to write them in exactly the same way and use the same materials and assignments that she would use.
LACK-OF-SUPPORT	When I asked specific questions, such as how long it should take to teach a specific concept (just to get a general idea), I was told to figure it out for myself. When I figured it out for myself, I was told the lesson or activity was "too short" or "too long." When I asked about what to do in certain situations with some of the students who were giving me problems, she would shrug her shoulders and not offer any advice. She doesn't talk with me much. She has another job and leaves as soon as school ends each day.

Apprenticeship

Apprenticeship, according to its traditional definition, involves working for someone who is skilled in a trade or craft in order to learn that trade or craft. Erdman (1983) points out that in some field-experience programs, a narrowly defined apprenticeship perspective can result in miseducative experiences. "The apprenticeship perspective construes the role of the preservice teacher as a helper who primarily assists the cooperating teacher," (p. 8).

Study participants who were placed in situations where the apprenticeship perspective dominated tended never to assume the roles and responsibilities of a classroom teacher. Rather, they continued to serve as helpers or assistants to the cooperating teacher throughout their classroom assignment. (For example, they were required to keep all student attendance records and grade all papers.) When they were permitted to teach, most of their instruction was tutorial with one or two students or small groups of students. Student teachers were expected to emulate the cooperating teacher's lesson planning, classroom management style, and instructional style. In the apprenticeship model, the cooperating teacher's conferences with the student teacher were nonreflective but rather focused on establishing the next day's routine and explaining the cooperating teacher's reasons for certain classroom practices.

Basic Mentorship

In Homer's *Odyssey,* Mentor was the person entrusted with the task of educating and caring for the son of Odysseus. The term *mentor* is now commonly used to refer to a veteran professional who provides guidance, support, and encouragement to a younger person entering the profession. Butler (1987) recommended that the mentor take a developmental approach in the relationship with the novice teacher and modify his or her role as needed in the novice's developmental process. Huling-Austin and Murphy (1987) provide a list of fourteen mentoring tasks, which include such areas as helping the novice locate materials, orientation to the school and school policies, lesson planning, and student behavior management. Their list is similar to Copas' (1984) fourteen critical requirements for cooperating teachers that affect student teachers (see Table 1).

In the case in which the basic mentorship type was played out, the student teacher followed the cooperating teacher as an exemplary teacher and trusted advisor. The cooperating teacher guided and supported the student teacher through the various roles of a classroom teacher, with induction into full teaching responsibilities occurring during the final one or two weeks of student teaching. The cooperating teacher encouraged the student teacher to observe and model the cooperating teacher's classroom instructional and management styles and permitted the student teacher to use instructional activities if those activities did not deviate from the cooperating teacher's teaching style. Throughout the field experience, the cooperating teacher worked with the student teacher in writing lesson plans and in making decisions about supplementary materials and equipment.

In addition to lesson planning and instruction, the basic mentorship–cooperating teacher assumed most responsibility in dealing with disruptive student behavior, directing the student teacher in all actions. Conferences held with the student teacher primarily centered around developing lesson plans and discussing why certain teaching and management styles "worked." Unlike the apprenticeship type, the basic mentorship arrangement allowed the student teacher to be much more actively involved in the classroom teaching process.

Professional Partnership: Mentoring Beyond Guiding and Supporting

The greatest amount of involvement occurred when a student teacher was placed in a professional partnership arrangement. Erdman (1983) has written that a "partnership perspective toward preservice teaching more readily addresses the complexity of teaching" (p. 28). Where a partnership was in operation in the field experiences of the study participants, the student teacher initially modeled the cooperating teacher in a manner similar to the basic mentorship relationship. However, the support and guidance did not stop there but moved forward to something more. The cooperating teacher encouraged the student to integrate effective teaching techniques with the student teacher's personal teaching style, and to experiment with various activities and instructional methods and then to evaluate the effectiveness of each. During conferences, the cooperating teacher discussed teaching and learning processes and the effects of various classroom practices upon students' intellectual and social development. For the student teacher, there was a sense of working with a peer—a "professional partner"—in the classroom. "We work together as a team," one student teacher said. Alternative classroom management patterns were explored together, with the cooperating teacher encouraging the student teacher to integrate her ideas about management with the cooperating teacher's program.

Cooperating teachers in the professional partnership category sometimes adapted some of the student teacher's instructional and management techniques into their own classroom programs. These cooperating teachers included the student teacher in classroom decision making, lesson development, and management. By the fourth week of student teaching, they permitted the student teacher to assume all the roles and responsibilities of teaching. "We used different approaches in teaching and discipline, but she allows me to try out different methods that I think will be effective," one student teacher said of her work with a "professional partner" cooperating teacher. "After a lesson or at the end of a school day, we discuss at length things that worked or didn't work and why. I feel like I am an important part of the classroom—a teacher."

Lack-of-Support

In situations where the lack-of-support interaction type prevailed, the cooperating teacher did nothing more than give the student teacher a sample lesson plan and teacher-edition textbook, providing no input about instruction except criticisms at the ends of lessons or in reports to the supervisor. Little or no suggestions were provided on dealing with disruptive student behavior. When a student teacher asked for suggestions on dealing with disruptive behavior, the cooperating teacher either told her to figure it out for herself or simply shrugged her shoulders and walked away. Lack-of-support cooperating teachers did not assist student teachers in locating supplementary materials for instruction, although they did not object to the students' using such materials. Likewise, assistance was not provided in developing tests. However, the cooperating teacher criticized most tests developed by the student teacher as being "too hard" or "too easy." Lack-of-support teachers held no conferences with the student teacher other than quick remarks when a lesson ended. Lack-of-support cooperating teachers requested that the supervisor talk with the student teacher but would not attend conferences between the supervisor and student teacher. One student commented that her field experience under such a cooperating teacher left her feeling "drained."

Rigidity

In this type of cooperating teacher-student teacher interaction, innovation has no place. The rigid cooperating teacher required that the student teacher teach the cooperating teacher's lesson plans and model the cooperating teacher's teaching and management style. If the student teacher deviated from any of these, the cooperating teacher would interrupt. The cooperating teacher required the student teacher to use textbooks and no supplementary materials or audio-visual equipment. "I was not allowed to use the overhead projector," said the student who was assigned to a rigid teacher. "She told me that I spent too much time *explaining* material rather than *covering* the material, that I have to learn that I can't reach everybody. Mrs. _____ told me to just cover the material and go on. Otherwise, these kids are going to go wild." At the same time, the cooperating teacher refused to permit the student teacher to have individual conferences with students. Rather, the student teacher was to report to the cooperating teacher any comments she wished to make, which would then be passed on to the child. The cooperating teacher did, however, hold daily conferences with the student teacher to tell her what and how to teach the next day.

IMPLICATIONS FOR TEACHER EDUCATION

Erdman (1983) concluded that the student teacher serves primarily as a classroom helper, assisting the cooperating teacher in an apprenticeship relationship. Implied here is that, even though the student teacher plans lessons and conducts class instruction, in most cases the preservice teacher never fully assumes the roles and responsibilities of a classroom teacher. The *apprenticeship* type, by not fully involving the student teacher in teaching and learning interactions with the children, may not provide the opportunity to experience any significant independence in the classroom. Based on the data provided by the student teacher placed in this type, the adequacy of the student teacher's preparation for first-year teaching could be questioned.

Moreover, some studies indicate that the first-year teacher is likely to continue modeling the cooperating teacher's lesson planning, classroom management, and instructional style (Zimpher, deVoss, & Nott, 1980; Richardson-Kohler, 1988). When the novice's modeling of the cooperating teacher is combined with the inadequate classroom experience of the apprenticeship type, the question to ask is: How prepared is the first-year teacher to manage the unpredictability of the classroom dynamics with situations for which she or he has no experience base from which to draw?

On the other hand, if a student teacher encounters a cooperating teacher whose method fits the *rigidity* type, the student teacher may teach only from the cooperating teacher's lesson plans using the cooperating teacher's instructional style. Moreover, the student teacher may remain under the cooperating teacher's close supervision and scrutiny and not have experience developing lesson plans and developing a personal instructional and classroom-management style. Based on the report of the student teacher in this type, the *rigidity* relationship and student teaching experience can be little more than scripted modeling that the cooperating teacher fully directs and manages. The student teacher may leave the field experience ill-prepared to assume fully the roles and responsibilities of a classroom teacher and may, as in the case of the student teacher in the apprenticeship type, lack an experience base to deal with unpredictable classroom events. If it is true that student teachers model their cooperating teachers' instructional and management styles (Richardson-Kohler, 1988; Zimpher, deVoss, & Nott, 1980), then, as first-year teachers, these student teachers would likely assume the "rigid" behavior they observed in their cooperating teachers.

A student teacher who experiences a *lack-of-support* relationship with the cooperating teacher may be no better off than the student who is in a *rigidity* relationship. In this study, the student teacher in a lack-of-support situation reported that she received no help, no guidance, and no support. The cooperating teacher who not only does not adequately guide and support the student teacher, but also provides primarily negative feedback, as reported by the student teacher in this type, places the student teacher in a trial-and-error position. This is analogous to sink-or-swim water training without the benefit of the watchful instructor to provide direction, safety, and assurance that the beginning swimmer will not drown. There may be at least two outcomes implied in the *lack-of-support* relationship: (a) a preservice teacher who is inadequately prepared for first-year teaching; and (b) pupils in the student teacher's assigned classroom who will likely receive diminished learning experiences from a student teacher who is not helped by—and may be hindered by—the cooperating teacher.

On the other hand, the *basic mentorship* relationship provides an expanded classroom role for the cooperating teacher and the preservice teacher. In this study, the cooperating teachers in the basic mentorship type expected the student teachers to model their instructional and classroom management styles. In addition, each student teacher reported that she and the cooperating teacher worked together developing lesson plans and other classroom experiences for the pupils. The student teachers suggested learning activities and other classroom procedures, but the cooperating teachers made all final decisions. Since this relationship type includes a time for the student teacher to assume full classroom responsibilities, the *basic mentorship* relationship potential may provide adequate preparation for the novice's first teaching year.

Likewise, the *professional partnership* relationship may provide the help, guidance, and support that is conducive to the preservice teacher's successful transition to first-year teaching. In addition, the *professional partnership* may be expected to increase the student teacher's involvement in the classroom to an even greater extent than does the *basic mentorship* relationship. In this study, each student teacher in the professional partnership type became a partner with the cooperating teacher in the pupils' educative experiences. The student teachers were encouraged to make decisions about virtually all classroom procedures, including alternative instructional processes and classroom management strategies. Of the five relationships types discussed in this study, the *professional partnership* may have the best potential to foster student teaching as a reflective process in the teacher-preparation program. For example, the student teacher might experiment with different instructional strategies and investigate the educational benefits for the pupils. Or the cooperating teacher and student teacher might examine ways to improve interactions between the pupils and the student teacher.

The potential of the *professional partnership* relationship may be realized only when cooperating teachers have been trained to become effective in preparing and relating to student teachers. Copas (1984) suggested that the critical requirements that she listed for cooperating teachers could provide a curriculum for cooperating teacher inservicing (see Table 1). Odell (1987) recommended a mentor-teacher training program that would include information about novice teacher requirements and apprehensions, supervision strategies, instructional effectiveness, learning theory, and adult and teacher development.

Closer examination of the cooperating teacher-student teacher relationship types suggests that a developmental approach might be appropriate during the preservice teacher's field experience. A developmental approach would include the *basic mentorship* relationship, in which the student teacher serves initially as a supervisee, with movement into a *professional partnership,* in which the student teacher becomes an active partner with the cooperating teacher. Unlike a *helper,* who provides supportive assistance to the cooperating teacher in an *apprenticeship* arrangement, the *supervisee* in the *basic mentorship* type would be guided through the learning and teaching process to emerge as a principal *partner* in classroom decision making, instruction, and managing classroom dynamics.

Further research is needed to examine this developmental supervisory approach to field experience and the cooperating teacher's role. If a pre-student teaching practicum is not a curricular component of preservice teacher education, a developmental approach to student teaching that includes the *helper, supervisee, partner*★ sequence is likely to provide the student teacher with the help, guidance, and support in the crucial aspects of interactions, induction, and socialization into the teaching professional. It is further suggested that cooperating teachers receive inservice preparation that includes discussion of Copas' critical requirements for cooperating teachers that affect student teachers (see Table 1). Facilitating the student teacher's development into a full partner is likely to provide a positive foundation for the novice's transition to the classroom teacher role and lead to a first-year teaching experience that advances development of a career teacher.

★My thanks to Dr. Eugene Anderson, University of Minnesota, who suggested these terms to clarify the explanation of the proposed typology.

REFERENCES

Bunting, C. (1988). Cooperating teachers and the changing views of teacher candidates. *Journal of Teacher Education, 39*(2), 42–46.

Burgess, R. G. (1984). *In the field: An introduction to field research.* Boston: Allen & Unwin.

Butler, E. D. (1987, February). Lessons learned about mentoring in two fifth-year teacher preparation-induction programs. Paper presented at the annual meeting of the Association of Teacher Educators, Houston. As summarized in L. Huling-Austin, Teacher induction programs and internships. In W. R. Houston (Ed.), *Handbook of research on teacher education* (pp. 535–548). New York: Macmillan Publishing Company.

Copas, E. (1984). Critical requirements for cooperating teachers. *Journal of Teacher Education, 35*(6), 49–54.

Eddy, E. M. (1969). *Becoming a teacher: The passage to professional status.* New York: Teachers College Press.

Erdman, J. I. (1983). Assessing the purposes of early field experience programs. *Journal of Teacher Education, 34*(4), 27–31.

Firestone, W. A. (1987). Meaning in method: The rhetoric of quantitative and qualitative research. *Education Researcher, 16*(7), 16–21.

Huling-Austin, L., & Murphy, S. C. (1987). Assessing the impact of teacher induction programs: Implications for program development. Paper presented at the annual meeting of the American Education Research Association, Washington, DC. (ERIC Document Reproduction Service No. ED 283 779).

Kuehl, R. (1976). A taxonomy of critical tasks for supervising teachers (A research study). (ERIC Document Reproduction Service No. ED 179 507).

McIntyre, D. J. & Killian, J. E. (1987). The influence of supervisory training for cooperating teachers on preservice teachers' development during early field experiences. *Journal of Educational Research, 80*(5), 277–282.

Odell, S. J. (1987). Teacher induction: Rationale and issues. In D. Brooks (Ed.), *Teacher Induction: A new beginning* (pp. 69–80). Reston, VA: Association of Teacher Educators.

Richardson-Kohler, V. (1988). Barriers to the effective supervision of student teaching: A field study. *Journal of Teacher Education, 39*(2), 28–34.

Zimpher, N., deVoss, G., & Nott, D. (1980). A closer look at university student teacher supervision. *Journal of Teacher Education, 31*(4), 11–15.

CHAPTER 6

First-Year Teachers' Assignments, Expectations, and Development: A Collaborative Investigation

ALAN J. REIMAN
BARBARA M. PARRAMORE
North Carolina State University

ALAN J. REIMAN is a Clinical Assistant Professor who works jointly in the Departments of Curriculum and Instruction and Psychology at North Carolina State University and in the Wake County Public School System. He currently is at work on an eight-year study of preservice teacher education and teacher induction.

BARBARA M. PARRAMORE is a Professor in the College of Education and Psychology at North Carolina State University, and first head of the Department of Curriculum and Instruction, 1975–1985. She directed the department's development and accreditation of its undergraduate and graduate programs. She is currently participating in a longitudinal study of preservice and inservice experiences of an initial group of North Carolina teaching fellows.

ABSTRACT

This paper is a report of survey data from an ongoing eight-year longitudinal study of traditional and nontraditional students entering their first year of teaching. Questions were raised about the reasonableness of first-year teaching assignments, expectations of the first year and relationships among concerns (Fuller, 1969), and developmental stages. After a discussion of the results, three implications for teacher educators and policymakers are presented.

INTRODUCTION

The purpose of this study was to describe the first-year experience of beginning teachers during the academic year 1991–92. The research questions emerged from a review of recent literature and research findings on teacher induction and teacher development. The study was a collaborative venture between faculty in the Department of Curriculum and Instruction and a clinical assistant professor, working jointly between the university and the public schools. The study was supported by the Model Clinical Teaching Program (MCTP) that has as its goals: 1) to prepare a cadre of school-based teacher educators through long-term professional development experiences; 2) to support joint IHE/LEA clinical instructor appointments; and 3) to initiate innovative approaches to organizing "seamless" teacher preparation that has IHE/LEA collaboration as its hallmark.

The results of this study are from a continuing eight-year longitudinal study of a nontraditional group of undergraduate teacher education students at North Carolina State University called the teaching fellows. This study also includes a traditional group of beginning teachers graduating the same year as the teaching fellows from the same institution.

THE PROBLEM

Beginning teacher-induction programs with mentors in key roles refer to a "planned program intended to provide systematic and sustained assistance, specifically to beginning teachers for at least one school year" (Huling-Austin, 1990, p. 536). Nationally, most induction programs have the goals of improving teacher retention and improving the instruction of new teachers (Odell, 1986). But there is a gap between the rhetoric of induction and the reality of induction. Both large urban school systems nationwide (Colbert and Wolff, 1992) and rural school systems often place the most inexperienced teachers in the most difficult and challenging classrooms. Even with more successful programs, controversy exists on whether these programs promote new teachers' personal and professional growth and development or simply contribute to their surviving and adapting to the established structures of school life (Little, 1990). The relationship between personal growth and development and learning to teach may be a vital one. Investigations (Haberman, 1991; Huling-Austin, 1992; Reiman & Thies-Sprinthall, 1993; Sprinthall & Thies-Sprinthall, 1983) have observed that teaching requires a level of maturity in which attention and care are given to guiding the growth of others. If new teachers are still too focused on concerns about self, they are less able to give thought and care to the ultimate challenge and responsibility of guiding the learning and growth of their students.

Also unclear is the role that preservice teacher education programs play in ameliorating or constraining new teachers' transition to the first years of teaching. Zeichner and Tabachnick (1981) explored sources of discontinuity and abruptness in the induction phase, examining whether school experiences produce "reality shocks" that erode the *presumed* effects of preservice teacher education programs. Veenman (1984) extended this analysis in his research review of eighty-three studies of beginning teachers. Yet, there are no recent attempts at further exploration of the role of teacher education programs on the first year of teaching. Our research questions emerged from this corpus of research. Three questions were raised:

1. Assuming that statewide attention given to beginning teachers may be marking the end of "sink-or-swim" socialization, are first-year teaching assignments reasonable?

2. Comparing a traditional and nontraditional group of teacher education alumni, are there differences in expectations about the first year of teaching?

3. Drawing on Fuller's seminal work (1969) and recent findings in cognitive-developmental psychology (Sprinthall, Reiman, & Thies-Sprinthall, in press), what concerns are dominant for first-year teachers at differing cognitive-developmental stages?

METHOD

Sample

Respondents for this study included all graduates of a teacher education program at North Carolina State University in May and August, 1991, who had received a teacher's certificate from the state. This is a report of the results of the fall and spring surveys. As part of a continuing eight-year study of teacher preparation and induction, teachers in their first year of employment were surveyed twice regarding their assignments and work. The first survey was distributed to seventy-four beginning teachers and included all alumni of North Carolina State University who had been recommended for certification the previous summer and who were employed in a North Carolina public school in September 1991. The fall survey was designed to determine the reasonableness of first-year teachers' assignments. The sample also included alumni who were teaching fellows and had been awarded a four-year fellowship by the state. The teaching fellows had participated in a modified teacher-preparation program that stressed summer internships and formal and informal cohort activities during all four years of undergraduate study, and focused inquiry and reflection on current educational issues. The second survey was conducted in the spring of the beginning teachers' first year with forty alumni who had indicated a willingness in responding to the fall survey, to continue with the study. Teacher education programs included middle and secondary certification programs; no elementary education programs are offered by the institution. Table 1 shows that seventy-four alumni constituted the sample for the fall survey with forty-six responding. Forty, as shown in Table 2, agreed to participate in a later survey and a total of thirty-two returns were received.

MEASURES

First-year teachers were surveyed in the fall and spring to investigate the induction process. The two surveys were designed to secure information about beginning teachers' teaching assignments during their first year of teaching. Each mailing included a cover letter explaining the purpose and nature of the study, the survey, and a postage-paid envelope for the survey's return. Both surveys also included several open-ended questions, two in the fall and three

TABLE 1.
First-year teacher survey population, Fall 1991

	Fall surveys	Number & returns	%
Alumni	40	23	57.5
Alumni:T.F.	34	23	67.6
Total	74	46	62.1

TABLE 2.
First-year teacher survey population, Spring 1992

	Spring surveys	Number & returns	%
Alumni	21	16	76.2
Alumni: T.F.	19	16	84.2
Total	40	32	80.0

in the spring to elicit concerns (Fuller, 1969). All responses to the open-ended statements were independently rated at self, task, and impact by both investigators. Interrater reliability was .82 percent.

In addition, the second survey included twenty-nine items to be rated with respect to a respondent's perceptions of actual and desirable situations for a beginning teacher and a rating of the importance of each. The spring survey yielded a discrepancy analysis, a rating of importance of the twenty-nine items, and a report and analysis of responses to the three open-ended questions. These items are a subset of a larger group of items used in a pilot study (Reiman and Edelfelt, 1991). The twenty-nine items used in the study were found to be sources of significant discrepancy for beginning teachers in the pilot study.

In addition to the surveys, developmental assessments were available on the teaching fellows, completed when respondents were freshmen and repeated four years later when they were seniors. Justice reasoning was measured by the Defining Issues Test or DIT (Rest, 1986). The DIT assesses how people analyze six social-moral dilemmas and judge appropriate courses of action. Scoring involves calculating a principled-thinking score (P score), that indicates the relative importance attributed to principled moral considerations in making decisions. A shorter three-dilemma version (used for this study) may also be given when an overlapping assessment design has been initiated. Scores of respondents ranged from 20.0 P to 80.0 P. Post-test scores from 20.0 to 39.0 were classified as low "P" scores; scores from 40.0 to 50.0 were classified as moderate "P" scores; and scores from 51.0 to 80.0 were classified as high "P" scores. These classifications are consistent with Rest's work (1986).

The Paragraph Completion Test (Hunt, 1971), was used to measure conceptual level (CL) of respondents' cognitive complexity and interpersonal maturity. This semiprojective test consists of six open-ended topic stems. Three assess how the individual thinks about conflict and uncertainty; the other three stems assess how the individual thinks about rule structure and authority. Post-test scores ranged from 1.5 to 2.7, with 1.5 to 1.7 classified as low CL, 1.8 to 2.2 classified as moderate CL, and 2.21 to 2.7 classified as high CL.

Results of the surveys are followed by a discussion and implications for teacher education. Data are reported for the total group and for each subgroup: alumni and alumni who are teaching fellows.

INTERVENTION

The intervention involved a reframing of the undergraduate program for students identified as teaching fellows. The overall approach was to ensure that these students had more frequent opportunities to become acquainted with one another and to work as a team. As freshmen they were required to live on campus and were housed in the same dormitory. They participated in special activities during three summers. They enrolled in seminars during freshman and senior years and were expected to reflect continuously on crucial issues in education throughout their four years. All of the fellows had opportunities for additional significant new experiences in summer internships in education, and a smaller number of fellows participated in additional tutoring experiences (Reiman & Parramore, 1993). All fellows were required to participate in and report multicultural experiences on a regular basis.

The objective of the intervention was to apply five conditions that a larger body of research and theory has reported as promoting psychological growth of learners (Sprinthall & Thies-Sprinthall, 1983). Among these are: participating in significant new, complex humane helping experiences; being guided in reflection on those experiences; having a balance between experience and reflection; experiencing support as well as challenge through the program, and assuring that continuity in the previous conditions exists.

SPECIAL CIRCUMSTANCES

This study, part of a larger, eight-year longitudinal study, relied upon volunteers who had relatively high levels of motivation and commitment. The participants in the intervention were nontraditional. They had been attracted to participate in the teaching fellows program through a unique scholarship program provided by the state legislature. It requires a high school senior to make a teaching career decision before entering a college or university. Upon completion of a teacher education curriculum, the teaching fellow must teach a minimum of four years. In return, the state provides a scholarship of $5,000 per year for each student for four years. The students selected were often among the top 10 percent of their high school classes. The respondents in this study were among the initial group of teaching fellows to enroll at North Carolina State University.

RESULTS AND DISCUSSION

The first research question asked the following: Assuming that statewide attention given to beginning teachers may be marking the end of sink-or-swim socialization, are first-year teaching assignments reasonable for novice teachers? A reasonable teaching assignment for a novice (not to be confused with an ideal assignment) is defined as having: no more than two instructional preparations; at least one planning period per day; no extracurricular assignments; no more than five classes; an assigned classroom; and a mentor who is on-site and trained for the role. Results from the fall survey were summarized to answer the question. Both the teaching fellows (n = 23) and alumni not connected with the fellows program (n = 23) responded to the survey. Also, questions on the survey requested information on the following: number of preparations; number of classes; extracurricular duties; number of planning periods; assigned classroom; assignment of mentor and, when the assignment was made; proximity of mentor; and types of services rendered by the mentor. A summary of the fall survey follows.

The number of preparations ranged from one to five with 2.6 being the average. The beginning teacher with five preparations taught foreign languages. Five teachers had a single preparation; twenty had two preparations (43 percent); and fifteen had three preparations (33 percent). Forty-two (91 percent) of the teachers had five class sections or more. Thirty-six (78 percent) of the respondents had extracurricular duties; and of the thirty-six teachers, twenty-two (48 percent) had two or more major extracurricular duties. Examples of duties included: yearbook, cheerleading coordinator, and coaching. All but one of the forty-six respondents had one planning period per day. Out of the forty-six respondents, fourteen (30 percent) reported not having their own classroom. Instead, they carried their curriculum and lessons on carts and "floated" to available classrooms. All of the first-year teachers except one reported having a trained mentor.

In regard to their work with trained mentors, twenty-five (55 percent) of the forty-six alumni who had mentors received assistance during the first week of employment. The remaining mentors were assigned by the third week of employment. Respondents in school systems that had the North Carolina State Department of Public Instruction's twenty-four contact hour mentor training program implemented over two weeks cited mentor services that included administrative support, psychological support, and assistance with lesson planning. Respondents in school systems electing to participate in a ninety contact-hour mentor education program organized by North Carolina State University's Department of Curriculum and Instruction, and implemented during one year, reported mentor services that included administrative support, psychological support, and assistance with lesson planning. They also received coaching with instructional strategies, formative observations, and help with resources. This more extensive mentor preparation included a supervised practicum for participants. Finally, in follow-up interviews with eleven first-year teachers (Heathcoat, 1992), all informants said they worked with challenging students.

When the fall survey results are looked at as a whole, one finds first-year teachers facing several curriculum preparations, large numbers of classes, challenging students, burdensome extracurricular duties, and, for 30 percent of the respondents, no classroom to call their own. In light of these results the answer to the first question of the study is a resounding "no." First-year teaching assignments assessed in this study were unreasonable. Many of the beginning teachers surveyed may have had assignments that were more challenging than those of their more experienced colleagues.

The second inquiry focused on the comparison of a traditional and a nontraditonal group of teacher education alumni with regard to their expectations about the first year of teaching. Results from the spring survey were summarized to answer this question and included the item-by-item mean responses and differences of first-year teachers to the questions of "what is" and "what should be" and the items' mean degree of importance as rated by the respondents. Responses are given for the sixteen alumni, the sixteen alumni who are teaching fellows, and for the total group of thirty-two respondents.

Each item was responded to in three ways. The first was by a rating scale of 1 to 4, from "never or hardly ever" to "always or almost always" in terms of "what actually had happened during the first year of teaching." The second response was by a rating scale of 1 to 4, from "never or hardly ever" to "always or almost always" in terms of what the respondent thinks should happen with beginning teachers. Finally, the third response was with regard to the importance attached to each item on a scale of 1 to 10, from "of little importance" to "exceedingly important."

A frequency count was made of all items by respondents' ratings. Then, the frequencies were multiplied by weighted ratings and divided by the number of respondents to yield means for each item for each of the three ratings: "what is," "what should be," and "importance." A few respondents omitted an occasional response; these were entered as a 0 in the frequency count.

Table 3 shows those items with discrepancy means of 1.0 or greater. A discrepancy of 1.0 or greater on the 4-point scale warrants attention. Nineteen of the twenty-nine items are included. Alumni had sixteen items with 1.0 or greater discrepancies and the teaching fellows alumni had ten with the total group showing eleven of the twenty-nine items of 1.0 or greater discrepancies. The patterns of responses for alumni and teaching fellows are similar. However, the alumni tended to have greater discrepancies between "what is" and "what should be" than the teaching fellows alumni.

Eleven of the twenty-nine items with discrepancy means of 1.0 or greater dealt mainly with instructional matters and school climate. For the total group these were: adequate planning time; assistance in developing teaching style and repertoire of teaching strategies; adequate materials for

TABLE 3.

Items with discrepancy means of 1.0 or greater by first-year teachers regarding "what is" and "what should be," Spring 1992

Item	Alumni N=16	Differences 1.0 + Alumni:T.F. N=16	Total N=32
1. Have adequate time to plan.	1.1875	(.9375)	1.06250
2. Have adequate clerical support.	(.7500)	1.0625	(.90625)
3. Helped to develop teaching style.	1.3750	1.3750	1.37500
4. Been helped to develop a repertoire of teaching strategies.	1.3125	1.1250	1.21875
6. Have materials needed for teaching.	1.5625	1.2500	1.40625
7. Have opportunities to visit and observe exemplary teachers.	1.2500	(.9375)	1.09375
9. My mentor provided assistance with classroom management.	1.0625	(.7500)	(.90625)
15. Feedback and encouragement were received from my principal.	1.1250	(.7500)	(.93750)
16. My teaching assignment was realistic for a beginner.	1.3125	(.5000)	(.90625)
17. Teacher training prepared me to work with racially diverse student groups.	1.0000	(.8750)	(.93750)
18. Have time to reflect on my teaching.	(.8125)	1.2500	1.03125
19. I find satisfaction in teaching.	1.0625	(.6250)	(.84375)
20. I feel a part of the school community.	1.3125	(.6250)	(.96875)
21. Climate in our school supports a good learning environment.	1.4375	1.0625	1.25000
22. Climate supports a good learning environment for me as a beginning teacher.	1.1250	1.0000	1.06250
23. Climate in our school supports exchange of ideas with colleagues.	1.0000	1.3750	1.18750
24. I participated in school policy decisions.	1.0000	1.1875	1.09375
25. Teaching is what I thought it would be.	.8750	.0000	.43750
26. Technology used to great advantage in our school.	1.3125	1.2500	1.28125
Total items with 1.0 or greater discrepancy	16	10	11

Note: Discrepancies less than 1.0 are reported in parentheses when one of the subgroups showed 1.0 or greater discrepancy on an item.

teaching and advantageous use of technology; opportunities to visit and observe exemplary teachers and time to reflect on own teaching; school climate supporting a good learning environment (for students), for beginning teachers, and for exchange of ideas with colleagues; and participation in school policy decisions.

Items 9, 10, 11, and 12 related to mentors and their roles with beginning teachers and 13, 14, and 15 are related to feedback from others regarding teaching effectiveness. More congruence between "what is" and "what should be" was evident in the mean responses for these items.

With regard to importance of situations given in the twenty-nine-item survey, eight were rated as 9.0 or greater on the 10-point scale. No items had a mean response of less than 6.0. Of most importance to the entire group were: adequate time to plan; having materials needed for teaching; helpful feedback from classroom observations; satisfaction in teaching; a good learning environment in the school; school climate supportive of a good learning environment for a beginning teacher; students responsive to teaching; and reasonable school rules and requirements.

The first-year teachers' responses to the survey as revealed by their ratings of "what is," "what should be," and "importance" for each of the twenty-five items provides evidence that they are most concerned with instructional effectiveness and relationships with students and a supportive educational environment for students and for themselves. Mentors' roles appear to be clear to beginners and mentors.

As mentioned previously, response patterns for alumni and teaching fellows were similar with three notable exceptions. Three survey items were expressly designed to identify global first-year teacher expectations. The three items were: My teaching assignment was realistic for a beginner; I find satisfaction in teaching; and, Teaching is what I thought it would be. Teaching fellows who entered the classrooms had significantly less discrepancy than their counterparts on each of these items. Their teaching assignments generally were what they had expected them to be, the level of satisfaction with teaching was relatively high, and their expectations of teaching were largely met. Table 4 shows the mean discrepancies on these three items for the alumni and the teaching fellows.

Results shown in Table 4 were somewhat surprising. It may be that the teaching fellows' program (intervention) with its emphasis on additional role-taking experiences such as internships and tutoring with guided critical reflection on those experiences, and continuity from the freshman through the senior year through networking in cohort groups, helped to ameliorate the "unrealistic optimism" found by Weinstein (1988). The Weinstein study suggests that novice teachers leave preservice programs and enter the profession believing that

TABLE 4.

Global first-year teacher expectations with discrepancy means for alumni and teaching fellows, Spring 1992

Item	Alumni N = 16	Alumni T. Fellows N = 16	Total N = 32
My teaching assignment was realistic for a beginner.	1.31	(.50)	.90
I find satisfaction in teaching.	1.06	(.62)	.84
Teaching is what I thought it would be.	.87	.00	.44

"teaching is not all that difficult." Huling-Austin (1992) has underscored how induction literature and teacher education literature have practically ignored this phenomenon. The intervention described in this study may offer a theory-based plan for combating this tendency among first-year teachers.

The third and final question of the study addressed what concerns (Fuller, 1969) are dominant for first-year teachers at differing cognitive-developmental stages. Developmental assessments, as described above, were administered only to the teaching fellows in their freshman and senior years. The third question was explored by developing a matrix that portrayed dominant concerns of the teaching fellows in the spring of their first year of teaching and the post-test justice reasoning and conceptual level of the teaching fellows assessed during their senior year. Table 5 shows a comparison of the beginning teachers' concerns with their justice-reasoning scores. The teaching fellows are grouped by low, moderate, and high use of principles (P) in three social dilemmas.

TABLE 5.

Concerns matrix: principled reasoning and first-year teacher concerns for sixteen teaching fellows

Stage of Principled Thinking	Level of Concern		
	Self	Task	Impact
Low (20.0–39.0)	1	4	1
Moderate (40.0–50.0)	0	3	1
High (51.0–80.0)	1	1	4

Table 5 presents the first-year teachers' (teaching fellows) distribution of concerns according to their stages of principled thinking. Only at the highest stage of principled reasoning are a clear majority of the teachers focused on concerns about their students.

Table 6 shows the levels of concerns and the stages of conceptual complexity for the teaching fellows in the spring of their first year of teaching. There is a trend away from self concerns and toward impact concerns (students and colleagues) with increases in the conceptual level. These results, then, indicate that two independent assessments of developmental stage both correlate positively with movement on concerns measures. Information from the second matrix corroborates data in the first matrix and supports the need for continued investigation of relationships between cognitive developmental stages of novice teachers and their classroom attitudes and behaviors. The trend for first-year teachers at higher developmental stages is to express more concern for student learning and welfare.

IMPLICATIONS FOR TEACHER EDUCATION

Research in teacher induction needs to describe more accurately both the first-year teaching/learning process as it exists, and investigate experimental programs that show promise in changing how teacher induction might most effectively be practiced. The study of teacher induction is inexorably linked to researched programs to improve teacher education and schools. Therefore, the three questions raised in this study were based on research literature on teacher induction and teacher education, and included the following:

1. Assuming that statewide attention given to beginning teachers may be marking the end of "sink or swim" socialization, are first-year teaching assignments reasonable?

TABLE 6.

Concerns matrix: conceptual complexity (CL) and spring concerns of sixteen first-year teachers who are teaching fellows

	Level of Concern		
Conceptual Complexity	Self	Task	Impact
Low (1.5–1.7)	1	2	1
Moderate (1.8–2.2)	2	5	2
High (2.21–2.7)	0	1	3

2. Comparing a traditional and nontraditional group of teacher education alumni, are there differences in expectations about the first year of teaching?

3. Drawing on Fuller's seminal work (1969) and recent findings in cognitive developmental psychology, what concerns are dominant for first-year teachers at differing cognitive-developmental stages?

The findings indicate: that first-year teaching assignments continue to be unreasonable; that nontraditional first-year teachers who participated in a theory-based undergraduate program had less discrepancy between "what is" and what "should be" in their expectations about the first year of teaching; and that first-year teachers at higher cognitive-developmental stages had more concern for students and had fewer self concerns than teachers at moderate and low stages. In light of these findings, three implications for practice are made.

Perhaps the most important implication is for school/university/state partnerships to cooperate to reframe the assignments of first-year teachers. The litany of problems associated with unrealistic first-year teaching assignments is all too familiar. Until policy is adopted that changes, in a fundamental way, the demands placed on first-year teachers, promising beginning teachers will continue to leave a profession that needs them.

Second, the unique theory-based (cognitive-developmental) configuration of activities of the teaching fellows warrants closer inspection. Teacher education courses have been roundly criticized from all sides for their lack of theoretical coherence, and the trend has been to force teacher-preparation courses into the final two years of an undergraduate program. The program developed for the teaching fellows used seminars beginning in the freshman year. It placed emphasis on critical guided reflection, offered additional field experiences such as summer internships and tutoring, and encouraged the use of cohort groups for interaction *throughout* the baccalaureate program. The program built a strong *esprit de corps* through networking among the teaching fellows both on a campus and among campuses in the state program, which may have encouraged a more informed and realistic set of expectations about the first year of teaching. Comparable programs might be examined to determine whether similar outcomes are reached as alumni enter the classroom.

Finally, teacher education programs and district induction programs could benefit from examining the relationships between the cognitive-developmental stage of their preservice teachers and their behaviors as novice teacher/learners. The demands of the first year of teaching require a moderate-to-high level of psychological maturity. It may be that teachers' level of maturity is predictive of their ability to adapt realistically to the complexities of the classroom. Research (Reiman & Thies-Sprinthall, 1993) indicates that teachers who can reflect-on-action and reflect-in-action (Schön, 1987) are at higher cognitive-developmental stages.

Perhaps the goals of teacher education should address the cognitive-developmental growth of prospective teachers. The data in this study lend promising support to this goal. How first-year teachers acquire compassion and teaching expertise is of primary concern for teacher educators and policymakers. The results of this study suggest that undergraduate teacher education programs can pass on more realistic expectations about the first year of teaching, and, through encouraging development, prepare the first-year teacher to have the cognitive ability to affect his or her students. More research is needed on the intriguing question of whether first-year teachers are in a better position to learn from their experiences when they have more realistic expectations, experience less dissonance, and are at higher cognitive-developmental stages.

REFERENCES

Colbert, I. A., & Wolff, D. (1992). Surviving in urban schools: A collaborative model for a beginning teacher support system. *Journal of Teacher Education, 43* (3), 193–199.

Fuller, F. (1969). Concerns of teachers: A developmental conceptualization. *American Educational Research Journal, 6,* 207–226.

Haberman, M. (1991). The dimensions of excellence in programs of teacher education. Paper presented at the Conference on Alternative Certification, South Padre Island, TX.

Heathcoat, L. (1992). First-year teachers: Context, concerns, relationships, and rewards. Unpublished master's thesis. Raleigh: North Carolina State University.

Huling-Austin, L. (1990). Teacher induction programs and internships. In W. R. Houston (Ed.), *Handbook of Research in Teacher Education* (pp. 535–548). New York: Macmillan.

Huling-Austin, L. (1992). Research on learning to teach: Implications for teacher induction and mentoring programs. *Journal of Teacher Education, 43* (3), 173–180.

Hunt, D. (1971). *Matching models in education: The coordination of teaching methods with student characteristics.* Toronto: Ontario Institute for Studies in Education.

Little, J. (1990). The mentor phenomenon and the social organization of teaching. In C. B. Cazden (Ed.), *Review of Research in Education, 16,* 297–351. Washington, DC: American Educational Research Association.

Odell, S. J. (1986). Induction support of new teachers: A functional approach. *Journal of Teacher Education, 37* (1), 26–29.

Reiman, A. J., & Thies-Sprinthall, L. (1993). Promoting the development of mentor teachers: Theory and research programs using guided reflection. *Journal of Research and Development, 26* (3), 179–185.

Reiman, A. J., & Parramore, B. (1993). Promoting preservice teacher development through extended field experience. In M. O'Hair and S. J. Odell (Eds.), *Diversity and teaching: Teacher education yearbook I* (pp. 111–121). Fort Worth: Harcourt Brace Jovanovich College Publishers.

Reiman, A. J. & Edelfelt, R. (1991). The opinions of mentors and beginning teachers: What do they say about induction? *Technical Report 91-1.* Raleigh: North Carolina State University.

Rest, J. (1986). *Moral development: Advances in research and theory.* New York: Praeger.

Schön, D. (1987). *Educating the reflective practitioner.* San Francisco: Jossey-Bass.

Sprinthall, N. A. & Thies-Sprinthall, L. (1983). The teacher as an adult learner: A cognitive-developmental view. In G. A. Griffin (Ed.), *Staff Development:Eighty-second Yearbook of the National Society for the Study of Education* (pp. 24–31). Chicago: University of Chicago Press.

Sprinthall, N. A., Reiman, A. J., & Thies-Sprinthall, L. (In press). Roletaking and reflection: Promoting the conceptual and moral development of teachers. *Learning and Individual Differences.*

Veenman, S. (1984) Perceived problems of beginning teachers. *Review of Educational Research,* 54, 143–178.

Weinstein, C. S. (1988). Preservice teachers' expectations about the first year of teaching, *Teaching and Teacher Education, 4,* 31–40.

Zeichner, K. M. & Tabachnick, B. (1981). Are the effects of university teacher education"washed out" by school experience? *Journal of Teacher Education, 32* (3), 7–11.

Teacher Preparation: Implications and Reflections

KENNETH R. HOWEY
The Ohio State University

PROMOTING A CULTURAL PARTNERSHIP

As indicated in the prelude to these chapters, Holm and Johnson address a problem of major proportion: the multicultural education of teachers. The United States becoming even more diverse culturally can be viewed positively. However, the number of youngsters in poverty is dramatically increasing at the same time cultural diversity in the prospective teaching force is diminishing. Beyond that, the number of Anglo prospective teachers who indicate that they would prefer to teach in either urban areas (cities from 100,000 to 500,000) or major urban areas where poverty is more common, is very limited. In the 1988 Research About Teacher Education (RATE) Study, only 6 percent of prospective teachers indicated that they were interested in teaching in a major urban area. Thus, the problem is not only one of recruiting more quality minorities into the teaching force, but also recruiting and preparing teachers who are able and disposed to teach in the areas where the challenges to our educational system are the greatest.

In an effort to underscore the importance of multiculturalism in teacher preparation and teaching, the authors chose to use the term *cultural partnership*. They wish to emphasize that to enable understanding and appreciation of cultural similarities and differences, one has to share with others firsthand. For Holm and Johnson, cultural partnerships are relationships that grow from, and are nourished by, the integration of knowledge of other cultural backgrounds combined with a pluralism in *practice* and belief.

This reviewer takes the position that laboratory and clinical activities can be designed to provide an *incremental* engagement with persons in cultural settings different than one's own. For example, one could begin with cases wherein multiple perspectives are shared in an environment that safely fosters clarification and reflection on these differences. An appreciation of multiple perspectives can be one of the explicit purposes in engaging a group of prospective teachers to deal with cases having multicultural content. Tillman (1992) in her research employed the case methodology for such purposes and had moderate success.

The Holm and Johnson study also is to be commended for its grounding in previous scholarship. For example, drawing on the work of McDiarmid and Price (1993) and Irvine (1985), they were able to focus on previously identified patterns of beliefs of preservice teachers relative to ethnic and racial differences. Likewise, in the framing of their study, they provide a perspective for dealing with the cultural beliefs and concerns of prospective teachers. They take the position that if teacher education is to redress cultural inequality in schools, it will be necessary for prospective teachers to understand the various societal forces that shape our current cultural beliefs and thus preservice students need to be made aware of the contribution in disciplines such as linguistics, history, and cultural anthropology.

THE INQUIRY

In order to gain some understanding of the current cultural beliefs of prospective teachers, Holm and Johnson interviewed 12 preservice teachers during their student teaching. Eight of these novices were Anglo and four were African American. However, all 12 volunteers grew up in mainstream, white neighborhoods.

Not surprisingly, each of the participants was able to speak to both covert and overt forms of discrimination within the context in which they were raised. Several of them also were able to articulate the frustration they encountered in trying to alter cultural beliefs and perspectives that were prevalent in their formative years. One surprising result of the pilot study interviews was that none of these future teachers recalled participating in multicultural curricula in their elementary and secondary education. Since there are formal curriculum and instruction efforts in most schools, however, that focus on multicultural concerns and issues of social justice, it is unclear why none of the students encountered such. In this regard, while the program description for the teacher education program in which these students were enrolled suggested that multicultural education was infused *throughout* their program, these particular students did not view this to be the situation. They were able to identify a specific course that focused on multicultural education and another on children's literature which was generally viewed as helpful. However, the idea of a major thematic focus that would manifest itself repeatedly in both the didactic and experiential aspects of the program was simply not familiar to these prospective teachers.

INSIGHTS INTO THE BELIEFS OF PRESERVICE TEACHERS

In the program design and development work that this author and Nancy Zimpher (1989) have engaged in, one of the attributes of effective programs we have identified is a limited number of themes—typically 6 to 10, which are derived from some conception of schooling and, in turn, teaching and learning. These explicit conceptions and derivative themes provide the guideposts for developing a curriculum scope and sequence in a program. Surely it would seem that a concern for social justice, manifold cultural understandings, and a respect for pluralism would be manifest in a theme in any program preparing teachers in our multicultural society. Nonetheless it was *not* thematic to these prospective teachers.

The results of the inquiry by Holm and Johnson provide considerable food for thought and, in many respects, are sobering. They report that: (1) these prospective teachers are willing to acknowledge their cultural intolerance but simply are not prepared to resolve the various conflicts which they experience in this regard; (2) diversity for these students is defined basically in terms of African-American students; students from other ethnicities, social class, gender, and religion are rarely referenced when diversity is discussed by these potential teachers; (3) correspondingly, minority groups are viewed in a largely undifferentiated manner—not even language differences are mentioned by the respondents. In a dualistic manner, their pupils are viewed as either mainstream or minority; (4) students believe that it is difficult for white teachers to deal with black students and have, as indicated earlier, a host of preconceptions and in many cases misconceptions about these youngsters in inner-city settings and the challenge or problems they would present in the classroom; (5) it is not so much a matter of diversity that is viewed as a problem, but rather the attitudes and behaviors they view as accommodating minority youth. (As the authors report: "Some of our preservice teachers want a suburban middle class type of diversity.") Thus, we see that "culture shock" may better be defined as "class shock" or at least a combination of the two in several instances.

POSSIBLE PROGRAM DIRECTIONS

Holm and Johnson reported these preservice teachers believe that they receive information in various courses to address multicultural goals but lack the *experiential* activities that accompany the didactic portion of their preparation to develop and refine their understandings and abilities. They further indicated that the lack of exemplary teacher role models who represented cultural differences was a major problem. Thus, in addition to a thematic strand on equity, social justice, and cultural differences with multiple experiential opportunities and laboratory, and clinical experiences incorporated within it, multiple opportunities for students to interact with people different from themselves are needed.

The position taken by this reviewer is that more consideration should be given to what would be a reasonable progression of activities. Short term *preservice student* cohorts, as heterogenous as possible, could be introduced over time to create increasingly sophisticated cultural understandings. For example, prospective teacher cohorts could take advantage of the variety of cultural activities that occur in most college and university settings beyond the college of education. They could, for example, participate in activities such as a cultural food fair. They could move next to a structured interview, with persons from different cultures and accompanied by formal study of a culture and finally immersion experiences in different cultural settings. The full resources of the campus and the community could be employed in this regard. A multicultural program then would include developmental activities with preservice students working closely together in activities, ranging from the development of intrapersonal skills and better understanding and appreciation of multiple perspectives to immersion experiences over time. The lack of laboratory and clinical opportunities interspersed with didactic instruction is a universal problem in teacher education and a multicultural focus suggests several means by which students can engage in experiential activities. Laboratory and clinical preparation need not denote highly sophisticated facilities based on state-of-the-art equipment, although surely teacher education is remiss in this regard. Rather, it suggests a structured set of experiential activities to accompany sound scholarship, many of which can be instituted with relative ease in existing campus settings.

Finally, Holm and Johnson report these prospective teachers made no mention of wanting to develop a special interest in what their pupils had to say, what they had experienced, and what they indicated that they needed or desired. They had no particular interest in trying to ascertain the beliefs of the individuals, especially a culturally different pupil. Perhaps one reason for this is because teacher education has been remiss in addressing the beliefs of prospective teachers. Recall that these scholars had the laudable goal of attempting to shape a *cultural partnership* but it appears that the students they interviewed fell far short. It should be underscored that a prevalent contemporary conception of teaching and learning is rooted in constructivist principles. Knowledge is socially constructed in groups, where learners and teachers have to make explicit their beliefs and what they understand to others, and just how they arrived at those understandings. A variety of powerful methodologies are evolving for pupils to better monitor efforts to learn, not only as individuals, but also in groups. These novice teachers are at some conceptual distance from this and it may very well be that ultimately much of the problem in our ignorance of and insensitivity to cultural differences is rooted in our limited conception of teaching and learning to settings where cultural diversity exists.

Holm and Johnson are to be commended for providing us with further insights into the beliefs and perceptions of prospective teachers regarding a critically important concept. Their findings reaffirm that bold and imaginative new directions are needed in how we prepare our teachers.

COOPERATING TEACHER/STUDENT TEACHER RELATIONSHIP

The Bowers chapter examines relationships in activities between student teachers and the cooperating teachers who guide them. Some excellent in-depth qualitative studies are beginning to be reported in the literature relative to the interactions between these two parties and in several instances the person from the school or college of education responsible for providing this supervision as well. Much remains to be done however in understanding the nature and impact of this critical aspect of preservice teacher preparation. Thus, Bowers is to be commended for her focus in this regard.

Bowers employed multiple methodologies in collecting information and data pertaining to five student teachers during a 14-week student teaching period. Her data gathering instrumentation and methodology included survey questionnaires, a focused essay, classroom observations accompanied with interviews, and an interactive seminar wherein specific topics of interest were probed individually and collectively. She reports that the student teachers completed nine different instruments although the nature and focus of these were not included in the chapter as reported herein.

Bowers grounded her work in the efforts of two earlier studies. One was undertaken by Copas (1984), who examined student teachers from more than 30 different programs and asked them to describe what they believed to be effective and ineffective practices and behaviors by those teachers who were assisting them in this preparation phase. Copas eventually reduced the many practices and behaviors identified in her inquiry to 14 basic supervisory functions that were further broken down into six categories: orienting, inducting, guiding, reflecting, cooperating, and supporting. The second investigation

Bowers drew from was that of Kuehl (1976), who developed a taxonomy of critical functions for supervising teachers, ranging from the orientation of a student teacher in the classroom to the development of core instructional strategies. Kuehl eventually recommended that the 40-some "critical" tasks he derived be employed as selection criteria for cooperating teachers.

RELATIONSHIP TYPES

Based on the information accrued in her interactions with these five student teachers and, in turn, their experiences with two different cooperating teachers, Bowers developed her own typology of what she refers to as "interaction types." Among the types of student teacher/cooperating teacher interactions she identified are: a professional partnership, a mentorship, an apprenticeship, a lack-of-support type, and finally, a rigidity type. Eventually and understandably, Bowers calls for a combination of a professional partnership and a mentorship arrangement and more attention to a thoughtful developmental sequence over time in terms of the instructional support and guidance provided to beginning teachers. The interaction styles of lack of support and rigidity are rejected. One of the major findings in her study from this perspective is that, in more than half of the instances, highly questionable guidance is provided by cooperating teachers to prospective teachers.

Even the apprenticeship notion has major limitations in terms of learning to teach. As this writer suggested in the introduction to these chapters, the essence of learning to teach is a sustained, structured discourse about teaching and learning. This dialogue is guided by looking at teaching and learning through the lenses of scholars in various fields as well as the expertise of experienced teachers. Apprenticeships characterized by a good deal of observation of veteran teachers followed by directions to emulate what was observed will accomplish no more than a person, assuming she or he could become an expert medical diagnostician by observing a physician in the course of an examination and then attempting to emulate this. While there are indeed legitimate apprenticeship functions, especially in terms of being enculturated into a particular setting, the nature of learning to teach surely goes beyond an apprenticeship as Bowers underscores in her treatise.

Bowers argues for an emphasis on professional partnerships and mentorships. The professional partnership, as defined by Bowers, appears more concerned with the relationship between the two parties than with any particular set of methodological strategies or orientation toward learning to teach. Bowers is concerned rather with achieving some equity in the relationship. While there must be mutual respect and a good deal of reciprocity in these critical working relationships, from this perspective it is misguided to view the two parties as equals, especially in terms of their abilities in the classroom. We have tended to underestimate the complexity of learning to teach, and the novice teacher is placed with more experienced teachers primarily to learn. The conceptual distance between more expert and novice teachers suggests at times than an intermediary is called for to interpret dialogue or to identify their differences in technical language. Notwithstanding licensure practices, the first year teacher and the veteran teacher are not equals nor should they be viewed as such.

NEEDED CHANGES IN TEACHER PREPARATION

The trend in several states is to provide for an internship or residency at the completion of what is now construed as initial or preservice preparation. Initial licensure is deferred for at least a year while the *reasoning* ability and teaching "performance" of beginning teachers is assessed more continuously and with greater veracity. The position taken here is that the profession is better served by a more protracted and rigorous educative and evaluative experience extending into the first year of teaching. Such arrangements promise greater quality control and more accurate assessment. In this more seamless extension of teacher education, the graduate in the first year or two of teaching would be better characterized as a *resident* or *intern* teacher.

Likewise, while mentoring arrangements are to be commended, it is difficult to structure the relationship characterized as *mentoring* and all this entails. Mentoring, as Bowers points out, is a manifold relationship that takes on dimensions of role modeling, personal guidance, individual support, and typically deep personal investment. Where such relationships evolve and protégés develop as a result of this investment, both parties are richly rewarded. This is obviously rare, however, in terms of the enculturation processes, which occur in most school settings or the broader socialization or the lack thereof that occurs in the preservice setting. Rather, what appears to be needed is a variety of educative functions vested more appropriately in titles such as *consulting* or *clinical* teacher or *advisor.*

A robust program of preparation for these consulting teachers—preferably designed by outstanding practicing professionals and those in the teacher education community—could draw upon a corpus of understandings embedded in several disciplines to make the role an instructional one with the needed clinical abilities to assist beginning teachers. In leadership programs which Nancy Zimpher and I (1989) have helped develop for cadres of teacher leaders, we have drawn upon the general leadership literature, studies of developmental patterns of beginning teachers, the ever-expanding literature on learning and teaching, insights from both adult development and studies of psychological maturity of college-aged students, multiple ways of analyzing teaching and learning interactions, and in engaging in dialogue and discourse about these through arrangements currently referred to as conferencing and coaching. The essence of the relationship is the ability to engage in highly intellectual discussions about the commonplaces of the school and classroom. Unfortunately, the selection and preparation of cooperating teachers and the reimbursement for an acknowledgment of their efforts can only be characterized as embarrassing.

In summary, Bowers is to be commended for her focus on these critical interactions, a phenomenon that is not well understood, and for calling our attention to the types of relationship that exist between prospective teachers and veteran teachers, especially the problems that very much need to be redressed.

BEGINNING TEACHER PROGRAMS: A RATIONALE

The final chapter in this trilogy is concerned with what transpires with teachers during what is referred to as an induction or first year experience for graduates in teacher education at North Carolina State University.

Reiman and Parramore are the investigators in this study. At the outset they make the case for induction programs by underscoring the goals of not only enhancing the quality of instruction for new teachers but also improving teacher *retention* given the high dropout rate of beginning teachers. This reviewer suggests there are other reasons for a focus on the critical first year(s) of teaching. Surely we should be concerned about finding ways to ensure that *quality* beginning teachers are not deterred from pursuing a career in teaching by a lack of support or needed further education in these early years. However, we should be concerned that we can identify and counsel teachers who, in fact, do *not* have the disposition and abilities to provide a quality educative experience for youth. The evaluative responsibility cuts both ways.

The fundamental rationale for assistance programs for beginning teachers should be rooted in quality instruction provided for students in their classrooms. Without sustained assistance for these beginning teachers, as called for in the Reiman and Parramore paper, one could argue that pupils in many classrooms of new teachers are considerably disadvantaged compared to pupils in more experienced classrooms.

Obviously enculturation is needed for many beginning teachers, especially given the anemic and in many cases even negative socialization which occurs in their preservice preparation generally. This need also argues for entry year(s) programs. Finally, there is the matter of the retention of outstanding veteran teachers; many of whom leave teaching at the peak of their careers. Providing leadership roles for exemplary veteran teachers to work with beginning teachers in an expanded instructional capacity in preservice programs is a desired future direction and some clinical faculties are now evolving. In these situations, joint appointments for outstanding teachers are negotiated wherein they maintain a classroom assignment but have some of their time allocated to the clinical preparation of beginning teachers. Such arrangements can be a powerful *retention* factor for outstanding *experienced* teachers who desire a change and might otherwise leave teaching.

A GROUNDED STUDY

To the credit of Reiman and Parramore, they ground their study in prior scholarship and conceptual work along two dimensions, which examine patterns of beginning teachers' concerns and which look at their conceptual development. A major difference in this prior research on concerns between novice and more experienced teachers is where they focus. Many novice teachers are concerned with their actions and the sense of who they are in the interactive engagements of teaching and learning. On the other hand, many veteran teachers are able to focus more squarely on their students' success or lack thereof. "Expert" teachers can speak more fully to the relationships between what they contribute to these endeavors and what their students take away. There appears to be a major developmental difference in terms of expertise and maturity between a focus primarily on self and a focus on relationships to student learning.

Similarly, the ability of teachers to move beyond dualistic interpretations and to embrace multiple perspectives in their interpretations of complex phenomena considerably differentiates teachers. The latter ability is similar to the main concern raised in the Holm and Johnson chapter; how do we acquire not only the habit, but as John Dewey suggested, the *taste* for dialogue and listening, especially to people who may act and believe differently than ourselves? By grounding their study of beginning teachers in constructs that have the potential to yield fuller understanding of the developmental patterns of beginning teachers, this joint inquiry has the potential for informing a type of teacher education that can both accommodate and rectify *patterns* of teacher development that are unnecessarily protracted, stabilized, or misdirected.

Reiman and Parramore report on two studies embedded in a broader, eight-year longitudinal study of teacher education students educated in two distinctively different programs. Longitudinal studies of teachers over time can be very informative. Such investigations, however, are difficult to sustain and these scholars deserve credit for their efforts in this regard.

Also I would encourage them to further elaborate in the literature on the program designed to promote cognitive development. The prospective teachers in the program live together on campus, and are housed in the same dormitory. They participate in special experiential activities during the summers between their formal teacher education studies. They are expected to reflect in a continuing manner on critical issues in education and they have multiple opportunities for multicultural interactions. Building on the pioneer work of Sprinthall and Thies-Sprinthall (1983), elements in this program are specifically designed to promote conceptual complexity. They include: new and complex helping experiences, a balance between experiential activities and guided reflection, continuing challenges to present views and beliefs as well as sustained support accompanying challenges, and finally thematic continuity of adult development throughout the program.

NEEDED CONDITIONS TO SUPPORT BEGINNING TEACHERS

The first major question these two investigators are concerned with is whether teaching assignments for their graduates are reasonable; they emphasize that reasonable is not to be confused with ideal. Their construal of reasonable conditions includes: no more than two instructional preparations, at least one planning period per day, no extracurricular assignments, no more than five classes total, an assigned classroom, and a mentor who is prepared for the role and is in the same school (the authors' concern is with secondary teachers). These indeed seem to be germane criteria and should serve as a departure for further discussion, especially in the policy arena, regarding what constitutes a reasonable assignment for a beginning teacher. Other factors which might be considered include: class size, type of student, the degree and quality of instructional materials available and their consonance with the preparation the first year teacher had in her or his preservice teacher preparation, the amount of release time for interaction between first year teacher and her or his mentor, and the extent and quality of these educative experiences during the first year for the beginning teacher. Similar concerns can be raised about the preparation and selection of the veteran teachers who will assist them.

Thus, Reiman and Parramore have addressed a problem of considerable magnitude. Entry year programs are typically viewed as some peripheral nicety and not as a *needed extension* of the education of teachers into the critical and formative first year(s) of teaching. The policy arena needs to be informed by studies such as theirs, in order to structure the kinds of assignments and experiences first year teachers should have.

Not surprisingly this research team found that the assignments of beginning teachers are *not* what they should be. For example, the number of preparations ranged from one to five, and approximately a third of nearly fifty respondents reported they did not have their own classroom. While all of these first year teachers, with the exception of one, reported having a mentor, there is no discussion of the amount of time nor the type and quality of interaction between these two parties, as Bowers began to probe in her chapter. Further studies are needed, including a focus on pupil success in beginning teacher classrooms.

CONCEPTUAL COMPLEXITY

A second aspect of their inquiry focused on the comparison of the teacher education program designed to promulgate more conceptual complexity and multicultural sensitivity with the more diversified secondary teacher education program. Among other matters they wished to examine was the possible gap between expectations of these beginning teachers about what they could encounter in their initial assignments and their perception of that reality once they had been in the assignment for some time. Beginning teachers often bring overly romanticized and idealized perceptions of teaching with them to their initial teaching assignments and hence encounter unnecessary "reality shock" (Weinstein, 1988).

Their findings indicate that the program—which focused on the promotion of conceptual complexity and was structured over a four-year period and provided multiple opportunities for experiences in community, school, and classroom settings—left their students with a smaller discrepancy between what they thought would be the situation as a first year teacher and what the reality was. Similarly, these beginning teachers had a smaller discrepancy in terms of how satisfied they thought they would be and how satisfied they were.

A second major issue was whether there appeared to be any relationship between stages of principled thinking and conceptual complexity as measured through different instruments among students enrolled in the teacher education program and the nature of the concerns they expressed about their experiences as first year teachers. This pilot study involved 16 teaching fellows. Reiman and Parramore found some modest correlations between indices of higher stages of principled thinking and conceptual complexity and students who tended to focus on *impact* or student concerns as opposed to *self* and *task* concerns. Their inquiry is provocative and this reviewer encourages further study in terms of the nature and structure of the teacher preparation program and the multiple measures which might be employed to assess both principled thinking and student concerns.

One of the obvious inferences one can make from the data shared is that only six of the sixteen students were characterized at the highest stage of principled thinking and only four of the sixteen at the highest stage of conceptual complexity. Hence, we still have much to learn in terms of how to promote the kinds of reasoning and behavior in our prospective teachers that is principled and likely representative of the complexity of classroom instruction.

Reiman and Parramore call for research into teacher induction or entry-year programs that describe more in-depth and accurately what occurs in these various programs. They underscore the need to investigate programs that show promise in how teacher *education* during this critical first year of teaching can be most effectively sustained. This reviewer wholly concurs with this. What is first needed, however, are more thoughtful and substantive programs of initial teacher education that are extended in a thematic and seamless fashion into the first year(s) of teaching. Unfortunately, such programs are rare at this time.

REFERENCES

Copas, E. (1989). Critical requirements for cooperating teachers. *Journal of Teacher Education, 35,* 49–54.

Howey, K. R., & Zimpher, N. L. (1989). *Profiles of preservice teacher preparation.* Albany: State University of New York Press.

Irvine, J. J. (1985). Teacher communication patterns as related to the race and sex of the student. *Journal of Educational Research, 78,* 338–345.

Kuehl, R. (1976). A taxonomy of critical tasks for supervising teachers. Washington, DC, ERIC Document Reproduction Service, No: ED 179507.

McDiarmid, G. W., & Price, J. (1993). Preparing teachers for diversity: A study of student teachers in a multicultural program. In M. J. O'Hair and S. J. Odell (Eds.), *Diversity and teaching: Teacher education yearbook I* (pp. 31–57). Fort Worth: Harcourt Brace Jovanovich.

Sprinthall, N. A., & Thies-Sprinthall, S. (1983). The need for theoretical frameworks in educating teachers. A cognitive-developmental perspective.

In K. R. Howey and W. E. Gardner (Eds.), *The education of teachers: A look ahead* (pp. 79–97). New York: Longman.

Tillman, B. A. (1992). A study of the use of case methods in preservice teacher education, Ph.D. dissertation, The Ohio State University.

Weinstein, C. S. (1988). Preservice teachers' expectations about the first year of teaching, *Teaching and Teacher Education, 4,* 31–40.

DIVISION III

Partnerships in Defining and Improving Communication in Schools

Communication: Overview and Framework

CARL D. GLICKMAN
H. JAMES MCLAUGHLIN
University of Georgia

VALERIE MILLER
Five Forks Middle School
Lawrenceville, Georgia

CARL D. GLICKMAN is Professor in the Department of Educational Leadership and chair of the Program for School Improvement at the University of Georgia. Most recently, he has been the founder and head of various university–public school collaborations. The collaborations have involved more than eighty elementary, middle, and secondary schools representing thirty-seven school districts focused on school renewal through democratic governance.

H. JAMES MCLAUGHLIN is Assistant Professor in the Middle School Program at the University of Georgia. His teaching and research interests include early adolescence and middle school curriculum and teacher education program development. Dr. McLaughlin is participating in an action research project with Valerie Miller and her team to study students' conceptions of learning.

VALERIE MILLER is a sixth grade English teacher at Five Forks Middle School in Gwinnett County, Georgia. She has taught for three years and is currently working on a Master's degree. Ms. Miller is part of a two-year project in which her team of teachers will progress to the next grade level with the same students.

INTRODUCTION

Upon accepting the invitation to be respondents to the 1994 ATE Yearbook, we decided to take the challenge of providing an introduction and conclusion to the research studies on communication in the same spirit as the title of this yearbook, *Partnerships in Education*. The three of us are partners in education trying to fulfill our different responsibilities to a program in educational leadership (Carl Glickman), a program in middle-school teacher education (Jim McLaughlin), and a public school program of team teaching more than a hundred adolescent students (Valerie Miller). We will each view the articles in this chapter through different lenses, and write about what we might learn from them for our own practice. We share a belief that collaboration between universities and public schools can help us realize the essential purpose of public education. At times, we speak in separate voices, but at the end, we speak together about what should be the focus of communication in education.

Fishbein and Ajzen (1975) described a classic paradigm for studying communication: Who says what, how, to whom, and with what effect? We want to highlight also the "why" of communication in education, which can be found in the original purpose for public schools. Public education was derived from Thomas Jefferson's notion that democracy and education are interdependent. The mission of publicly supported schools (primary, secondary, and higher) should be to enable students to become powerful, proactive citizens of the larger democratic society. In most discussions about public school and teacher education reform, what is omitted is the understanding of *why* schools and teacher education institutes exist. Instead, most discussions focus on the shortcomings of students' subject matter achievement, or the deficiencies of schools and teacher education institutes in raising student achievement with the goal of becoming more competitive in the global market.

The study of communication in education should be different from the study of communication in other settings. The "what" being communicated between teachers, teacher educators, and students should not be about organizations or competitive products, but rather about how school interactions can help or hinder the development of all students toward taking their rightful and responsible places in society. What is refreshing about all three of the following studies is that they address topics closely connected to higher purposes.

As the three of us analyze, interpret, and draw implications from these studies, we will attempt to make explicit how the research may relate to the purposes of public education and teacher education institutions. In addition, we will consider what the articles have to say about the contexts, texts and subtexts of communication, which we believe are essential to understanding the meaning and effects of interpersonal communication. The participants in schooling—teachers, students, parents, and administrators—all meet within the complex confines of school. We believe that contextual issues lie at the heart of any research aimed at a deeper understanding of communication in educational settings. To clarify how contexts are examined (and not examined) in writing about communication, we will provide an overview of several representative pieces authored by K–12 classroom teachers and university educators. This introductory section will be somewhat brief, because our intent is simply to alert the reader to our focus as reviewers, and to pose questions for the reader to ponder. In our responses to the articles, we will explain more fully what we take to be the outcomes of this sort of research, and our thoughts on important issues of context and purpose.

CONTEXTS, TEXTS, AND SUBTEXTS OF COMMUNICATION

Textual Questions

When studying communication, researchers can examine the context, the text, and the subtext of a given situation. The context consists of the characteristics woven into a certain interaction that give meaning to the communication. Contextual questions, which are an elaboration of Fishbein and Ajzen's ideas, include:

- Who is communicating? Research may be concerned with dyadic communication or with group interactions, and it may also portray communication from one person's perspective or from multiple angles. The "who" does not simply name the participants; the participants' beliefs and interpretations of past experiences are also a key contextual factor.
- What is the setting within which people communicate? The description of setting is not merely physical; it might incorporate the expressed rules or tacit guidelines that circumscribe action.

- Why are people communicating? This is a matter of one's intentions when communicating with others.

If we metaphorically think of the context as the "ground" in a scene, then the text is the "figure." The text is made up of the explicit messages that are being communicated. Textual questions include:

- What are the people communicating about? This is a question of the domain, the explicit subject, of communication.
- How do they communicate? This "how" question must be asked alongside the "what." Our ways of communicating, verbal and nonverbal, are just as much part of the text as the words we speak.

The subtext of any communication includes our hidden or unconscious intentions and the meanings we attach to the interaction. Subtexts are formulated in conjunction with the text. From moment to moment we are expressing ourselves and trying to maintain communication with another person, even as we try to determine what the communication means to us. Questions related to subtext might be:

- What is *not* being expressed? What we don't say is often as vital as what we say.
- What are the hidden messages being transmitted or received during the interaction? The traditional "sender-receiver" metaphor of the preceding sentence doesn't quite convey the interpretive nature of the subtext. In discourse, we are constantly interpreting what someone might mean, or what lies behind the meaning (to insert another metaphor). A researcher, then, interprets the subtext of a communication by speculating about what a communicative interaction *means* to the participant and to a wider audience.

In the next section we will summarize five studies of communication in education. Our purposes are to exhibit the diversity of approaches to this line of research, and to provide examples of how different writers deal with the context, text, and subtext of communication. We have purposely chosen studies that involve participants similar to those described in the articles to follow (for example, teacher-to-teacher communication).

Research about Teacher-to-Teacher Communication

Andrew Hargreaves (1984) described a group of British teachers' communications with one another in decision-making meetings and interviews. The stated purpose of the meetings was fundamentally to revise the school curriculum. Hargreaves was curious about what the text would be and about whether the context of different settings, one "public" and the other "private," would alter the text of the communication. He found that the conversations in both settings revolved around teachers' interpretations of their classroom experiences with students. In the interviews, but not in school meetings, the teachers talked also about personal influences on their thinking as a teacher. In neither setting did they discuss what they were reading, or educational theory, or their current theoretical beliefs related to teaching and learning. The teachers seemed to appeal to a "shared cultural assumption," a "taken-for-granted, educational consensus" that relied on personal tales of experience (p. 247). In Hargreaves' interpretation, the subtext of the communications was that theoretical talk, or even public talk about influences on one's thinking, was "culturally inadmissible" (p. 248). What they were not communicating was vitally important to understanding the school culture. The difficulty that the teachers had in devising a curriculum that addressed major societal issues was related to their unwillingness to examine their beliefs and social theories.

Hargreaves' discussion was important because he saw that changing school conditions, to encourage a teacher culture that was more inviting to nonclassroom interpretations of experience, was a key to improving teaching and learning. The central subtextual issue was what was absent, not what was present in the communications.

Research about Teacher-and-Student Communication

McNeil (1986) wrote about how teachers' curriculum can be a means of control. The context of her study involved four secondary schools, and she centered on classroom communication of subject matter content. Although the text of this communication was about the "content," NcNeil believed that the teachers utilized "defensive teaching strategies" to control students' actions. "They chose to simplify content and reduce demands on students in return for classroom order and minimal student compliance on assignments" (p. 158). The causes of this subtext of classroom communication "lay in the tension between the teachers' professional roles within the school and the administrative context within which they worked" (p. xix). It was, in essence, the tension between responding to students' learning needs and working within the bounds of a bureaucratic institution.

Jackson (1992) offered a more positive description of how one teacher displayed her concern for students (pp. 37–56). On a regular basis, this teacher engaged in open communication with her students about their actions. Her intentions, a part of the context, were to get children to consider their own actions, and to "give them definition" (p. 49). The text of the communication thus centered on what students' actions *meant* in the life of the class. There were several subtexts to this sort of communication. The teacher believed that her semipublic conversations with misbehaving students were a means of teaching about commitment and responsibility. And Jackson believed that the blurring of the private and the public "encourage[d] listeners *to place themselves* in relation to the content of the conversation" (p. 47). Individual action was not isolated from other participants in the class.

Research about Teachers Communicating with Students and Adults

This example was written by a preschool teacher, Cynthia Ballenger (1992). It concerned her efforts to learn better how to teach Haitian immigrant students. Ballenger's communications took place with many people, within diverse settings. She conversed with North American colleagues in a teacher-researcher seminar, with Haitian teachers and parents in her preschool, and with a Haitian co-teacher of a college course in child development that was intended for Haitian day-care providers (p. 200). In the classroom she tried out what she was learning, so she was also communicating with her students, although she wrote little about the discourse. In her talks with other adults, Ballenger soon came to see the importance of the "language of control." Her intention in these various settings became to learn what Haitian teachers and parents said to the children that increased the children's participation in class activities and their adherence to class norms.

What we have just described is the context of the communication. The text involved Ballenger's notes of classroom conversation and observations as she shared them with the numerous participants. They would then talk about how the communication patterns of Haitians and North Americans differed, and posit reasons for the differences (pp. 202–203). The subtext of the communication for Ballenger, who was acting as a teacher-researcher, was that we can better understand how to teach if we understand another culture's orientations toward adult-child interactions. In this case, Ballenger learned from the communication—and her subsequent teaching experience that year—that sometimes reprimands can be confirming, and that North American classrooms need a "moral community" to augment our "powerful individualism" (p. 207). These gleanings constituted a portion of the meaning of her communication with the other adults. Her writing is a reminder of the cultural complexity of caring and controlling, and of the benefits of careful observation and thoughtful talk with colleagues about dilemmas we face in classrooms.

Research about Principal-and-Teacher Communication

Stephen Ball (1987) has tried to "map out the micropolitics of school life" (p. 7). His book analyzed several studies of the political structures and processes of British secondary schools. The communication was among teachers, and between teachers and the school head. The studies collected data in classrooms, teachers' workrooms, school meeting rooms, and other settings. Communication was both formal (faculty meetings, for example) and informal (casual hallway conversations). After describing these varied contexts, Ball concluded that four "leadership styles" ran through the studies. Teachers reacted to these styles in different ways, and their interactions with the head constituted a central dynamic in each school. Examining these styles shows the text and subtext of communication in each case.

Heads with an "interpersonal" style (pp. 88–95) communicated through personal relationships and face-to-face contact with teachers. The text, then, centered on individual concerns. Informal networks with the teachers emerged; public meetings to create policies were rare. The subtext of this style of communication served to value individual autonomy and personal support and to devalue collective decision making.

In a "managerial" style (pp. 95–104), school heads communicated with teachers via committees, memos, and other formal procedures. The texts of communication were likely to be written, and in any case public. Ball speculated that the communicative subtext (in our terms) was that policy is more important than person, and that the first priority of a head is to be responsible for the school as a system, a set of responsibilities, and duties.

In Ball's scheme, there was a "political" style that had two components. The first, an "adversarial" style (pp. 104–108), used the text of public debate to establish school policies. Adversarial heads "relish[ed] argument and confrontation" (p. 120). The subtext of this approach was that autonomy and support had to be earned through a powerful and persuasive argument. In the other political style, called "authoritarian" (pp. 109-117), school heads used public and private statements or edicts as the primary means of communication. The texts of communication were one-way, from the head to the teachers, and the language was didactic. The subtext was that no argument was to be discussed in public, and that the only recourse for teacher involvement in decision-making would come through closed-door discussions with the head. As with the interpersonal style, personal loyalty to the head was central to wielding influence.

Ball then noted one overarching subtext: Regardless of the style, in these schools autonomy was not a right but a privilege to be granted by the head, dependent on certain conditions. "In other words, autonomy is a set of freedoms to act which are set within firm limits and which may be withdrawn or curtailed if limits are infringed . . . . Autonomy is in effect an illusion . . . [It is] a major compromise between freedom and control" (p. 122). Heads strove to achieve control and commitment, and their underlying intention was to maintain political stability in the organization (p. 120). In this work, Ball drew a vivid portrait of the texts and subtexts of the micropolitical communications in schools.

TO THE READER

As you read the following studies, you might find useful the lenses or categories that we used as university faculty and public school practitioner. We read for contexts, texts, and subtexts to inform our interpretations of, and applications to, each of our settings. Chapter 7, authored by Judith Ponticell, focuses on a professional development project in which teachers designed a program where professional interaction could occur between teacher colleagues and where teachers could work together through cycles of videotaping and peer coaching. McKay, Powell, and Jarchow follow in Chapter 8 with their case study research of preservice and experienced teachers' communication in multicultural learning environments. Finally, in Chapter 9, Stanford explores the experiences and perspectives of elementary and middle school teachers identified as having high morale and lengthy teaching careers.

REFERENCES

Ball, S. J. (1987). *The micro-politics of the school.* New York: Methuen.

Ballenger, C. (1992). Because you like us: The language of control. *Harvard Educational Review, 62*(2), 199–208.

Fishbein, M., & Ajzen, I. (1975). *Beliefs, attitude, intention, and behavior.* Reading, MA: Addison-Wesley.

Hargreaves, A. (1984). Experience counts, theory doesn't: How teachers talk about their work. *Sociology of Education, 57,* 244–254.

Jackson, P. W. (1992). *Untaught lessons.* New York: Teachers College Press.

McNeil, L. M. (1986). *Contradictions of control.* London: Routledge and Kegan Paul.

CHAPTER 7

Seeing and Believing: Using Collegial Coaching and Videotaping to Improve Instruction in an Urban High School

JUDITH A. PONTICELL
Texas Tech University

JUDITH A. PONTICELL is Assistant Professor in the College of Education at Texas Tech University and served as Director and Principal Investigator of the Panhandle-South Plains Center for Professional Development and Technology. Dr. Ponticell has served in teaching, research, and administrative positions in two universities. Her school experience includes elementary and secondary classroom teaching and high school administration. Primary research interests are belief systems and their relation to classroom and school practices, adult cognition and its relation to learning, change processes, and professional development.

ABSTRACT

A teacher-designed, professional development project using collegial peer coaching and videotaping proved to be effective in improving classroom practices in a large, inner-city high school.

Inventories, videotapes, participant observation notes, and semi-structured interviews provided the data for this study. Data were analyzed using frequency of responses to interpret inventories and to compare pre- and post-project data, together with constant comparative analysis to identify changes in teachers' attitudes and classroom practices.

Teachers' experiences with videotaping and collegial peer coaching broke the professional isolation they felt. Increased collegiality resulted in increased value for exchanges of ideas, shared problem solving, and support for risk-taking. Teachers' perceptions of a need to change increased dramatically after they viewed the first videotapes made of their classrooms. Three areas in particular became important for self-assessment and group problem solving: 1) shifting from teacher-centered to student-centered instruction; 2) praising student success; and 3) providing more teaching time per class period.

INTRODUCTION

In recent years, literature on urban education, particularly at the secondary level, has consistently painted a picture of uninvolved, "at risk" students who fail to perform adequately and who find few incentives for serious academic study (Cuban, 1989; Goodlad, 1984; Sirotnik, 1983; Sizer, 1984).

Likewise, urban teachers, particularly those with ten or more years of teaching experience in urban schools, have been characterized as overworked, undersupported, and devalued (Bird & Little, 1986; Frymier, 1987; Maeroff, 1988). Traditional methods of staff development and teacher evaluation, along with varying efforts at school reform, have effected little change in teaching practice (Cuban, 1984; Darling-Hammond, Wise & Pease, 1983; Sirotnik, 1983).

In addition, recent literature on teacher renewal and professional growth suggests that many urban teachers need support to rebuild lost confidence, renew their sense of purpose, and recapture their belief in students' ability to learn (e.g., Bolin & Falk, 1987; Levine, 1989; Maeroff, 1988).

But how? Staff development programs in schools have largely been "one-shot, quick-fix" episodes of teacher inservice training. Supervisory efforts in schools are often characterized by few and far between classroom observations for summative evaluation. Both attempts at teacher change and growth have played a small and ineffectual role in the professional growth of teachers (Busching & Rowls, 1987; Howey & Vaughn, 1983; Karant, 1989; Zimpher, 1988). Opportunities for teachers to engage in ongoing renewal have existed more frequently in the theoretical constructs of researchers than in practice (Bolin & Falk, 1987; Levine, 1989; Little, 1986; Schon, 1983; Sergiovanni, 1985).

These were the considerations that led to a proposal to the University of Illinois at Chicago Center for Urban Education Research Development for a professional development project in a Chicago public high school. The project began in August 1991 with cautious expectations for positive effect on teacher self-perception, knowledge, attitudes, and classroom behavior. Within a year, the project produced changes in teachers' assessments of their need to change classroom practice, knowledge of and experimentation with new teaching strategies, and attitudes toward collegiality and shared problem solving for instructional improvement.

This chapter presents a description of the project objectives; the theoretical framework upon which the project was built; data collection and analysis methods; findings related to changes in teacher perceptions, attitudes, and practice; and a discussion of implications of the findings.

PROJECT OBJECTIVES

The objectives of the project were determined by the teachers involved. They talked extensively about desired outcomes, expectations for working together, professional development activities that have successfully supported teacher change, and possibilities for follow-up and extension of the teachers' work on the project.

Teachers expressed a desire to engage in activities that would give them a motivational "shot in the arm." They wanted to know more about teachers' experiences in urban schools, together with their collective experiences in this urban high school. In addition, they expressed a need to look at new teaching strategies. As one teacher explained, "Most of us have been teaching for fifteen years or more. What worked then is not helping now." Teachers hoped that they would learn ways of looking at their own classroom practices and working with colleagues to help solve their common problems.

The teachers' most important goal was to search for "commonality." Working with colleagues was seen by these teachers as a way to "enlighten one's daily spirit, lighten the burden, and widen the vision." With these considerations in mind, four objectives were defined:

1. To provide teachers with increased opportunity for collegiality through peer coaching;

2. To provide teachers with increased opportunity for self-analysis of their teaching practices through videotaping and professional dialogue;

3. To provide teachers with skills in classroom observation and problem-solving dialogue; and

4. To increase teachers' knowledge of, and experimentation with, effective teaching strategies.

Together, teachers designed a program that began with a professional retreat. Here, initial collegial learning relationships were built. Although teachers had taught together in the same school for years, they had never worked together collaboratively. Together they learned the goals and processes of peer coaching and videotape analysis. They developed a model for reading and discussing current educational research, together with a strategy-setting framework for practicing research-based teaching strategies in the classroom.

The retreat allowed teachers to talk seriously and substantively about teaching. The retreat renewed their interest in what is new in teaching; focused their attention on self-directed examination and improvement of teaching practice; valued collaborative, critical, and intellectual examination of teaching; and built comfort with the videotaping and peer coaching processes.

Project components were designed to create a collegial culture in which teachers talked about common classroom concerns and designed and implemented plans for experimenting with new teaching strategies. More specifically, new strategies were discussed in monthly professional seminars at which teachers read research-based articles related to their specific classroom concerns and identified teaching strategies that made sense in relation to their expressed common concerns. A strategy was defined, and an operational plan was designed to enable teachers to experiment with the strategy in their own classrooms.

After these seminars, teachers worked together through cycles of videotaping and peer coaching. The videotaping enabled teachers to watch themselves trying something new and to refine their teaching strategies. The peer coaching enabled teachers to gain feedback and support from other teachers engaged in experimentation. Videotapes further enabled teachers to engage in group problem solving.

THEORETICAL PERSPECTIVES

The teachers' positive expectations for their participation in the project were, nevertheless, couched within a context of powerful obstacles. Isolation, absence of intellectual discussions about teaching, absence of useful feedback on teaching, little support for teacher renewal or experimentation, and "useless" experiences with staff development were cited as deterrents to teacher innovation and instructional change. These deterrents are also reflected in the theoretical perspectives that shaped the project's intent and design.

Individuals learn and grow when the need for learning and growing starts from within (Levine, 1989), in response to, or in concert with, perceived "cues" from the environment (Katz & Kahn, 1978; March & Simon, 1958). Thus, as Levine (1989) suggested, teachers who work in the same building will most likely have very different experiences of school and teaching and very diverse perceptions of what they mean. They will also vary in their ability and disposition to learn in the environment in which they teach (Joyce & McKibbin, 1982).

Teaching is complex, draining, and isolating in its nature, particularly at the high school level (Goodlad, 1984). Teachers are required to give of themselves continually in a role in which "getting is elusive and infrequent" (Levine, 1989). As Lieberman and Miller (1984) noted, in order to deal with contradictions and demands, teachers develop a professional identity that, once defined, "may be militantly protected and defended" (p. 2). Thus, new learning and new ideas meet with frequent resistance.

Organizational structures of schools tend to contribute to the isolation and separation of the adults who work in them (Bird & Little, 1986; Buchmann, 1986; Little, 1982). In high schools, classroom space allocation and time scheduling separate teachers and provide little time for interaction, let alone collaborative problem solving. As a result, teachers tend to focus inward, relying on their own classroom experiences (Hargreaves, 1984). It is not surprising, then, that as Smylie (1988) noted, "individual perceptions of self as influenced by experiences within classrooms and with teaching colleagues" are related to teacher learning and change (p. 24).

The norms of teaching, and accompanying lack of professional support, tend to be more conducive to discontent and dissatisfaction (Lieberman & Miller, 1984; Little, 1982). Teachers do not share their expertise, customarily visit each others' classrooms, create and evaluate teaching strategies together, or talk analytically about the practice of teaching. Yet, studies (e.g., Rosenholtz, 1989) show that such behaviors promote norms of experimentation and collegiality, enhanced professionalism, and teacher and school improvement.

Current educational reform efforts have focused considerable attention on the problem of creating conditions for continued learning, growth, and self-renewal in schools (Krupp, 1987; Levine, 1989). As Rosenholtz (1989) discovered, "learning-impoverished schools" are characterized by sameness, routine, and self-reliance. On the other hand, "learning-enriched" schools exhibit qualities of continuous improvement, continuous learning, collaborative relationships, and information-rich communication.

Evans (1989) suggested that if we intend to pay attention to the needs of teachers as learners, four coping needs deserve emphasis. These are: 1) growth, through opportunities that "stimulate teachers' awareness of choice and exploration"; 2) recognition, through opportunities that "counter the tendency to take veteran staff for granted"; 3) experience-enhancing roles, through opportunities that "create job variety and enrichment"; and 4) collegiality, through opportunities that enhance mutuality, support, and collaboration.

In essence, feedback, support, and follow-up are essential to teacher learning and development (Guskey, 1986). They are also largely missing from learning opportunities typically provided for teachers in schools. Key elements involved in feedback, support, and follow-up are norms of active participation;

mutual trust, acceptance, and helpfulness; ongoing and constructive feedback; and peer support (Parry, 1990; Ponticell & Ewing, 1989; Schafe & Willis, 1978; Smylie, 1990).

Long-term efforts in real classrooms, together with attention to helping teachers integrate new ideas into their understandings of how schools and teaching work, appear to have greater success. Perspectives on transfer of training (Parry, 1990) indicate that adult learners enter into any learning opportunity with previously acquired knowledge, skills, attitudes, conceptions, and dispositions. For new knowledge and skills to be integrated into teachers' existing understandings of teaching, teachers must be able to apply and improve in what they have learned through immediate use, together with feedback and support.

From the perspective of change theory (e.g., Benne, 1961), growth involves the increased ability of individuals to face and solve their problems. Successful professional development programs (Bird & Little, 1986; Glatthorn, 1984; Griffin, 1987; Guskey, 1986; Oja, 1990; Shroyer, 1990; Sparks, 1983) are 1) context sensitive, providing specific discussion of teaching practice; 2) knowledge-based, providing strong conceptual, theoretical, and research information; 3) participative and collaborative, enabling teachers to define desired outcomes, share ideas, observe peers and be observed in their work, and to collaborate on strategies; 4) ongoing; 5) developmental, attending to the learning, psychological, and developmental supports essential to growth; and 6) reflective and analytical, to facilitate knowledge and skill restructuring.

DATA COLLECTION AND ANALYSIS

Ten teachers in a large, inner-city high school in the Midwest participated in this study. Data were collected in several ways. At the beginning of the project, participating teachers were asked to complete three inventories: an inventory of perceived problems of teachers at the school; a 14-item collegiality inventory based upon an instrument created by McPherson & Rinnander (1988); and a self-assessment inventory of perceived teaching problems.

During the project, teachers were videotaped four times and completed four videotape self-analysis inventories. In addition, participant observer notes were kept as the researcher observed the teachers' peer coaching conferences, professional dialogue seminars, and group problem-solving seminars.

At the end of the project, teachers completed a second collegiality inventory and self-assessment inventory of perceived teaching problems. In addition, semistructured exit interviews were conducted with project participants to capture their perceptions of their experiences with peer coaching and videotaping; their perceptions of changes in their classroom practices; their under-standings of the new teaching strategies implemented in their classrooms; and their estimate of the effectiveness of the project in supporting teachers as they work to improve classroom instruction.

Frequency of responses was used to interpret the results of the inventories and to compare pre- and post-project data. Constant comparative analysis was used to identify changes in teachers' practices as captured on videotapes, and to interpret interview responses and participant observation notes.

FINDINGS

Collegiality

When teachers described their experiences with peer coaching and videotap-ing, they spoke of changes in their relationships with colleagues and the degree to which these relationships broke the "professional isolation" that they felt.

Pre- and post-collegiality inventories asked respondents to indicate the frequency with which various aspects of collegiality were experienced in in-tradepartmental and interdepartmental relationships. Table 1 presents the fre-quency of teachers' responses, grouped in four categories, representing aspects of collegiality. These four dimensions are: sharing ideas; colleague-to-colleague relations; shared problem solving; and seeing colleagues as professionals.

Table 1 indicates that teachers perceived a free, nonjudgmental flow of ideas among their colleagues as a result of the project. Value-for-idea ex-change increased perceptions of the need for adequate time for frequent ex-changes. Comfort with discussions of sensitive subjects or criticism was increased. Also, respondents reported increased thoughtful listening and feel-ings of responsibility toward colleagues.

Respondents also perceived increased shared decision-making among their colleagues, together with an increased ability among colleagues to iden-tify and risk dealing with problems. Colleagues came to be viewed as profes-sionals who encouraged learning and growth among their peers.

Perceptions of the Need to Change

Probably one of the more dramatic findings related to teachers' perceptions of the need to change their own classroom practice. An inventory of perceived problems of teachers at the school, together with a self-assessment inventory of perceived teaching problems, was completed by the project participants before they viewed the first videotapes made in their classrooms. The inventories asked

TABLE 1.

Frequency of Responses on Collegiality Inventory (N=9)

		1 Hardly ever	2 Not often	3 As often as not	4 Quite often	5 Almost always
SHARING IDEAS						
1 IDEAS VALUED	PRE	1	1	2	4	1
	POST	1			4	4
2 JUDGED ON MERIT	PRE		1	3	1	3
	POST				4	5
9 TAKING TIME TO TALK	PRE	2	1	2	1	3
	POST	1			6	2
13 LISTENING ACTIVELY	PRE		1	1	3	4
	POST				3	6
COLLEAGUE-TO-COLLEAGUE RELATIONSHIPS						
3 SUGGESTIONS MADE	PRE	1	1	3	3	1
	POST			5	2	2
7 ADVICE GIVEN	PRE		2	4	1	2
	POST			2	3	4
10 CRITICISM ACCEPTED	PRE	2	3	2		2
	POST	6	3			
11 SHARED COMMITMENT	PRE	1	1	3	2	2
	POST				4	5
14 SHARED AUTHORITY	PRE		1	3	2	3
	POST				3	6
SHARED PROBLEM SOLVING						
4 PRETENSE DROPPED	PRE	2	1	2	2	2
	POST	2	3	2	1	1
6 SHARED PROCESSES	PRE	2	1	2	2	2
	POST	3	5	1		
12 IDENTIFICATION	PRE		1	3	2	3
	POST				4	5
COLLEAGUES AS PROFESSIONALS						
5 RESPECT	PRE		1	1	3	4
	POST				2	7
8 LEARNING COMMUNITY	PRE			2	4	3
	POST				4	5

teachers to rank on a scale of 1 (low frequency) to 4 (high frequency) forty concerns associated with teaching problems. They were asked to respond to one inventory as if they were ranking the problems they believed other teachers at the school would evidence in their classrooms. On the second inventory, they were asked to rank the problems they believed would be evidenced in their own classrooms.

Overall, before watching themselves on videotape for the first time, participating teachers believed that few changes were needed in their classroom teaching, but they anticipated serious problems with other teachers in several areas noted in Table 2.

After viewing the first videotape made in their classrooms, teachers were asked to complete the self-assessment of perceived problems again. Table 3 indicates that the videotape changed teachers' perceptions of what they needed to improve. Generally, teachers were much more concerned with the images of teaching that they projected to students (for instance, the lack of excitement/ energy projected); their relationships with students (for

TABLE 2.
Teachers' Perceptions of Teaching Problems

Areas in Which I Need Improvement

TIME MANAGEMENT

CLASSROOM ORGANIZATION

Expectations for Sources of Help

SELF-HELP

Areas in Which My Colleagues Need Improvement

SUBJECT CONTENT

INSTRUCTIONAL STRATEGIES

MATERIALS AND TECHNOLOGY

CLASSROOM MANAGEMENT

CLASSROOM ORGANIZATION

Expectations for Sources of Help

SELF-HELP

OTHER TEACHERS

DEPARTMENT CHAIRS

ADMINISTRATORS

Table 3.

Teachers' Perceptions of Teaching Problems

Areas in Which I Need Improvement

Organization and planning

Excitement/energy in teaching

Patience with students' needs

Increased subject knowledge

Increased repertoire for presenting subject material

New teaching techniques

Strategies for involving students

Strategies for addressing individual learner needs

Techniques in being more supportive of students

Attention to clarity and purpose

Humor/enjoyment

Classroom organization

Expectations for Sources of Help

Self-help

Other teachers

University courses

instance, patience with students' needs); the need for new strategies, particularly those related to addressing student differences; and attention to clarity and purpose in their lessons.

Teachers' Perceptions about Their Experiences with Peer Coaching and Videotaping

Generally, teachers were surprised to discover that observing their own classrooms and being observed by colleagues could be "positive" and "non-job performance in nature." Teachers' only experiences with classroom observation had been related to teacher evaluation. Their skepticism about the worth of assessing classrooms was replaced by genuine appreciation for the power and worth of the videotaping and peer coaching processes. This is captured in several teachers' comments:

> The importance of the videotaping and coaching process . . . was its purpose . . . improving one's *own* classroom instruction.

The program made me look inside myself and ask not just what I'm doing but why. This facilitates improvement.

Seeing growth over time—videotaping and coaching allow you to see the growth, to look inward and re-examine oneself.

We *really* talked to each other about teaching . . . Observing, exchanging information and views with others, intellectual discussion with teachers . . . we learned we don't have to work alone.

In seeing myself, I could put myself in the students' seat. It made me more thoughtful about how I respond to them, how tired they must get of sitting. I'm working on ways to get students more active; I let them work together; I go to those not interested. I spend more time teaching and paying attention to positive rather than negative things.

I think we were all afraid of videotaping . . . I still am, but it's important that we really look at ourselves. I don't think I'm as good as I should be. Having another teacher to work with has given me support and encouragement to change. Seeing—through my eyes and theirs—is believing.

Changes in Teaching Practices

Teachers perceived a "possible" link between their own growth as teachers and their students' achievement. When teachers saw teaching strategies being implemented and worked collaboratively on common problems, they received needed support for risk taking. Feedback from colleagues' observations, problem-solving discussions, and "learning from my own example" were viewed positively as "useful for teacher growth and change."

Classrooms at the outset of the project were, in most cases, predictable. Teachers took attendance and attended to a good many administrative tasks in anywhere from five to fifteen minutes at the beginning of class; asked whether anyone had done the homework; lectured or did demonstration problems at the board; and assigned seatwork (sometimes for twenty minutes or more in a forty-minute class period). Discourse was largely teacher-initiated. Questions were usually answered by five or six "key students" who could be counted on to give correct or approximately correct answers, so that the "lesson could move along."

Students were generally pleasant and nondisruptive. Many simply "did other things" during the lesson, other than attending to task or teacher. Classes were described by teachers as usually going well "when students are quiet and most are working on assignments." Teachers frequently commented, "I teach the ones who want to learn."

In general, teachers "covered" textbook pages and interacted with those students who signaled that they wanted to be part of the lesson. These students were the barometers of success. If they "knew the right answer," then the lesson was perceived as going well. Lack of student homework and poor performance on tests was attributed to "lazy, unmotivated kids."

Videotapes and discussions of classroom observations revealed three common changes in classroom instruction: 1) shifting from teacher-centered to student-centered learning; 2) praising student success; and 3) providing more teaching time per class period.

Student-Centered Learning

Strategies most frequently added to instructional practice during project participation were related to increasing student involvement in the lesson. Teachers called on more students; they stuck with students who were attempting answers. Teachers more frequently asked for students' ideas and opinions and were more willing to let students grapple with a problem, rather than answering it themselves and moving on.

Teachers also employed peer and cooperative learning strategies, encouraging students to verbalize what they knew and to learn concepts together. Many teachers developed games and rewarded team competitions. The constructive noise level of classrooms increased in many cases, and teachers were less comfortable with silence.

Praising Student Success

It was not uncommon at the outset of the project to spend forty minutes in a classroom and never hear students praised for doing something well. Verbal encouragement was rare. Teachers became more aware of the effects of "positive stroking." In particular, teachers gave specific attention to telling students when they had done something well, telling them *why* what they had done was good, discouraging negative student-to-student comments, and modeling simple courtesy.

Teachers discovered that praise and encouragement were particularly important for students in seatwork. Teachers practiced moving about the classroom and monitoring student work, not to determine whether students were working, but to determine how they were working. Teachers practiced giving specific encouragement or help to students as they moved about the classroom monitoring student work.

Teachers also experimented with peer tutoring to provide more intense help and immediate encouragement for students who needed more time and instruction.

Increased Teaching Time

Teachers' attention focused on "wasting less time" in the classroom. Many teachers devised ways to use the first five minutes of class in warm-up or retention activities. This enabled them to take attendance, check with late or previously absent students, and set a pattern for early student participation. In talking with their students about the change in late arrivals after the warm-up routines had been established, some teachers discovered that students made no effort to get to class on time "because nothing was happening."

Teachers also worked at structuring their lessons more with clear review, objectives, demonstrations, practice time, and monitoring. Teachers generally agreed that "better routines" and "better structure to lessons" helped them to "get students involved." In addition, students' listening to other students proved to be an untapped resource for reteaching/repeating concepts. Teachers observed that they could use student explanations as quick assessments of levels of understanding and as springboards for clarifying or reteaching.

DISCUSSION AND IMPLICATIONS

The ten urban high school teachers who participated in this project saw and believed that their instruction had changed, and that those changes affected students' participation. They came to value more interactive, student-centered strategies. Their attitudes toward their students, their teaching, and their own professional growth had changed.

What factors motivated these urban teachers to change attitudes and practice? Observing one's own teaching, observing others' teaching, being observed, learning how to talk about and make sense of the classroom, and sharing in problem solving were powerful motivators for these teachers.

Teachers became aware of their professional isolation. They discovered that chats in the teachers' lounge or lunchroom did not constitute professional interaction. Teachers described being "isolated from intellectual criticism" of their own teaching and "from any professional interaction" with their teaching colleagues. Teachers' new professional dialogue broke down the walls of isolation and opened doors to new ways of looking at and working with colleagues.

Showers (1985) suggested that "the practice of public teaching; focus on the clinical aspects of teaching; development of common language and understandings; and sharing of lesson plans, materials, and problems contribute to school norms of collegiality and experimentation" (p. 46). Findings here suggest similarly that when isolation is broken, renewal takes place—a kind of rekindled desire to reflect upon the quality of one's own efforts in the classroom and, more important, to improve them.

This new, open door policy, in many cases, validated teachers' own teaching successes but more so encouraged risk taking in critical examination of practice. This extends Smylie's (1988) findings that "through interactions with colleagues, teachers may develop a body of technical knowledge about what teaching practices are likely to be effective. That body of knowledge may be confirmed by classroom experience and by other teachers through continued interaction" (p. 24). Findings in this project suggest that videotaping and peer coaching, together with substantive, problem-solving oriented discussions about teaching, provided sustained collegial interactions that enabled teachers to move past the phase of validation into challenging the routines of practice.

Teachers commonly stated that videotaping and peer coaching made them look inside themselves to probe what they were doing in their teaching and why they were doing it. Teachers valued attention to the individual teacher's context. Shulman and Carey (1984) had noted the "boundedly rational" nature of teacher knowledge. This suggests that teachers combine new information with what they already know, restructure it, and fit it to their perceptions of the "reality" of their working environment. Further, teachers' thinking appears to change in relation to the "sensibleness" of an innovation (Duffy & Roehler, 1986). This project confirmed that teachers tried new strategies in their classrooms because they had learned them in their own context, and thus it made sense to experiment with them in their own classrooms.

The findings of this study also suggest that teachers' initial lack of specific knowledge about the effects of their own teaching, together with feelings of ineffectiveness, changed largely because of their experiences with being successful with at-risk students. This confirms findings in previous studies of efficacy (Bandura, 1977; Ponticell, 1991; Smylie, 1988) that suggested teachers are more likely to change classroom practice to improve effectiveness if they believe themselves to be instrumental in promoting student learning.

It should be noted that effects in this project were greater over time. Teachers gained momentum in trying out new strategies and in gaining comfort, and indeed enjoyment, from studying their own teaching. Teachers perceived themselves functioning as professionals. They became willing to engage in dialogue about schools, students, and teaching practice. Trust in collegial relationships built over time. Interaction and support from peers had both the time and context in which to pass beyond the safety of an initial "lifting of spirits" to the professional work of examining practice.

The typical "one-shot" workshop approach to staff development, most common in these teachers' experiences, lacked the continuity necessary for "seeing growth over time." The current reform focus on the professional model of teaching (Busching & Rowls, 1987; Karant, 1989; Lieberman, 1986; Zimpher, 1988) suggests that teacher professional development must be an ongoing discovery in practice where teachers engage in interaction and inquiry. In this study, teachers expressed appreciation for "learning from one another" in a context of discussion and problem solving for the purpose of helping the individual teacher "to look inward and re-examine oneself."

Also key to the professional view of teaching is the view of teachers as "reflective practitioners" (Schon, 1983). The process of reflection recognizes individual differences among teachers and reverences them, working "with" teachers, as opposed to "on" them. Teachers in this study expressed faith in the videotaping and coaching processes largely because of their direct experiences in "being able to get an idea of how I was coming across" to students, along with strategies developed through peer problem solving that "made sense" to use in the individual teacher's classroom.

Teachers' professional growth can be seen as a tool or strategy for attaining schoolwide improvement (Shroyer, 1990). Indeed, emerging views (Garman, 1986; Holland, 1988; Smyth, 1988) suggest that teachers grow through an interactive process in which they learn from one another by teacher-initiated, -developed, and -sustained "critical learning communities" within individual schools (Smyth, 1988).

Urban schools are not generally characterized as "critical learning communities," nor are urban teachers often characterized as "reflective practitioners." However, despite the generally accepted hostile professional environment of the urban school teacher, these urban teachers did, in fact, critically examine and change instructional practice with peer support.

Frymier (1987) has suggested that one solution for large urban school systems that have "lost the centrality" of teachers is "to empower teachers, to help them develop an internalized locus of control" (p. 14). The results of this study of videotaping and peer coaching in an urban high school suggest that these tools can be a powerful impetus for empowerment and renewal, for changing teacher attitudes about instrumentality in promoting successful student learning, and changing instructional behavior. In addition, teachers observing their own and others' teaching, and engaging in critical dialogue around common classroom concerns, presents a successful strategy for renewing beliefs and for rekindling teachers' willingness to risk rethinking their own instructional routines.

REFERENCES

Bandura, A. (1977). Self-efficacy: Toward a unifying theory of behavioral change. *Psychological Review, 84*(2), 191–215.

Benne, K.D. (1961). Deliberate changing as the facilitation of growth. In W.G. Bennis, K.D. Benne, & R. Chin, (Eds.), *The planning of change: Readings in the applied behavioral sciences.* New York: Holt, Rinehart & Winston.

Bird, T., & Little, J.W. (1986). How schools organize the teaching occupation. *Elementary School Journal, 86*(4), 493–511.

Bolin, F., & Falk, J. (1987). *Teacher renewal.* New York: Teachers College Press.

Buchmann, M. (1986). Role over person: Morality and authenticity in teaching. *Teachers College Record, 87*(4), 529–543.

Busching, B., & Rowls, M. (1987). Teachers: Professional partners in school reform. *Action in Teacher Education, 9*(3), 13–24.

Cuban, L. (1984). *How teachers taught: Constancy and change in American classrooms 1890-1980.* New York: Longman.

Cuban, L. (1989). The "at-risk" label and the problem of urban school reform. *Phi Delta Kappan, 70*(10), 780–801.

Darling-Hammond, L., Wise, A.E., & Pease, S.R. (1983). Teacher evaluation in the organizational context: A review of the literature. *Review of Educational Research, 53*(3), 285–328.

Duffy, G., & Roehler, L. (1986). Constraints on teacher change. *Journal of Teacher Education, 37*(1), 55–58.

Evans, R. (1989). The faculty in midcareer: Implications for school improvement. *Educational Leadership, 46*(8), 10–15.

Frymier, J. (1987). Bureaucracy and the neutering of teachers. *Phi Delta Kappan, 69*(1), 9–14.

Garman, N.B. (1986) Reflection, the heart of clinical supervision: A modern rationale for professional practice. *Journal of Curriculum and Supervision, 2*(1), 1–24.

Glatthorn, A.A. (1984). *Differentiated supervision.* Alexandria, VA: Association for Supervision and Curriculum Development.

Goodlad, J.I. (1984). *A place called school.* New York: McGraw-Hill.

Griffin, G.A. (1987). The school in society and social organization of the school: Implications for staff development. In M.F. Wideen and I. Andrews, (Eds.), *Staff development for school improvement: A focus on the teacher.* New York: The Falmer Press.

Guskey, T.R. (1986). Staff development and the process of teacher change. *Educational Researcher, 15*(5), 5–12.

Hargreaves, A. (1984). Experience counts, theory doesn't: How teachers talk about their work. *Sociology of Education, 57*(October), 244–254.

Holland, P.E. (1988). Keeping faith with Cogan: Current theorizing in a maturing practice of clinical supervision. *Journal of Curriculum and Supervision, 3*(2), 97–108.

Howey, K., & Vaughn, J. (1983). Current patterns of staff development. In G. Griffin (Ed.), *Staff development: Eighty-second yearbook of the National Society for the Study of Education,* Part II. Chicago: University of Chicago Press.

Joyce, B., & McKibbin, M. (1982). Teacher growth states and school environments. *Educational Leadership, 40*(3), 36–41.

Karant, V.I. (1989). Supervision in an age of teacher empowerment. *Educational Leadership, 46*(8), 27–29.

Katz, D., & Kahn, R. (1978). *The social psychology of organizations.* New York: John Wiley and Sons.

Krupp, J.A. (1987). Understanding and motivating personnel in the second half of life. *Journal of Education, 169*(1), 20–46.

Levine, S.L. (1989). *Promoting adult growth in schools: The promise of professional development.* Niedham Heights, MA: Allyn and Bacon.

Lieberman, A. (Ed.). (1986). *Rethinking school improvement: Research, craft, and concept.* New York: Teachers College Press.

Lieberman, A., & Miller, L. (1984). *Teachers, their world, and their work.* Alexandria, VA: Association for Supervision and Curriculum Development.

Little, J.W. (1982). Norms of collegiality and experimentation in the workplace. *American Educational Research Journal, 19*(3), 320–340.

Little, J.W. (1986). Seductive images and organizational realities in professional development. In A. Lieberman, (Ed.), *Rethinking school improvement: Research, craft, and concept.* New York: Teachers College Press.

Maeroff, G.I. (1988). *The empowerment of teachers: Overcoming the crisis of confidence.* New York: Teachers College Press.

March, J.S., & Simon, H.A. (1958). *Organizations.* New York: John Wiley and Sons.

McPherson, R.B., & Rinnander, J.A. (1988). Collegiality: Its meanings and purposes. Independent School, 41-44.

Oja, S.N. (1980). Adult development is implicit in staff development. *The Journal of Staff Development, 1*(2), 9–56.

Parry, S. (1990). Ideas for improving transfer of training. *Adult Learning, 1*(7), 19–23.

Ponticell, J.A. (1991, April). What's possible: Teachers' beliefs about teaching excellence and possibility. A paper presented at the Annual Meeting of the American Educational Research Association, San Francisco.

Ponticell, J.A., & Ewing, M. (1989, November). Teachers' perceptions of supervisory relationships: A view toward differentiated practice. A paper presented at the Annual Conference of the Illinois Association of Teacher Educators in Effingham, IL.

Rosenholtz, S.J. (1989). *Teachers' workplace: The social organization of schools.* NY: Longman.

Schafe, K.W., & Willis, S.L. (1978). Life-span development: Implications for education. In L.S. Shulman, (Ed.), *Review of research in education.* Itasca, IL: Peacock.

Schon, D.A. (1983). *The reflective practitioner: How professionals think in action.* New York: Basic Books.

Sergiovanni, T.J. (1985). Landscapes, mindscapes, and reflective practice in supervision. *Journal of Curriculum and Supervision, 1*(1), 5–17.

Showers, B. (1985). Teachers coaching teachers. *Educational Leadership, 42*(7), 43–48.

Shroyer, M.G. (1990). Effective staff development for effective organizational development. *Journal of Staff Development, 11*(1), 2–6.

Shulman, L., & Carey, N. (1984). Psychology and the limitations of individual rationality: Implications for the study of reasoning and civility. *Review of Educational Research, 54*(4), 501–524.

Sirotnik, K.A. (1983). What you see is what you get—consistency, persistency, and mediocrity in classrooms. *Harvard Educational Review, 53*(1), 16–31.

Sizer, T.R. (1984). *Horace's compromise: The dilemma of the American high school.* Boston: Houghton Mifflin.

Smylie, M.A. (1988). The enhancement function of staff development: Organizational and psychological antecedents to individual teacher change. *American Educational Research Journal, 25*(1), 1–30.

Smylie, M.A. (1990). Teacher efficacy at work. In P. Reyes, (Ed.), *Teachers and their workplace: Commitment, performance, and productivity.* Newbury Park, CA: Sage.

Smyth, W.J. (1988). A "critical" perspective for clinical supervision. *Journal of Curriculum and Supervision, 3*(2), 136–156.

Sparks, G.M. (1983). Synthesis of research on staff development for effective teaching. *Educational Leadership, 41*(3), 65–72.

Zimpher, N.L. (1988). A design for the professional development of teacher leaders. *Journal of Teacher Education, 39*(1), 53–60.

CHAPTER 8

Profiles of Communication in Multicultural Learning Environments: Case Studies of Preservice and Experienced Teachers

JOANE McKAY
University of Northern Iowa

RICHARD POWELL
ELAINE JARCHOW
University of Nevada, Las Vegas

JOANE McKAY is Associate Professor in the Department of Teaching at the University of Northern Iowa. Her primary research interests are teachers of the year, international education, and multicultural education.

RICHARD POWELL is Assistant Professor in the Department of Instructional and Curricular Studies at the University of Nevada, Las Vegas. His research focuses primarily on the relationship between biography and teacher development in preservice and novice teachers. Other areas of interest include science teacher development, cultural diversity in school classrooms, gender and ethnic issues in science teaching, and middle school teaching.

ELAINE JARCHOW is Associate Dean and Director of Teacher Education at the University of Nevada, Las Vegas. Her research areas include international education, curriculum development, and teacher education.

ABSTRACT

Changing cultural demographics in the United States have given rise to intercultural communication problems in school classrooms that were relatively unknown only a few decades ago. Teachers in many schools do not have the same cultural backgrounds as their students, especially in teacher preparation experiences, such as international student teaching. This study focuses on classroom communication patterns of two student teachers and one experienced teacher who were teaching in classrooms that were richly multicultural. Teachers' classroom communication patterns were found to be highly idiosyncratic and context specific. These patterns were also found to be linked to prior professional experiences and to personal biography. Implications for teacher education are reported.

BACKGROUND AND PURPOSE

With rapidly changing cultural demographics in schools today, teachers are being challenged with intercultural communication problems unknown a few decades ago. For example, classrooms with students representing over a half dozen different cultures are now common in schools that were previously mono or bicultural (Bennett, 1990; Nieto, 1992). Consequently, teachers in such schools do not have the same cultural backgrounds as many of their students. This is especially true for international schools and international student programs (Cole & Knowles, 1992; Jarchow, 1991; Gutek, 1993), thus illuminating the need for greater cultural awareness among teachers.

Banks (1992) holds that one of the goals of multicultural education is to help teachers and students develop effective cross-cultural communication skills and view themselves from the perspectives of different groups. Because effective teaching in multicultural and international learning environments requires proficiency in cross-cultural communication skills, the need for teacher education programs to focus on multicultural and intercultural communication has never been greater. Similarly, the need for research examining ways that teachers communicate with students in multicultural classrooms has also increased.

Although teacher educators and classroom teachers would probably agree that communicating content is central to teaching, the social complexity of multicultural classrooms requires teachers to communicate other things to students. Teachers are expected, for example, to communicate positive attitudes toward learning and authority so that content can be taught more effectively (Feimen-Nemser & Floden, 1986). As another example, Joyce (1980) reported that effective teachers establish routines quickly and communicate them consistently and equitably to students (see also Bullough, 1989).

The purpose of this chapter is to report on research that explored communication patterns of three educators teaching in multicultural classrooms. An assumption for our research was that all teachers bring to the classroom unique personal histories (Knowles, 1988) and previously established patterns for communicating with others socially and professionally (Powell & Riner, 1992; Powell, 1992). From this assumption, and from the need for studies exploring communication in multicultural classrooms, we were able to generate questions that provided the initial framework and the purpose for our study. In rather broad terms we asked: How do educators learn to communicate with students in multicultural classrooms? What established communication patterns, if any, do educators transfer to these classrooms? How do these transferred patterns influence classroom instruction? Given that some educators in the initial stages of their teaching careers have difficulty becoming effective teachers (Bullough, Knowles, & Crow, 1991), what patterns of communication are demonstrated in the classroom by successful teachers and less successful teachers?

THEORETICAL FRAMEWORK

Our study was conducted in three multicultural classroom contexts and focused on the communication patterns between teachers and students. The theoretical perspectives we used to explore how classroom communication patterns developed and changed for the teachers included symbolic interactionism (Blumer, 1972; Charon, 1985) and schema theory (Anderson, 1984; Neisser, 1976). (See also Bullough, Knowles, & Crow, 1991.) About symbolic interactionism Blumer (1972) notes, "Human interaction is mediated by the use of symbols, by interpretation, or by ascertaining the meaning of one another's actions" (p. 145). Following Blumer (1972) we held the view that teachers and students who interact over time in a classroom create a shared set of symbols that provide unique patterns of communication. These symbols are verbal, such as specific ways students address the teacher, and nonverbal, such as proximity control and room arrangement. To develop a fuller understanding of classroom communication, we carefully tracked how interactions between teachers and students shape the classroom context (c.f., Bullough & Knowles, 1991).

Our study was also embedded in cognitive psychology, specifically schema theory. Following Neisser (1976) (see also Howard, 1987) we understood schemata to be a set of personal anticipations, that is, "the medium by which the past affects the future" (Neisser, 1976, p. 22). We also viewed schemata as changeable mental structures, particularly during accommodation of new environments and events. We assumed, then, that teachers' past experiences shape their ways of communicating with students. Examples of these experiences include: professional work settings (Powell & Riner, 1992); schooling experiences (Novak & Knowles, 1992); and family attitudes, values, and beliefs (Bullough, 1989; McKay, 1990). Because teachers are unique and because students are unique individuals with specific needs, we expected that patterns of classroom communication would be unique among teachers in this study, not only between teachers and individual students, but between teachers and whole classes of learners.

METHODOLOGY AND DATA COLLECTION STRATEGIES

The methods we used to explore classroom communication were those associated with long-term field studies (Erickson, 1986). These methods were necessary to examine the teachers in their natural context and to study the ongoing interactions of teachers with their students. These methods also enabled us to develop an intuitive understanding of the classroom climate that teachers and students created and shared, and to capture the nuances of classroom communication. Strategies deemed appropriate for gathering data were: case study methodology (Yin, 1989); participant observation (Spradley, 1979); theoretical sampling (Strauss, 1987); and constant comparative data collection and analysis (Glaser & Strauss, 1967; Strauss, 1987).

Participants and Research Context

Our study of classroom communication patterns centered on the teaching activities of three educators who were teaching in different school contexts. Using theoretical sampling (Strauss, 1987) and a case-study design (Yin, 1989), we purposely selected educators who we believed would provide interesting and useful profiles of classroom communication, and whose narratives would furnish teacher educators with descriptive cases of development of communication skills. Elizabeth, James, and Beverly[1] were selected because they were in varying stages of professional development and were in different multicultural settings. They also represented both elementary and secondary classrooms. Moreover, James and Beverly demonstrated different levels of

---

1 Real names have not been used in this chapter.

proficiency in communication skills, thus illuminating more successful and less successful patterns of classroom communication.

As an elementary teacher education student, Elizabeth was completing her student teaching assignment in New Zealand at the time of this study. Like Elizabeth, James was a student teacher. However, James was student teaching in an urban high school in the desert Southwest. Beverly, who was an experienced secondary teacher, was a recipient of a Teacher of the Year award. For this study, Beverly was viewed as an experienced ESL teacher who would probably demonstrate high levels of proficiency in communicating with culturally diverse students.

Classroom Communication Patterns

Three types of classroom communication patterns were selected as the foci of this study. Patterns were selected if they were found to be essential elements for effective teaching and successful entry into the professions, and if they were reported to be central to initial teacher development. Two tasks, which were extant in the literature, were: (1) communicating content to learners (Feimen-Nemser & Parker, 1990; Shulman, 1986); and (2) communicating boundaries for behavior (Veenam, 1984). Communicating content referred to ways that teachers taught content to their students. Boundaries for behavior referred to teachers' efforts to establish limitations for learner behavior in the classroom, thus maintaining classroom management and discipline.

We inductively generated a third communication pattern during data collection (Strauss, 1987). This pattern was communicating empathy to learners, which was demonstrated in varying degrees by all teachers. Empathy was observed when teachers, either explicitly or implicitly, responded with a caring attitude to learners' feelings and/or personal needs. However, not all teachers in our study successfully demonstrated empathy for students' needs. Nonetheless, communicating empathy was consistently salient so that it was included as an individual task in this report. Moreover, communicating empathy was linked to all other teaching actions and contributed significantly to the tone of each teacher's classroom climate.

Data Collection

To gain different perspectives of classroom communication in multicultural learning environments and to establish internal validity (Mathison, 1988), we individually gathered multiple sources of data throughout the study. The primary sources were observations of classroom teaching, informal conversations and formal interviews with teachers, and the teachers' personal journals.

Teachers were observed biweekly in their classrooms. These observations and corresponding field notes, along with teachers' personal journals, became an important basis for developing insights and theoretical propositions about classroom communication. We spoke informally with teachers throughout the study, and conducted interviews at the beginning and at the end of the study. For James and Elizabeth, formal interviews were held at the beginning and end of student teaching. For Beverly, formal interviews were held at the beginning and end of the first semester. Interviews were taped and transcribed whenever possible. Interview transcripts provided a rich source of data and preserved the integrity of teachers' perceptions of their interactions with students.

Data Analysis

Using the constant comparative method (Strauss, 1987), we began data analysis during our first interactions with teachers and continued throughout the study. We began coding field notes and journal entries for communicating content and communicating boundaries for behavior. All interview transcripts and notes from informal conversations with teachers were similarly analyzed.

Following constant comparative data analysis, we maintained a consistent pattern of comparing newly collected data with prior data. From this process, the third form of communication (communicating empathy to students) was identified early in the study. As we continuously explored data we combined key quotes from teachers with our recorded insights to develop a rich data base for describing our three patterns of classroom communication.

PROFILES OF COMMUNICATION

Elizabeth: An Elementary Student Teacher Profile

A forty-nine year old single mother of two, Elizabeth listed bowling, horses, reading, flower arranging, camping, and gardening among her interests. Her employment record included working at the telephone company and the local library, running a housecleaning company, and assisting in an office. Although she described herself as an average student, she twice won a library publication award and a $500 library scholarship. Her interest in a Chrysanthemum Club prompted her to make two trips to New Zealand in the early 1980s.

Elizabeth dreamed of being a "darn good teacher" but postponed her dream to raise a family. She sought to complete student teaching in New Zealand because she wanted to observe the whole language curriculum, revisit old friends, participate in a chrysthanemum festival, and "have an adventure." Because her finances were limited, she sold her house to finance the international experience.

Communicating Content. Elizabeth formulated several rules for herself before she arrived in New Zealand. One of these was to keep negative comments to herself. She followed the instructional suggestions of her mentor teacher, even though she did not always agree. She had hoped to teach a dinosaur unit but was quickly informed that "dinosaurs had been done the year before." Although her Native American unit was well received by the students, she often struggled with a lack of familiar resources for planning and delivering lessons.

Worried about making mistakes, Elizabeth tested her ideas about communicating content through reflection and trial and error.

> I'm scared to death of making mistakes. I must learn to relax. In math, the bright kids catch all my mistakes. I feel dull-witted at times.

After the children had taken some tests, Elizabeth tried to teach two poems. "They were not a hit," she reflected.

> Maybe the kids are tired from taking their tests. What can I do differently before a lesson starts to ensure its success?

Elizabeth exercised her ability to think about larger issues related to instruction. After she read an interesting story to the class, she noticed that the children were bored. They told her that the story had too many long words and no pictures. Elizabeth asked, "Are we smothering their imagination?" She was concerned also that students criticized her chalkboard writing and did not understand her directions. "I must break directions down into small units so that the students will understand them."

She developed another strategy that worked well. She wrote problems on the chalkboard and encouraged students to debate the answers. Sometimes, she deliberately made mistakes and taught the students to challenge the teacher politely. Summarizing her experiences with communicating content, Elizabeth concluded, "I just need experience to find the right balance."

Communicating Empathy. Elizabeth's rules for herself extended into her relationships with students and staff. Elizabeth noted,

> Be appreciative and sensitive to people. Use your good sense of humor. Keep a positive attitude toward your experience. Smile outwardly—cry or complain to no one but yourself. Respect your students' opinions.

Armed with these caveats, Elizabeth described herself as far from a "fresh-faced, wide-eyed typical student." She was a mature woman ready to encounter New Zealand children.

The indigenous people of New Zealand, the Maoris, come from a Polynesian background and make up twelve percent of the population. As a people, they are trying to preserve their heritage and language. Elizabeth worked hard to pronounce their names correctly. She noted that Te Aroha and Ke Ho were troubled when she did not pronounce their names correctly.

Of particular interest to Elizabeth was a Chinese student named Ke Ho. She noted that his name was pronounced "Gha Ho." He struggled to be accepted by his peers but was often rebuffed. During a five-day outdoor camping experience, Ke Ho was given a "Camp Buddy" who refused to associate with him. "How painful life is for wallflowers," Elizabeth reflected. She spent much of her camp experience working on English words with Ke Ho. As she drew him out, Elizabeth remarked: "Hooray. He seems to have taken a liking to me."

Elizabeth learned to use "Kiwi" expressions and found that her students warmed to her more and more. She tended to conclude each day's journal with goals for herself. Frequently, her goal was, "Learn to praise more . . . and more."

Communicating Boundaries for Behavior. Elizabeth's repertoire of student behavior strategies was thoroughly tested as she joined a school culture in which establishing boundaries for behavior and maintaining student discipline differed from any she had previously experienced. She reflected upon common practices in New Zealand.

> The teachers discipline the students right out loud. They call out the student's name, denounce the behavior, and announce the punishment. I remember what happened to John when he talked in class. John's teacher said, "John was chatting right out loud during the whole song. He can write out the words of the song since he wasn't paying attention." Children move in and out of the room a lot. Discipline is lax. No one worries about being sued here.

Little by little, Elizabeth had an opportunity to try to manage the class.

> As I try to fit into someone else's rules, I continually ask myself how I will manage my own classroom. Should I notice everything or ignore everything and get on with the lesson? There must be a middle ground somewhere. Do I clip the fuse before the situation disintegrates or after it has become full blown?

One practice Elizabeth developed was to focus on the children as individuals.

> How could I have helped Adam? He has a chip on his shoulder, low es-
> teem—he's a bully. I know that he wants to be liked. Brandon is jealous
> because I don't give him as much responsibility as Kevin.

Elizabeth also worried about seeking help from other teachers for establishing
class boundaries for behavior.

> There is no way I can become effective if other teachers don't back me
> up. I hate to ask other teachers for help with discipline problems. They
> will think that something is wrong with me.

Toward the end of her experience, she concluded: "I am getting better
and better with class management. The students see me more each day as a
teacher and are responding well." She reflected upon the five-day outdoor
camping experience and its superb opportunity to teach appropriate behavior,

> Children learned how to be a buddy, how to handle responsibility for
> their own gear, courtesy, following directions, setting goals, undertaking
> personal challenges, teamwork, verbal and written expression, and rec-
> ognizing the rights of others. They didn't learn these to perfection, but
> they will know them when they bump into these learnings again.

From her student-teaching experience in New Zealand, Elizabeth learned
about the cross-cultural dimensions of classroom management. Toward the end
of student teaching, Elizabeth noted in her personal journal: "New Zealand
children learn to be responsible. Rules are nearly the same everywhere."

James: A Secondary Student Teacher Profile

James, a twenty-eight year old bachelor, was entering teaching as a second career. He reported that his past work was not rewarding, and he chose teaching
because of the influence of a former high school coach. James was a quiet person, rarely inviting a conversation or offering an opinion. He was from a small
family and has only one brother. Although James' past work was people-
centered, it wasn't group-oriented. James noted: "The job I had the longest
was in customer service. I was working one on one [with other persons] most
of the time in that job." Before entering teaching, James had few opportunities to be in front of groups or take a teaching role. In addition, he had only
limited experience working with adolescents.

Communicating Content. Foremost among James' concerns with becoming a teacher and with student teaching was imparting content effectively to learners in a clear and effective manner. James felt underprepared to teach history, his primary teaching field, and consequently he lacked confidence in front of students. Regarding his preparation in history James noted:

> Part of the problem is that I only have a limited amount of history credits. I have enough to be certified by the state, but I could see I would be much better prepared if I had a degree in history rather than the minimum amount of credits.

Another factor that interfered with James' ability to communicate content effectively was his limited awareness of the learning styles and academic potential of his students. This seemed to be especially true for students who had cultural backgrounds different from James'. In the third week of student teaching, James' comment reflects the frustration he was experiencing in trying to communicate content to students whose ethnicity was different than his.

> I'm just not sure how some of these kids learn. The diversity is really overwhelming. I have kids with so many different cultural backgrounds that I never realized I would have this kind of teaching to do. I thought I knew how to teach a class like this when I came to [the classroom] but now I just don't know. And its hard for me to teach kids with so many different backgrounds. They're good kids, so don't get me wrong on what I'm saying here. But it's like I just don't know how they need the content presented to them.

Communicating Empathy. Throughout student teaching, James voiced an empathetic concern for learners. In week three of student teaching he noted: "It's important to get to know students' interests and what is important to them. You can relate to them better if you know their interests." However, James had difficulty "becoming more comfortable in the classroom situation and getting rid of those initial inhibitions." These inhibitions, which remained with James throughout student teaching, may have been partly why he appeared unable, either explicitly or implicitly, to be empathetic with learners, especially during the early stages of student teaching.

Moreover, James initially viewed students as hindering his progress in student teaching, even referring to students as "the enemy." James viewed students as a barrier to his success, especially students with different cultural background. However, as James got to know his students and as he became more familiar with how to teach students with different cultural backgrounds, his fear began to dissipate. Indeed, in the last few weeks of student teaching James began viewing students as part of his progress and professional growth.

Communicating Boundaries of Behavior. James was aware of the importance of establishing various kinds of boundaries with learners when he began student teaching. Yet establishing and maintaining boundaries remained a formidable challenge for him throughout student teaching. James' students often talked to one another out loud about personal matters at inappropriate times, and they were observed walking toward other students in the middle of the lesson to carry on personal conversations.

James' repertoire of strategies for establishing and maintaining clear boundaries was limited, especially for two of his classes that had the greatest ethnic diversity. When asked about managing his classrooms and when asked to compare the boundaries for behavior he tried to establish, James reported that he was unsure how to manage a class of ethnically diverse students.

> I'm not sure how to get all this [classroom discipline] stuff under control especially for second and fourth periods. I know it's too noisy all the time in those classes, but how do I get them to be quiet and get on task? I seem to have better luck with my other classes, but I always feel sort of afraid in second and fourth periods.

Although James had continuous supervision throughout student teaching from his cooperating teacher, he nonetheless had difficulty establishing class-room boundaries in those classes (second and fourth periods) that were pre-dominantly minority students.

Beverly: An Experienced Secondary Teacher Profile

Beverly, married and the mother of two college-aged daughters, taught Eng-lish as a Second Language (ESL) at a large high school in the Midwest. She grew up on a farm in the Midwest and was educated in rural schools. She de-scribed her growing-up years as being part of a "very close family" that "still writes letters to one another every week." One of her earliest memories of an awareness of "a bigger world" came at the age of five when her father told her about Chiang Kai-shek.

Beverly's teaching experience spanned twenty-five years and included al-ternative school settings, graduate assistant experiences and administrative du-ties. She also founded the ESL program at her school. She accrued an excellent academic record including a baccalaureate and two masters degrees, all with highest honors.

Communicating Content. Because of the nature of her classroom, Beverly believed that it was important for her students to write and to speak about things that had special significance for them. For example, the students were invited to choose a favorite color and write a poem about it. An Asian student wrote:

> Excited is the color golden.
> It is not [name of school] golden.
> It is not Hawkeye golden.
> It is summer sun golden.

Beverly indicated that part of her effectiveness in communicating content to newly immigrated students came from displaying interest not only in their academic welfare, but in their lives as newcomers to the United States. She said, "It's a great learning experience for me, too, because these students bring a new way of thinking and a new attitude from different cultures and different perspectives." Beverly related a success story from her class. One of her students, a young man, escaped from Vietnam with his older brother. The student traveled on a large fishing boat with eighty-five others for three days and three nights before reaching Thailand, only to have the boat he was riding in captured by the Thais. Eventually, the two young men entered a refugee camp, and in 1983 arrived in the Midwestern community where Beverly taught. Beverly noted this about the young man: "I not only had to teach [him] ESL, but this young man wanted to be an electrical engineer, so we had to help him understand course content in many subjects."

Beverly was always searching for ways to make the content more relevant to her students. One of the ways she did this was to discuss what the local newspaper had printed about a soccer game. She explained that soccer had more meaning to her culturally diverse students than a sport that might be seen as typically North American (for instance, football).

Reflecting on her belief about communicating content, Beverly concluded:

> We deal a lot with trying to build up self-esteem and to talk about all the things they're doing that other kids never do. Nursing and parenting are part of our teaching. A major part of communicating our content is really counseling as we learn the language together.

Communicating Empathy. During classroom observations Beverly was observed continuously voicing an empathetic concern for learners. From her extensive experience teaching ESL, she was aware of cultural differences among students and of the language barriers that existed in her classroom. Beverly demonstrated a warm and caring attitude at the beginning of each class, asking students daily about their activities outside her classroom. One of her assignments included having students write about their cross-cultural relationships with other students and about their activities outside school. For some assignments, Beverly also invited students to write about important personal topics.

Beverly also demonstrated patience with students, always encouraging them to participate in class activities. For example, one afternoon Beverly noticed a student with his head down on his desk. Approaching the student, Beverly kneeled down and said, "We need you."

Communicating Boundaries for Behavior. Beverly was especially sensitive to students' needs for personal space in her classroom, and her classroom arrangement reflected this sensitivity. Classroom observations of Beverly revealed this classroom arrangement:

> Beverly's classroom was a very small . . . but cheerful room. The concrete block had been painted green . . . and yellow. There were bulletin boards all around. One bulletin board said, "May is Asia month. Is the war in Southeast Asia over?" Pictures about Vietnam were on the board. On the back bulletin board were things about the Chinese New Year. There were three rows of desks and three desks per row. Students sat in unassigned seats. Unlike some homogeneous classrooms, Beverly's classroom was clearly heterogenous. The students were from Iran, China, Japan, Taiwan, Venezuela, and Vietnam.

Beverly explained that she often had to think of the children's cultural needs in the arrangement of the classroom (that is, in setting boundaries for student behavior). For example, Beverly allowed one female student from Iran to sit in the back of the room, where she felt more comfortable. Beverly also permitted another female student from China, who was eager to assimilate North American culture, to sit in the front of the classroom. In both cases, Beverly tried to help students feel comfortable with the boundaries they established for themselves.

Beverly's respect and concern for the class were evident in her treatment of her students and in her relationships with students in the crowded hallways of high school during passing time. Beverly was consistently observed positively interacting in a social way with students during these times.

In establishing classroom rules and routines, Beverly frequently solicited students' opinions. Realizing the cultural differences in her students, she always tried to give them choices that aligned with their cultural preferences.

Beverly also tried to establish an environment of camaraderie and teamwork, in which students from different cultures would have to cross cultural boundaries to work together in academically positive ways.

IMPLICATIONS FOR TEACHER EDUCATION

Juxtaposing our theoretical framework for the study with the profiles of communication described for the three teachers, we have drawn four implications for teacher education. First, teacher education should implement reflective activities, such as journal writing, that help preservice and inservice teachers carefully consider communication patterns of culturally diverse classrooms. Because Elizabeth did her student teaching in an international setting far away from her university supervisors and professors, she wrote freely and thoroughly each day in her personal journal. In this reflective mode, asking questions of herself, Elizabeth constantly reminded herself of progress and failure, and continuously reassessed her teaching goals in light of the cultural diversity she experienced. Moreover, when Elizabeth combined her deliberate reflection on practice with her maturity, empathy, and experience as a mother (see also Bullough, 1989), she gained insight into the adjustment problems of a Chinese student.

Second, teacher education programs, most especially those in large multicultural populations, must help preservice teachers to become more aware of issues surrounding multicultural learning environments before classroom teaching. James, for example, completed his student teaching in a culturally diverse high school. Two of his classes during student teaching contained predominantly minority students. James expressed his lack of confidence in teaching history, was observed as having limited skills for communicating empathy to students, and had difficulty establishing classroom boundaries for student behavior. Moreover, when he began student teaching, he had limited knowledge of cultural learning styles and ethnic diversity in the classroom. Consequently, when he was confronted with cultural diversity, James voiced his fear of the students, seeing them as the enemy. Had James been better prepared in his teacher education program, he might have been initially more confident to teach diverse students and to draw clear boundaries for behavior.

Third, teachers and students alike need to develop cross–cultural dependency and view themselves from the perspectives of different groups (see also Banks, 1992). Beverly, a teacher with twenty-five years in the classroom and recipient of a Teacher of the Year award, recalled that learning at home early in her life about Chiang Kai-shek introduced her to a "bigger world out there." This helped her to begin viewing the world as a place to be explored and investigated. Consequently, her success in culturally diverse classrooms could be what Banks

(1992) advises when he states that one of the goals of multicultural education is to help teachers and students explore, understand, and appreciate cultural diversity.

For a final implication, this study points out the importance of teacher education programs in helping all teachers to develop a greater awareness of cultural differences in school classrooms. James, who lacked an awareness of cultural differences and who was mostly unfamiliar with cultural learning styles, experienced fear of his students and consequently had difficulty establishing clear boundaries for student behavior. Beverly, on the other hand, who had experience working with students from diverse cultures, acknowledged diversity and demonstrated empathy for students' needs. Elizabeth was open to learning about different cultures, and had contracted a student teaching assignment in another country, in part to expand her awareness of cultural diversity. James' difficulty with cultural diversity and his combined problems with establishing clear boundaries for learner behavior, when contrasted with Beverly's acceptance of cultural diversity and Elizabeth's earnest pursuit of cultural awareness, confirms the need for teachers at all stages of development to become aware of cultural diversity, and corresponding differences in learning styles. Teacher education programs that lack an emphasis on multicultural values and that do not foster an understanding of cultural diversity in school classrooms will limit the instructional potential of teachers in contemporary classrooms.

CONCLUSIONS

Garcia and Pugh (1992) believe that teacher education programs at the preservice and inservice levels must cease providing teachers with a predominantly monocultural view of classroom instruction. This study is consistent with that view, and further suggests that teacher educators introduce beginning and experienced teachers to innovative ways for teaching students from diverse cultures. These case studies of Elizabeth, James, and Beverly illuminate the challenges teachers face with classroom communication in multicultural learning environments. Also highlighted in the studies is the dynamic interaction between the classroom content and teachers' predispositions for communicating with ethnically diverse students. Finally, this study provides evidence that effective communication with students in culturally diverse classrooms is crucial to teacher success.

REFERENCES

Anderson, R.C. (1984). Some reflections on the acquisition of knowledge. *Educational Researcher, 13*(9), 5–10.

Banks, J. (1992). Multicultural Education. For Freedom's Sake. *Educational Leadership, 49*(4), 32–36.

Bennett, C.I. (1990). *Comprehensive Multicultural Education* (2nd ed.). Needham Heights, MA: Allyn and Bacon.

Blumer, H. (1972). Society as symbolic interaction. In Manis, J., & Meltzer, B. (Eds.), *Symbolic interaction: A reader in social psychology* (2nd ed.) (145–154). Boston: Allyn and Bacon.

Bullough, R.V. (1989). *First year teacher: A case study.* New York: Teachers College Press.

Bullough, R.V., Knowles, J.G., & Crow, N.A. (1991) *Emerging as a Teacher.* London: Routledge.

Bullough, R.V., & Knowles, J.G. (1991). Teaching and nurturing: Changing conceptions of self as teacher in a case study of becoming a teacher. *Qualitative Studies in Education, 4*(2), 121–140.

Charon, J.M. (1985). *Symbolic Interactionism: An introduction, an interpretation, an integration.* (2nd ed.). Englewood Cliffs, NJ: Prentice-Hall.

Cole, A.L., & Knowles, G.J. (1992, April). Extending Boundaries: Narratives on Exchange. Paper presented at the annual meeting of the American Educational Research Association, San Francisco.

Erickson, F. (1986). Qualitative methods in research on teaching. In Wittrock, M.C. (Ed.), *Handbook of Research on Teaching* (3rd ed.) (pp. 392–431). New York: Macmillan Publishing Company.

Feiman-Nemser, S., & Floden, R.E. (1986). The cultures of teaching. In Wittrock, M.C. (Ed.), *Handbook of Research on Teaching* (3rd ed.) (pp. 505–526). New York: Macmillan.

Feimen-Nemser, S., & Parker, M. (1990). Making subject matter part of the conversation in learning to teach. *Journal of Teacher Education, 41*(3), 32–43.

Garcia, J., & Pugh, S.L. (1992). Multicultural Education in Teacher Preparation Programs: A Political or an Educational Concept? *Phi Delta Kappan, 74*(3), 214–219.

Glaser, B.G., & Strauss, A.L. (1967). *The discovery of grounded theory: Strategies for qualitative research.* Chicago: Aldine Publishing Company.

Gutek, G. L. (1993). *American Education in a Global Society.* New York: Longman.

Howard, R.W. (1987). *Concepts and Schemata: An Introduction.* London: Cassell Educational Limited.

Jarchow, E. (1991). Surviving the first year of teaching: Lessons from New Zealand. *Instructional Psychology, 189*(3), 211–216.

Joyce, B. (1980). *Toward a theory of information processing in teaching.* Michigan State University: The Institute for Research on Teaching.

Knowles, J.G. (1988, April). Models for understanding preservice and beginning teachers' biographies: Illustrations from case studies. Paper presented at the Annual Meeting of the American Educational Research Association, New Orleans.

Mathison, S. (1988). Why triangulate? *Educational Researcher, 17*(2), 13–17.

McKay, J.W. (1990). Iowa Teacher of the Year: A Case Study. Unpublished doctoral dissertation, Iowa State University: Ames, IA.

Neisser, U. (1976). *Cognition and reality.* New York: Meredith Publishing Company.

Nieto, S. (1992). *Affirming Diversity: The Sociopolitical Context of Multicultural Education.* New York: Longman.

Novak, D., & Knowles, J.G. (1992, April). Life histories and the transition to teaching as a second career. Paper presented at the Annual Meeting of the American Educational Research Association, San Francisco.

Powell, R.R. (1992). The influence of prior experiences on pedagogical constructs of traditional and nontraditional preservice teachers. *Teaching and Teacher Education, 8*(3), 225–238.

Powell, R.R., & Riner, P. (1992, April). The origins of teaching: A study of teacher development in secondary career-change preservice teachers. Paper presented at the Annual Meeting of the American Educational Research Association, San Francisco.

Shulman, L. (1986). Those who understand: Knowledge growth in teaching. *Educational Researcher, 5*(2), 4–14.

Spradley, D.L. (1979). *Participant observation: A methodology for human studies.* Newbury Park, CA: Sage Publications.

Strauss, A.L. (1987). *Qualitative analysis for social scientists.* New York: Cambridge University Press.

Veenam, S. (1984). Perceived problems of beginning teachers. *Review of Educational Research, 54*(2), 143–178.

Yin, R.K. (1989). *Case study research: Design and methods.* Newbury Park, CA: Sage Publications.

CHAPTER 9

A Spirit of Partnership: Qualities Conducive to Career Perseverance and High Morale in Teachers*

BEVERLY HARDCASTLE STANFORD
Azusa Pacific University

BEVERLY HARDCASTLE STANFORD is Professor and Associate Chair of the Education Department at Azusa Pacific University. She is co-author of the textbook *Becoming a Teacher*. She teaches education and human development classes. Her research interests include gender equity, teachers' perspectives, and life themes of the unempowered.

ABSTRACT

Using a grounded theory approach, the researcher explored the experiences and perspectives of elementary and middle school teachers identified as having career perseverance and high morale. The qualities of their school relationships that reflected a spirit of partnership emerged as the dominant explanation of their career perseverance and high morale. The teachers expressed needs for support of their administrators, autonomy in their work, appreciation from their colleagues, and shared perceptions of students and school. Through the perceptions of this valued group, educational administrators and teacher educators are offered insights into the significance of a spirit of partnership within a school and guidance that could enrich and extend the careers of teachers.

*This research report was funded by the Lyndon Baines Johnson Institute for the Improvement of Teaching and Learning, Southwest Texas State University, San Marcos, Texas. Special thanks are given to Deborah Coben, research assistant, Leslie Huling-Austin, director of the LBJ Institute, and the twelve teachers who participated in the study.

What qualities in school relationships are conducive to developing career perseverance and high morale in teachers? The study sought answers to this question and began asking other pertinent questions. Using a grounded theory approach to research, the researcher sought answers to the questions: Why do some teachers not only endure a long time in the field but do so with high morale? Why do they thrive through the years and seem to be increasingly satisfied and spiritually rewarded? What is it that promotes their continued enthusiasm for their work? Answers to such questions were sought to assist teacher educators in their efforts to orient new teachers to the field, to give administrators insights on ways to help restore vigor to weary veterans, and to guide teachers toward a lasting and rewarding career.

The results of the study were somewhat baffling. In addition to a sense of collegiality with fellow teachers, two equally clear but seemingly contradictory patterns emerged. The teachers with career perseverance and high morale expressed a deep need for their administrators' support in addition to expressing equally strong valuing of their own autonomy. They, clearly, were not dependent upon their principal's support if defined as the principal dictating what they should do. Yet, some nearly left the profession because a principal had not been supportive. From the perspective of today's climate of collaboration and partnership, the apparent contradiction makes perfect sense. Where else but in a partnership can teachers find both support and autonomy? Apparently what the teachers in the study valued were the qualities of their school relationships that reflected a spirit of partnership.

METHODOLOGY

Research Approach

Adopting a grounded theory approach (Glaser & Strauss, 1967), the researcher conducted in-depth interviews with experienced teachers regarded as having high morale. The interviews focused on the teachers' reflections on their career paths, their experiences of high morale, and the sources they drew upon for renewal.

Procedure

Selection of Participants. The participants were selected for this study on the basis of two factors: career longevity and high morale. For the latter, the researcher presented a descriptive profile (see Appendix A) of a teacher with high morale and career perseverance (ten or more years of teaching) to selected administrators and personnel in five elementary and middle schools in a school district. These individuals ranked their top nominees for each grade level, yielding twelve participants.

The Interview. The researcher met with each teacher individually one or two times over a three-week period for forty to sixty minutes.

During the interview sessions a number of instruments were used, including:

A Self-Anchoring Scale (Kilpatrick & Cantril, 1960)
An adult-years lifeline activity (Hardcastle, 1985)
Open-ended questions on teaching and life in general (Hardcastle, 1985; 1988)
School and Life Similes Questionnaires (Hardcastle, Yamamoto, Parkay, & Chan, 1985) (Appendix B)

Participants

All twelve teachers were married women aged thirty-four to fifty-one with children whose ages ranged from three to thirty-one. They had taught ten to twenty-one years, with the average being sixteen years. Nine had earned a masters degree. Three had taught only in their current district. All had taught at more than one grade level.

PATTERNS

The most significant patterns to emerge included support of administrators, need for autonomy, and appreciation of colleagues. The teachers clearly expressed needs for the support of administrators, especially the principal, and the need for autonomy in their work. In their responses to the *Self-Anchoring Scale Activity,* which called for teachers to imagine and describe their "ideal teaching life'" and "worst possible teaching life," the teachers used a total of 104 phrases to describe ideal conditions (seventy) and negative conditions (thirty-four). Of the total, over one-third (36%) of the phrases dealt with either support of administrators or autonomy. Seven teachers also referenced the support or interference of parents.

A third clear pattern that emerged was the teachers' appreciation of their colleagues and of a spirit of collegiality. Two additional patterns worth noting were the similarities in their perspectives on students and schools.

Support of Administrators

The teachers' appreciation for the support of school administrators was evident in their responses to the *Self-Anchoring Scale Activity* (see Table 1). In this they were asked to imagine a ten-step ladder stretching between their ideal teaching-life description and their worst possible teaching-life description. They designated where they would place themselves on the ladder for the present time, for five years in the past, and for five years in the future. When their answers revealed a different position, the researcher probed for the reasons for the change. Four teachers who reflected changes, three an upward change and one a downward, attributed the change to administrators.

When asked about their ideal teaching life, they mentioned having an administrator who recognized and encouraged creativity and who was supportive. Being directed, being told exactly what to do and when to do it were phrases mentioned in their descriptions of the worst possible teaching situation. These comments, which are noted in the following section as indicative of a need for autonomy, also reflect a resistance to controlling administrators.

When asked "What do you like especially about your school?" six of the teachers included "the administration" or "the principal" in their answers.

TABLE 1

References to Administrative Support in Descriptions of Ideal and Worst Possible Teaching Conditions

---

[expressed positively]

"administrator recognizes and encourages creativity" (Barbara)
"administrator who understands that children aren't robots" (Helen)
"support from principal, associate principal, through chain to superintendent" (Amy)
"supportive principal" (Rita)
"supportive administration" (Elizabeth)
"good leadership, principal" (Nancy)
"good leadership, good principal" (Lucy)
"administrator encouraged and rewarded innovation" (Laura)
"support from administration and parents" (Evelyn)

[expressed negatively]

"administration told you what to do" (Barbara—negative comment)
"no support from administration" (Evelyn)
"principal thought room should be silent, students in desks" (Mary)
"little cooperation from parents, administration, or principal" (Amy)

The answers for the remaining six could be interpreted as including the administration: "the people I work with" (four), "the positive climate" (one) and "given lots of opportunities" (one).

Need for Autonomy

In the *Self-Anchoring Scale* descriptions of ideal and worst possible teaching lives, all twelve participants included phrases that reflected a need for autonomy in their teaching (see Table 2).

For ideal teaching situations, they imagined conditions that would allow them to be creative, to use new ideas, and to have control. In their descriptions

TABLE 2

References to Autonomy

POSITIVE

"a chance to be creative" (Sylvia)
"to do things I feel the kids would benefit from" (Sylvia)
"independence" (Evelyn)
"administration encouraged and rewarded innovation" (Laura)
"more time for creative lessons—fun, relevant" (Elizabeth)
"new ideas, innovations" (Amy)
"creatively plan and teach" (Helen)
"opportunity to try new things" (Helen)
"administration that recognized and encouraged creativity" (Barbara)
"have control, free to do things" (Mary)

NEGATIVE

"held to teaching only certain things, certain ways" (Sylvia)
"being with strict rules you can't live with" (Nancy)
"being told when to do what, a certain page on a certain day" (Evelyn)
"having to conform to a certain mode of teaching" (Laura)
"no opportunity to use new ideas" (Laura)
"being stifled" (Star)
"someone else would have total control of what and how you teach" (Lucy)
"interfering parents" (Rita)
"told what I had to teach" (Helen)
"given a time schedule" (Helen)
"didn't feel you had any control" (Barbara)
"administration told you what to do" (Barbara)
"principal thought room should be silent, students in desks" (Mary)

---

of the worst possible teaching lives, they noted that being told what and how to teach would be characteristics.

Appreciation of Colleagues

A third pattern that emerged was the teachers' expressed appreciation for colleagues. This attitude was clear in responses to the question "What do you especially like about your school?" Five mentioned teachers specifically, four mentioned "the people I work with," and another said, "the positive climate." In their ideal teaching-life descriptions, four mentioned working with teachers who were cooperative and had similar goals:

"working with other teachers willing to take risks" (Barbara)
"other equally committed teachers who enjoy their work" (Rita)
"receptive people, staff, faculty" (Sylvia)
"working with unit of people with same goals" (Nancy)

The teachers had generally similar views on students and schools. Their answers to the question "What do you like most about teaching?" tended to reflect students, with nine of the twelve referring to their students (see Table 3). The words they most frequently selected in the simile questionnaire (see Appendix B) were *family* and *team*. They were told that they could select any number of answers for each simile question. The *family* simile was selected by the largest group of teachers (seven) and *team* by the second-largest group (six) for what being in elementary school should be like for children. The *team* simile was the most popular one (nine) for what being in school should be like for teachers, with the next most popular being *family* (four).

TABLE 3
What Teachers Like About Teaching

"the kids" (Sylvia and Laura)
"being with children" (Evelyn)
"the children" (Mary)
"the kids, their honesty and excitement" (Rita)
"being with the kids, watching growth" (Barbara)
"the outcome of students" (Annie)
"when someone finally learns" (Lucy)
"when I reach a misbehaving child" (Lucy)
"the hugs" (Paula)

DISCUSSION

The patterns that emerge in the reflections of these teachers with career persever-ance and high morale reflect a valuing of a partnership spirit in their schools. The support of their administrators, the collegiality of their peers, a respect for teacher autonomy, and the view of school as a family or team characterize such spirit.

The Principal's Regard

The teachers' expressed need for the support of their administrators emphasizes the crucial role that principals play in this partnership and reminds us of the power and influence that principals have on school climate and teacher morale. Frymier (1984), Sarason (1982, 1989), and Glasser (1990) have recognized the crucial importance of the principal in their analyses on school quality and process of school change. In a related study Denton (1981) discovered the sig-nificance of the principal's influence and termed the phenomenon the "Prin-cipal Effect." In her report on a field study of daily life in three fifth-grade classrooms, Denton concluded that "a remarkable principal can and does gen-erate and sustain a remarkable school environment." The teaching experience of the participants apparently did not make them immune to such an influence; on the contrary, for a number, feelings of high morale seemed to be tied di-rectly to their perceptions of their principals' support.

The administrative support that the teachers in this study valued appears to involve trust and respect. In Yamamoto's writings (1988) on mentorships, he discusses a similar attitude, that of *regard,* which he defines as "an acknowledg-ment of one's personhood as well as trust in what is and is to come." We can sense such a *regard* behind the words of the principal in Denton's (1981) study:

> You've gotta be caring but you have to step back and give them the aura that, 'I have confidence that you can solve your problem.' And so that's what I do here. I think that is as important as being a good listener be-cause I don't take the responsibility away from them. I keep pushin' it back at them (p. 184).

The Teacher's Sense of Control

The value that these teachers placed on autonomy may also be interpreted as their desire to be in control, especially in control of their teaching. They reacted strongly to being directed in their teaching, and they appreciated administrators who allowed them to be innovative. The theme of control was particularly evi-dent in their descriptions of the worst possible teaching situations: "someone else would have total control of what and how you teach," "held to teaching only certain things, certain ways," "didn't feel you had any control," "having to conform to a certain mode of teaching."

In another study, Kobasa (1979) found that a sense of control was one dimension of the quality of "hardiness" attributed to stressed but healthy executives. She determined that the group of hardy executives (high stress/low illness) had a sense of control over their actions and events; those who were not "hardy" (high stress/high illness) did not. Could the teachers in this study have been exhibiting their "career hardiness" because they had a sense of control over the ways they taught? Is this element of a partnership, the control given to each partner, crucial to longevity?

The School's Spirit of Partnership

The influence of their schools' spirit of partnership on the morale of the teachers may be the most significant discovery in this study. It offers an initial response to the hypothesis and challenge raised in a report on the professional life cycle of teachers:

> It just may be the case that there are institutional environments in which teachers do not disengage, do not end up tending uniquely their own gardens, do not feel the stale breath of routine after only 8–10 years in the profession. . . . If so, the research community is singularly well placed to identify them and to specify the conditions under which others, too, might play out their careers in such places as these. (Huberman, 1989, p. 54)

The themes that emerged in this study create a distinct picture of an institutional environment valued by teachers with career perseverance and high morale. They clearly valued a climate of partnership characterized by administrative support, teacher autonomy, collegiality, and a spirit of teamwork.

IMPLICATIONS

The messages from these teachers with high morale and career perseverance, teachers we want to keep in the field and in our schools, are deep and reasonable ones. They apparently thrive best and longest in a spirit of partnership with their principals and colleagues. They want to be free to teach in the ways they think best, and they want to do so with the support of administrators who believe in them and in the company of colleagues who share their commitment.

The implications of this study for administrators are obvious. Principals should examine their attitudes and behaviors toward teachers to see if they do indeed offer and express the type of support these teachers appreciated in their principals. They need to reflect on the climate of their schools to determine if it is characterized by a spirit of partnership.

Teacher educators may wish to share these findings with their students in order to encourage them to become active participants in building partnerships with their principal and colleagues. Beginning teachers may want to consider the insights of these teachers with career perseverance and high morale so that they move toward behaviors and attitudes that extend and enrich their careers.

REFERENCES

Denton, N. P. (1981). The "principal" effect: The dialectic between macro and micro ethnography in school. Paper presented at the annual meeting of the American Anthropological Association, Los Angeles, CA.

Frymier, J. (1984). *One hundred good schools.* West Lafayette, IN: Kappa Delta Pi.

Glaser, B., & Strauss, A. (1967). *The discovery of grounded theory.* Chicago: Aldine.

Glasser, W. (1990). *The quality school.* San Francisco: Harper & Row.

Hardcastle, B. (1985). Midlife themes of invisible citizens. *Journal of Humanistic Psychology, 25*(2), 45–63.

Hardcastle, B. (1988). Spiritual connections: Proteges' reflections on significant mentorships. *Theory Into Practice, 27*(3), 201–208.

Hardcastle, B., Yamamoto, K., Parkay, F., & Chan, J. (1985). Metaphorical views of school: A cross-cultural comparison of college students. *Teaching and Teacher Education, 1*(4), 309–315.

Huberman, M. (1989). The professional life cycle of teachers. *Teachers College Record, 91*(1), 31–57.

Kilpatrick, F. P., & Cantril, H. (1960). Self-anchoring scaling, a measure of individual's unique reality worlds. *Journal of Individual Psychology, 16,* 158–173.

Kobasa, S. (1979). Stressful life events, personality, and health: An inquiry into hardiness. *Journal of Personality and Social Psychology, 37*(1), 1–11.

Sarason, S. B. (1983). *Schooling in America: Scapegoat and Salvation.* New York: The Free Press.

Sarason, S. B. (1982). *The culture of the school and the problem of change.* Boston: Allyn and Bacon.

Yamamoto, K. (1988). To see life grow: The meaning of mentorship. *Theory Into Practice, 27*(3), 183–189.

APPENDIX A
PROFILE OF TEACHERS WITH HIGH MORALE

1. Positive   –in attitude
      never or rarely complain
      have can-do attitude
   –in treatment of others
      students
      fellow teachers
      parents
      staff-secretaries/bus drivers

2. Enthusiastic About Teaching Their Students, School, the Field
      –express it
      –show it in actions
      –attendance
      –have reputation for enthusiasm

3. Involved in Their Work
      –workshops
      –learning
      –professional organizations
      –not absent
      –graduate school
      –self-development activities

4. Are Themselves
      –confident
      –idiosyncratically creative
      –unique in style

5. Increasingly More Satisfied
      –beginning teachers: hesitant/scared
      –middle teachers: competent
      –long-term teachers: confident

APPENDIX B
SCHOOL SIMILES

For a child today, being in elementary school is like being:

___in a business
___in a circus
___in a crowd
___in a factory
___in a family
___in a garden
___in a hospital
___in a prison
___on a stage
___on a team
___in a zoo
___other (describe)

Why?

For a child today, being in elementary school should be like being:

___in a business
___in a circus
___in a crowd
___in a factory
___in a family
___in a garden
___in a hospital
___in a prison
___on a stage
___on a team
___in a zoo
___other (describe)

Why?

For a teacher today, being in elementary school is like being:

___in a business
___in a circus
___in a crowd
___in a factory
___in a family
___in a garden
___in a hospital
___in a prison
___on a stage
___on a team
___in a zoo
___other (describe)

Why?

For a teacher today, being in elementary school should be like being:

___in a business
___in a circus
___in a crowd
___in a factory
___in a family
___in a garden
___in a hospital
___in a prison
___on a stage
___on a team
___in a zoo
___other (describe)

Why?

Communication:
Implications and Reflections

CARL D. GLICKMAN

H. JAMES MCLAUGHLIN

University of Georgia

VALERIE MILLER

Five Forks Middle School
Lawrenceville, Georgia

Throughout our response, we will refer to the three articles you have just read in this order, using the name of the authors: Ponticell ("Seeing and believing: Using collegial coaching and videotaping to improve instruction in an urban high school"); McKay, Powell and Jarchow ("Profiles of communication in multicultural learning environments: Case studies of preservice and experienced teachers"); and Stanford ("A spirit of partnership: Qualities conducive to career perseverance and high morale in teachers"). To begin, we will summarize the methodological issues raised by the studies in paragraph and chart form. Then we comment on how the authors addressed issues of context, text, and subtext. Finally, each of us will sketch the meaning of the pieces for us, in our different roles.

METHODOLOGICAL ISSUES

Because all three studies primarily utilized qualitative methods of research, we will summarize their characteristics in chart form. First, however, it is necessary to make a few summary comments about the essential elements in reporting such studies.

Writers of any research piece should be compelled to establish their *theoretical underpinnings,* and to *review the pertinent research literature.* McKay, et al., summarize their beliefs about symbolic interactionism and schema theory, and Ponticell discusses "change theory," so that the reader can see more clearly why the writer makes certain judgments, and perhaps what the article does *not* concern. Stanford does not afford us that opportunity, even though there is a large literature on principals' roles and their ways of interacting with teachers.

The *criteria for selecting participants,* along with *biographical information* about the participants and some explanation of their roles, are important components of a study's description. The credibility of qualitative research depends on how well the reader knows *who* is part of a study, *why* they are in the study, and *what they do* in the process of the study. University researchers often assume different roles at different points in research, as do school-level participants: both may be facilitators of discussion, collectors and analysts of data, actors or observers in particular school scenes, and take many other roles. Two of the three studies detail the selection criteria for participants, but none of the studies fully clarified the roles of researchers and other participants. This represents a tacit acceptance of traditional assumptions that the researcher plays a singular, "objective" role. In most cases such an approach to reporting research fails to depict the complexity of interactions in a study.

In research about communication, the *unit of analysis* names the nexus of interactions: whose communication is being studied, and what sort of communication is it? Two of the studies focus on interpersonal communication; the Stanford study directly concerns teachers' thoughts, and does not describe active communication. The Ponticell study addresses *two-way* communication in which the relationships among teachers are explored. Researchers in communication need to consider whether one can faithfully capture the patterns of communication only from one participant's angle, or just from spoken words.

Data collection and analysis are not always carefully explained. Two of the studies are longitudinal and utilize a variety of data sources, so that they provide the reader with adequate information to make informed judgments about their conclusions. However, in the Stanford study of "partnerships" between principals and teachers, twelve teachers were interviewed once or twice each, over a three-week period. This is a short time period, and there was only one data source. It was difficult for us to determine why certain instruments were used, what questions were asked, how the data were analyzed, or what the "subjects" in the study had to say—there are no quotations from them. Likewise, the Ponticell study of peer coaching contains snippets taken from teachers' remarks, but no dialogue or full accounts of responses.

Finally, there is the seldom-noticed but essential issue of whether the authors report *discrepant data,* data that may not jibe with the study's prevailing conclusions. Such data allow for a *contrary analysis* to be developed, which is the basis for an alternative interpretation of what the participants meant, and affects the meaning that a reader might glean from the study. None of the articles incorporates a contrary analysis. Therefore, we don't know if they were omitted or simply did not exist.

SUMMARY CHART OF METHODOLOGICAL ELEMENTS

	PONTICELL	MCKAY, et al.	STANFORD
THEORETICAL PERSPECTIVE AND LITERATURE REVIEW	"Change theory" and literature on conditions of teaching summarized	Symbolic interactionism and schema theory	Little discussion of theory or literature
SELECTION CRITERIA	Not described	Well-described	Well-described
BIOGRAPHICAL INFORMATION AND ROLES OF PARTICIPANTS	No biographical data on the 10 teachers; Roles of teachers included determining objectives of research, but researcher's role not clarified	Biographical data on the 3 teachers; No information on roles of researcher and teachers	Brief biographical data on 12 teachers; Roles of researcher and teacher not discussed
UNIT OF ANALYSIS	Teacher-and-teacher communication	Teacher-to-student patterns of communication	Teachers' thoughts about relationship with principals
DATA COLLECTION AND ANALYSIS	Variety of sources: Pre- and post-inventories, observations, interviews, self-analysis inventories	Variety of sources: Observations, interviews, journals	Interview sources: including questionnaire and two scaled instruments
CONTRARY ANALYSIS OR DISCREPANT DATA INCLUDED	Not included	Not included	Not included

HOW THE STUDIES ADDRESS CONTEXTUAL, TEXTUAL, AND SUBTEXTUAL ISSUES

Context

We have already detailed the unit of analysis for each study, which outlines whose communication is being analyzed. Studies such as these three have generally focused on teachers' communications in school settings or classroom sites. Ponticell utilized multiple settings: a "retreat" site, school classrooms, and a "professional seminar" site. The teachers' intentions in these settings were to "search for commonality" through peer coaching; to use videotapes to examine their own teaching; to gain skills in classroom observation; and to increase their willingness to try new teaching strategies. McKay's research centered on the classroom: small group work between students, whole group discussions, and individual conferences with students. Stanford did not describe a setting.

Numerous other arrangements of participants and settings might be interesting to explore. For example, researchers could study teacher-and-parent interactions outside of school or in school conferences, student-and-parent interactions at home or in school conferences, or teacher-and-teacher interactions within team or departmental meetings. Studies of non-classroom communication, and how the purposes of communication vary, could enhance our understanding of how school participants attach meaning to educational experiences.

Text

The texts of communication differed in the three studies. Teachers in Ponticell's work talked with one another about their own and their colleagues' teaching. The McKay et al. study focused on how teachers communicated content, control, and concern for students. Stanford did not delve into the subject or process of principal-teacher communication, but centered on teachers' perceptions of their relationships with a principal.

None of the three studies offered full accounts of the language of communication. The McKay et al. study did give numerous examples of student teachers' statements, yet the authors did not indicate the interactive nature of communication by quoting dialogue. The type of language used by interacting participants, and their varying understandings of what the language means, are vital parts of the whole of an interaction.

Subtext

One explicit intention of the Ponticell study was to empower teachers by enabling them to determine the agenda of the project. At the same time, there was an implicit agenda—a subtext—from the outset. The conversations were intended to alter teachers' perceptions of the need to change their teaching practices, and to result in changes in "routine" practice. This seems to be a crucial issue to anyone who wishes to reform or restructure schools. Top-down management and "teacher-proof" curriculum packages have come under heavy siege recently, and now more emphasis is placed on teachers as curriculum developers and school leaders. But change will not occur unless teachers wish to reexamine their roles and responsibilities, or for that matter their teaching and learning practices. And if we pay heed to Hargreaves (1984), summarized earlier, perhaps communication needs to be broadened by accepting non-school experiences, including one's theoretical stances about education and learning, into the conversations of schoolteachers.

In the McKay et al. article, there was an assumption that we know the "essential elements for both effective teaching and successful entry into the professions." This was the *researchers'* subtext: "content" and "communicating boundaries for behavior" were deemed to be essential. Both of these elements could be critiqued for their narrow interpretations of learning: Is content a thing that teachers present *to* students, or is the content of an educational interaction socially constructed by students and teachers together? Are boundaries of behavior fixed, and is the establishment and maintenance of limitations related to learning? This is connected with a subtext in the student teachers' communication about their experiences. For Beverly, "learning together" was an essential component of effective communication with students. Conversely, James sometimes expressed fear and distrust of students. These student teachers held epistemological beliefs about the nature of learning and of learners that might cross ethnic lines. To gain more information about such underlying, often tacit beliefs, a researcher would need to include the missing text in this study: student voices and how the student teachers conversed with students about learning and knowing. Jackson's description of a teacher who believed in public discourse about students' actions, and Ballenger's eagerness to learn about the cultural components of caring and controlling, offer other examples of studies concerned with students and teachers learning together.

The Stanford study assumes that partnership is good. Therefore, one subtext of the researchers' communication with teachers was to ascertain what teachers "needed" to form a partnership with their principal. If one were to assume that school politics and decision making are conflictive, as did Ball (1987), and that administrators are searching for ways to balance control and the integration of teachers into school processes, then the sort of question asked and the responses might be markedly different. Perhaps there is no sense of negotiation and conflict because in the authors' depiction of partnership, the voice of the principal was absent. So there is a missing text; that of principals and teachers communicating about a range of school concerns.

INDIVIDUAL PERSPECTIVES
ON THE STUDIES' IMPLICATIONS

We will now each respond to the studies, and summarize what the findings might mean for our practice. Jim McLaughlin will offer some questions to consider; Valerie Miller will talk about how the studies might be useful for teachers; and Carl Glickman will examine how the authors address central purposes of public schools and teacher education.

Jim's Perspective: A Middle-School Teacher Educator

In this response I will ask myself questions designed to challenge my thinking—and actions. To begin, the Ponticell study shows the need for "feedback, support and follow-up," if teachers are to communicate consistently and openly about their teaching. How, then, should videotaping and peer coaching be used in preservice teacher education? (See Freiberg & Waxman, 1990, for support of videotaping techniques, and then Adelman, 1981, p. 96, for remarks about the dangers of mistaking videotapes for "reality.")

And what about learning? The foundation of Ponticell's research was teaching, with very little indication that the teachers discussed and studied students' conceptions of learning. We need to do a much better job of understanding and acting on our notions of how and why students learn (see Nicholls, 1979; Oldfather, in press). Perhaps action research can engage practicing teachers as well as prospective teachers in group problem solving and serious reflection about teaching and learning (Noffke & Zeichner, 1987). In addition, the combination of action research and peer coaching may alter how staff development needs are determined (Iwanicki & McEachern, 1984).

In teacher education, how might *all* field experiences incorporate action research and some form of peer coaching? To what extent should prospective teachers learn about research methodology and communication skills? Is there a need for some sort of gradual build-up in this process of learning how to observe and analyze one's observations?

McKay, Powell, and Jarchow have written a useful piece about establishing positive and knowledgeable relationships with students. The particularly salient points have to do with preservice teachers' inclinations to be culturally sensitive. The authors want to affect teacher education by increasing preservice teachers' awareness of the diversity of cultural groups in America, a worthy aim. But it is not just awareness and understanding from student teachers that is crucial. Journal writing and other means of reflection are important, but it is teachers' *actions* within a multicultural environment that are crucial to change. How do we better prepare preservice teachers, in spite of their proclivities to think in certain ways? McKay et al. have good ideas within the analytical summaries of each teacher, which could be synthesized within a framework or a set of principles to nudge our thinking. To bring out some key issues, let me now offer some questions that teacher educators might ask about the facets of communication the authors discussed.

To increase teachers' ability to communicate content, should we increase the number of arts and sciences courses? Should we provide better—or more—teaching methods courses? How can we enable students to reexamine various sorts of *texts* (I use the term broadly to connote material resources and also sets of ideas) in particular content areas? In that process of textual analysis, how can students take into account what we know and don't know about cultural differences?

With regard to communicating the boundaries for student behavior, how can we challenge teacher education students to reinterpret the meanings and metaphors of "classroom management"? The McKay article has a traditional individualistic, teacher-oriented approach to discussing students' actions. What part can *students* play in establishing flexible, sensible norms for action in the classroom and the school, which somehow take into account cultural differences while fostering unity of purpose? School governance and classroom governance are connected; how can our university students learn more about those connections?

I agree with the authors that communicating empathy is central to a teacher's success with students. They portray how teachers empathize, for example, by listening to students' stories (as with the Vietnamese student). Listening to students, and considering who they are as individuals and as group members, is the starting point for taking action. We need to help prospective teachers determine how teachers "invite" students to write, how they establish non-classroom relationships with their students, and how students can participate in classroom governance and make other choices.

One other point about this study must be made. I wonder how we can talk about teachers' understandings and actions related to cultural issues, without examining how students communicate with teachers. Shouldn't we conceive of classrooms as sites in which ever-negotiated dialogues are taking place, in complex patterns of communication? How can we acquaint future teachers with this sort of complexity? The McKay et al. study has performed a valuable function for me, because from reading it, I have once again seen how we need to approach communication from teachers' and students' perspectives.

The Stanford study, aside from its methodological limitations, relays a vital message to us: that support and autonomy are not separate, but are always intertwined. Support and autonomy are the centrifugal and centripetal forces that keep schools revolving. A sense of control has to do with one's participation in a setting, one's part in a social environment. Autonomy is not an individual matter; it results from socially constructed agreements about one's terrain, and how decisions will be made in that arena. "Power is something that is negotiated by the participants in the instructional process" (McCrosky & Richmond, 1993, p. 169). We are always seeking autonomy in a social setting that requires the support of others, or else we become outcasts, recluses. Lortie (1979) asserted that teachers already have the autonomy of working behind (mostly closed) doors, yet it is the conditions of support and communication within a school that encourage or suppress creativity. Many times, we have as much autonomy as we are willing to claim, but the autonomy cannot be sustained without support.

How do we educate prospective teachers to be "partners" with school administrators? The study did not clearly describe how one goes about developing a "spirit of partnership," because it reproduced the typical top-down model of school governance: principals do—or fail to do—something to teachers, thus affecting teachers' empowerment. Should we create seminars at which prospective administrators share an internship with teacher interns? How can we begin a conversation between teachers and administrators during, and not after, their preservice preparation? Will a collective endeavor enable administrators to examine their attitudes or reflect on the climate of their school, as Stanford urges teachers to do?

Valerie's Perspective: A Middle-School Teacher

Ponticell's article focuses on the change and growth in teacher instruction after the use of peer coaching and videotaping. Both strategies placed the teachers in objective roles and disclosed valuable material regarding instruction and teachers' perceptions. The teachers changed their instructional strategies to include more student praise, student-centered activities, and teaching time in class. At-risk students reacted well to the changes in instruction.

For educators interested in improving education, the article is encouraging. The idea of having us reflect on our own teaching obviously bears positive results. Teachers may use the framework of this study to develop their own reflection strategies. We could implement such dialogue and observation on a one-to-one level, in a team partnership, or at a grade level. Focusing on one or two specific aspects of teaching, and sharing dialogue journals about our own observations, would be helpful. I envision a scenario in which a small group of teachers plans goals and objectives, and then develops a long-term peer coaching schedule. It is also essential that teachers desensitize themselves from a personal reaction to others' observations, and closely observe communication patterns and the dynamics of the group.

The use of videotaping is perhaps the most effective way for teachers to view themselves objectively. Teachers could engage in this strategy without the help of other colleagues, but the benefits of group study are evident. Videotaping allows teachers to view and review segments repeatedly, to reflect on successes and needed changes. Videotaping could also be used to compare one's actions over time.

However, we must choose strategies that coincide with our comfort level. Teachers' perceptions of collegiality and their own teaching are as diverse as the teachers themselves. Many teachers thrive on research, change, and collegial relations, others are content without these three. Although many in the educational system search for ways to grow, some teachers are presently unwilling to do that. Yet it is unreasonable to assume that education will change without a concerted effort among teachers to improve instruction. To create the best learning environment for students and to empower them to succeed, teachers must be willing to risk their traditional methods. First, we must carefully review our attitudes toward students, toward the parents we deal with, and toward the curriculum. Second, we must review our instructional strategies, if not through videotaping, then through journal keeping, student evaluations, or research. Third, we must make changes based on our reflections, and continue to be reflective learners.

The purpose of peer coaching is not to ensure the teacher's personal gain, but to act in the students' best interests. Engaging in a study is rewarding and productive. Combining a group of teachers and perhaps using videotaping may open up new avenues for teachers to talk with one another. The question is whether teachers are ready to open up. We must begin to perceive teaching as a process whereby no one may become satisfied; rather, we constantly seek better ways to help our students succeed.

The McKay et al. article highlights that in every classroom, students have individual needs. Their needs are determined by their family, social, and academic backgrounds. We as teachers must be able to communicate effectively with each student according to the student's needs, keeping in mind the student's personal history. In a multicultural classroom, the individual needs run a larger gamut, and we must acknowledge the differences and communicate in such a way that all students are given an equal opportunity to succeed.

The article outlines three specific communication patterns that teachers need to use in the classroom. However, in a multicultural classroom, *communication* takes on a whole new meaning. Communicating content, empathy, and behavior management will undoubtedly reflect the teacher's own culture, as he or she uses gestures, slang and formal expressions, voice intonations and inflection, and other underlying cultural messages. For students of diverse cultures, such cultural communication techniques may or may not be deemed appropriate, or may not be understood. It is not just the terminology that is crucial to communication, but rather the way in which something is communicated, keeping in mind that students' backgrounds are different, which is vital to note in today's classroom.

According to Nelson Brooks, "deep culture" is most important in learning about other cultures. Deep culture entails the culture's view on humor, gestures and expressions of courtesy/rudeness, approval/disapproval, intonations of voice, and various other aspects that deeply affect intercultural relations. Teacher education programs and local school districts should not merely try to claim cross-cultural understanding through one-time workshops, but rather develop an ongoing process so that teachers become acculturated into various cultural experiences.

The three teachers in the article showed varying levels of communication skills, due to teaching experience and personal backgrounds. We all have our personal histories as teachers, which affect the learning environment. We must learn to confirm our views as we approach new multicultural experiences in the classroom. Personal reflection would be one way to determine our personal histories. Before attempting to understand and communicate successfully with students from varying cultural backgrounds, we must be comfortable with *our* deep culture. We must ask "Why do I make eye contact only the first few seconds I speak? Why do I make sure I am at least two feet away from a person when I am speaking? Why do I point to my chest when I am speaking about myself?"

Although the questions might seem absurd for us to ask, they are indeed the very questions asked by students unfamiliar with our cultural expressions. In the same way, we may ask why some students point to their nose when speaking of themselves or why other students look down when we speak to them. Once we engage in our own personal histories and are reminded that we are products of our environment, our communication with others will reflect not only our own culture, but a renewed sense of appreciation for others' culture.

Communicating content and behavior management are quite necessary in a classroom, but communicating empathy is what dictates success for diverse students. We must be willing to ask students what they do and do not understand. We must engage in real conversation, and ask them where they feel most comfortable sitting, just as Beverly did in her ESL classroom. We must ask them their preferences, fears, questions, and needs, and react to them. Students who discern the teacher's sincere efforts to be empathetic will probably become more capable of learning.

The article is not specific about how teachers should be taught about cultural differences. The awareness is first and foremost, and should be taught in educational programs. However, teachers need rich resources to inform them of the deep culture prevalent in every culture. Teachers must understand how eye contact, spatial relations, and social graces differ across and within societies. Do all Europeans look one another in the eye when speaking? Do all Asians create a minimal or maximal distance from one another? Then teachers must reflect on their own personal history. Communication with students from diverse backgrounds exists in every classroom, a dynamic environment of diverse learners. And whether the students are from across the street, town, county, or continent, teachers need to know that effective communication requires sensitivity to student diversity.

The Stanford study reminds us that in any profession, the need for both autonomy and support is paramount. It is with support as an individual that one becomes confident and willing to take risks. Although the article asserts that the need for both autonomy and support is a contradiction, it is almost necessary that the two exist together.

The worst teaching situations described as "little cooperation from parents, administrators, or principal" are universal. The ideal teaching situations described as "administrators recognizing and encouraging creativity" are accepted wisdom among teachers. It is obvious that administrative support or lack of support tremendously affects teachers' perceptions of their jobs, and their subsequent actions.

This article has far more implications for administrators and teacher educators than for classroom teachers, but it does allow teachers to reflect on the issues. For teachers, this article reiterates our sentiments. However, it does provoke us to take action based on what is reported. We must take this information and transform our own situation. For example, if we know our career perseverance and high morale stem from our collegial relations, then we must work to create such collegial relations. We must not sit and wait for administrators to take this step. In a middle school environment, the dynamics of teaming are conducive to building relations. Middle school teachers should make every effort to build strong collegial support throughout the year. Other school levels should do the same.

Although the article encourages reflection, collegial relations, autonomy, and administrative support, teachers' personal perceptions and actions in the classroom greatly determine their degree of career perseverance and high morale. Others around us affect our profession, but it is only how we react to our own situation that truly influences us. Teachers in the most supportive environment can be the least motivated, because of personal circumstances. What happens inside one's own heart and in one's own classroom often allows us to overcome difficult conditions.

In considering the need for a partnership among teachers and administrators to enhance teachers' perseverance and morale, I see the same needs for our students. Students seek a "spirit of partnership" in the classroom, teacher support, and most certainly autonomy. Perhaps teachers can use this article to reflect on how *all* members of a school community can persevere with high morale.

Carl's Perspective: A University Teacher in Educational Leadership

In reading these studies, I was struck by how far we've come and how far we need to go! "Seeing and Believing," "Profiles of Communication," and a "Spirit of Partnership" are robust in the professional discussions of teacher education and school reform. The positive results of urban high school teachers' using videotaping and peer coaching is not surprising. Peer-coaching programs are prevalent in many reform-minded schools. The awareness, experience, and learning of teachers about multicultural learning environments and the concomitant relationship with a) communicating content to students, b) communicating boundaries for behavior, and c) communicating empathy to the learner, make eminently good sense. The findings that "highly motivated" and committed teachers find a sense of collegiality with their peers and have deep needs for administrative support and autonomy are again part of a series of now mainstream studies about teachers, their work, and their schools.

It is most encouraging that the topics, studies, and results are not new. We accept that teacher education needs to accept a respectful and more comprehensive view of teachers, learners, and settings for communication between them. There are major efforts nationwide to create school renewal networks and new teacher education programs along these lines. These studies nudge us to continue these efforts.

But now, I must present my troubling disclaimers of "how far we still need to go." For example, shouldn't it be obvious that when teachers are accorded respect, given the support to be collegial, and allowed to formulate their own activities around professional deliberations about teaching and learning, that they will question and improve their own practice? These are the crucial *contexts* of schools, which foster communication. It should be obvious, but Grimmett (1992) and Smyth (1991; 1992) have pointed out that many of the staff-development programs to promote collegiality are contrived and politically, not pedagogically, motivated. Others decide for teachers how they will be brought together to discuss teaching (i.e., programs in clinical supervision, peer coaching, microteaching, and mentoring). Hierarchical authority is still the prevailing force in deciding how teachers are to be collegial.

There is a lack of fit between the idea of collegiality and the strategy for bringing it about, because we have not heeded the necessary contexts of communication.

The profile of multicultural communication is a wonderful portrayal of the uses of knowledge, sensitivity, and empathy to educate students from diverse backgrounds. But again, I'm troubled about how far we need to go. Dorris (1992) has eloquently depicted the cultural patterns of North America as a tapestry, begun by different Native American populations and augmented by people from Europe, Africa, and other places. It seems that only now do we find it important to be aware of and sensitive to, such diversity. This always should have been the case. It hasn't been because of the restrictive definition of who was considered a valid citizen.

"A Spirit of Partnership" is also encouraging and disturbing. There have been sincere attempts to decentralize educational decisions in schools and to "empower" teachers in collaborative decision making. Yet, in this article, a sample of persevering teachers with high morale still express regard for their principals for "giving" them support and autonomy. Although it is certainly better to have a patriarchal or matriarchal figure give competent professionals freedom and responsibility, why should there still be such dependency on a singular authority figure? Autonomy and decision making should be a right of a professional in an educational community, not a gift delivered by someone else.

In sum, these studies point out that coaching, multicultural understanding, and autonomy and collegiality should be the focus of professional work. That we still need to study these factors to provide "proof" of their effectiveness might mean that many of us are still not entirely convinced of their rightness. And this is where the implications from these studies swing full circle to confront those of us who prepare teachers and administrators. If teaching, coaching, multicultural understanding, autonomy, and collegiality are all important aspects of positive teacher communication in public schools, why don't higher-education faculty reflect those beliefs in their own actions, when interacting with one another and with students? These are not the sorts of questions generally raised in university faculty meetings. If we agreed on the findings of these studies and the underlying beliefs about teachers and the teaching/learning process, then our university preparation programs would incorporate some of the following:

1. Preparation programs designed so that university students learned to team with each other, to coach each other, and to be involved with faculty in decisions about their own programs. Prospective teachers would have classroom and field experiences in multicultural settings.

2. Teaching by university faculty would be done more in teams; faculty would coach each other, plan coordinated programs, and have multicultural experiences in a variety of schools and communities.

To say it another way, university undergraduate and graduate programs and the teaching norms of university faculty are often the antithesis of those theoretically advocated for students and public schools. Of course, there are healthy exceptions to the rule, but the rule still dominates. Our credibility depends on how we meld theory and practice about public schools in our own university practice.

CONCLUSION

Each of us has examined the communicative issues in these studies according to our roles in education. Whatever our differences, we agree that issues of context and purpose are central to understanding and encouraging communication. When all is said and done, the focus of communication in education is the dialogue among educators and students that prepares our next generation of citizens to be knowledgeable, wise, and dedicated to promoting a decent society. These studies point us in the direction of looking deeply at what are important factors in creating this dialogue. There can be no concept of the good life and no concept of the good society without a corresponding concept of good education. We all have much to talk about.

REFERENCES

Adelman, C. (1981). On first hearing. In C. Adelman (Ed.), *Uttering, muttering,* 78–97. London: Grant McIntyre.

Ball, S. J. (1987). *The micro-politics of the school.* New York: Methuen & Co.

Ballenger, C. (1992). Because you like us: The language of control. *Harvard Educational Review, 62*(2), 199–208.

Barnes, D. (1992). *From communication to curriculum.* Portsmouth, NH: Boynton/Cook.

Brooks, N. (1964). Language and language learning: Theory and practice. NY: Harcourt Brace.

Dorris, M. (1992). Beyond cliché, beyond politics: Multiculturalism and the fact of America. *The Georgia Review, 46*(3), 473–478.

Fishbein, M., & Ajzen, I. (1975). *Beliefs, attitude, intention, and behavior.* Reading, MA: Addison-Wesley.

Freiberg, H. J., & Waxman, H. C. (1990). Changing teacher education. In W. R. Houston (Ed.), *Handbook of research on teacher education,* 617–635. New York: Macmillan.

Grimmett, P. P., Rostad, O. P., & Ford, B. (1992). The transformation of supervision. In C. D. Glickman (Ed.), *Supervision in transition: The 1992 ASCD*

Yearbook. Alexandria, VA: Association for Supervision and Curriculum Development.

Hargreaves, A. (1984). Experience counts, theory doesn't: How teachers talk about their work. *Sociology of Education, 57,* 244–254.

Iwanicki, E. F., & McEachern, L. (1984). Using teacher self-assessment to identify staff development needs. *Journal of Teacher Education, 35*(2), 38–41.

Jackson, P. W. (1992). *Untaught lessons.* New York: Teachers College Press.

Lortie, D. (1979). *Schoolteacher.* Chicago: University of Chicago Press.

McCrosky, J., & Richmond, V. (1993). Communication: Implications and reflections. In M. O'Hair & S. Odell (Eds.), *Diversity and teaching: Teacher education yearbook I* (pp. 227–234). Fort Worth: Harcourt Brace Jovanovich.

McNeil, L. M. (1986). *Contradictions of control.* London: Routledge and Kegan Paul.

Nicholls, J. G. (1979). Quality and equality in intellectual development: The role of motivation in education. *American Psychologist, 34,* 1071–1084.

Noffke, S. E., & Zeichner, K. M. (1987). Action research and teacher thinking: The first phase of the action research on action research project at the University of Wisconsin-Madison. Paper presented at the Annual Meeting of the American Educational Research Association, Washington, DC, April.

Oldfather, P. (In press). What students say about motivating experiences in a whole language classroom. *The Reading Teacher.*

Seletsky, A. (1988). My name is Alice: A fifth grade story of naming and family history. In V. Rogers, A. D. Roberts, & T. P. Weinland (Eds.), *Teaching social studies: Portraits from the classroom,* pp. 10–18. Washington, DC: National Council for the Social Studies.

Smyth, J. (1991). International perspectives on teacher collegiality: A labour process discussion based on the concept of teachers' work. *British Journal of Sociology of Education, 12*(3), 323–345.

Smyth, J. (1992). Teachers' work and the politics or reflection. *American Educational Research Journal, 29*(2), 267–300.

Zisman, P., & Wison, V. (1992). Table hopping in the cafeteria: An exploration of "racial" integration in early adolescent social groups. *Anthropology and Education Quarterly, 23,* 199–220.

Partnerships in Curriculum Development and Evaluation

Curriculum: Overview and Framework

JANE STALLINGS
DONNA WISEMAN
GERALD KULM
Texas A&M University

JANE STALLINGS is Dean of Education at Texas A&M University. She has conducted numerous national studies focused on relationships between the teaching and learning processes. Current research is focused on research on school reform to improve education so all students can ultimately become productive citizens in a democratic society.

DONNA WISEMAN is Professor and Associate Dean of Teacher Education at Texas A&M University. Her specialty is reading/language arts (early literacy, readers' responses, and writing development). Recent research focuses on teacher education and the development of school-university partnerships. She is an Associate involved in John Goodlad's Institute for Educational Inquiry.

GERALD KULM is Professor of Mathematics Education at Texas A&M University. Areas of interest include mathematics and science assessment and evaluation, minority involvement in mathematics and science learning and teaching, and mathematics and science teacher preparation. Current research includes development of assessment instruments for at-risk learners in mathematics.

What should children learn in school? The answer to that question has changed over time, always reflecting the needs and priorities of society. For example, in 1957 fear of Russia's Sputnik and the United States losing the space race prompted the development of new science curricula at every grade level. These programs were developed primarily by scientists in universities, laboratories, and centers, and then implemented in schools.

The civil rights movement in the 1960s was the next social stimulus to curricular change. Again education laboratories and centers and colleges of education were the respondents to large scale federal government requests for proposals to initiate Head Start and Follow Through Planned Variation model programs. These grant recipients developed unique curricular models that held promise for improving the life chances of low-income children. A second part of the challenge was to develop a training system that could ensure consistent program implementation in schools serving diverse populations and in varied locations . . . urban, rural, north, or south. In both of the above curricular reforms, schools were the receivers of the good ideas developed by those outside the school system.

As it became evident during the 1970s that test scores of students at all grade levels were plummeting, society called for a stronger focus on basic skills. This time school districts as well as labs and centers and colleges of education responded with proposals for national programs to improve basic skills, bilingual, and special education programs. There was little collaborative design reflected in these programs or among institutions developing and implementing them.

Although test scores of basic skills improved, scores for higher order thinking skills did not. Thus, throughout the 1980s there has been a concern that our students are performing more poorly than their European and Asian peers. Particularly disturbing is the fact that German and Japanese economies, supported by the automotive and high-tech industries, have surpassed the United States. Disturbing social changes have occurred as our economy has become more fragile and unbalanced. Middle- and low-income families have lost sources of income and become homeless. Thirty-seven million Americans lack health insurance or coverage and twelve million are children. One in four pregnant women in the U.S. lacks care during pregnancy. Forty percent of the poor in our country are children, and poverty among children aged 5 and younger is increasing. There are fifteen million children being raised by single mothers and living within poverty. Only one-half of the children who qualify for Head Start are able to attend. The overall dropout rate is now reaching twenty-five percent and can be as high as forty to fifty percent in urban areas. In addition, one-fifth of our children report that they regularly bring guns to school; last year, 16,000 crimes at school were reported. The number of illiterate adults in our society is reaching 2.7 million.

Given these complex socioeconomic problems, the goals set forth in *America 2000* seek the health and welfare of children and families while promoting academic achievement, particularly higher order thinking. The main goal stipulates that all children will come to school ready to learn. If this is to happen, children must have healthy bodies, minds free from fear, and the support of a family. To achieve this, collaboration must occur among social service, health, and education agencies. For the health and education needs of children and families to be met, professionals who serve in these roles must be prepared in the context of the schools serving diverse populations. Education curricula developed that are not responsive to the school culture are not viable. With this realization, during the end of the 1980s, many colleges of education formed partnerships with schools to develop curricula and prepare teachers.

The answer to the question "What Should Children Learn in School?" has been greatly influenced in the 1990s by the technological revolution and the need for an educated, creative, problem-solving, flexible work force. The economy cannot be turned around if large segments of our population are in poor health and are poorly educated. To respond to this challenge educators, health providers, social workers, business, industry, and communities must forge partnerships committed to developing citizens who can participate, thrive, and contribute to a free and democratic society.

Few challenge the view that new curricula are needed for every subject area and grade level of schools and for the colleges that prepare the educators. Complex societal issues require integrated approaches to curricular development and delivery. This integration is occurring in some locations where college and school faculties teach and learn together with mutual respect. In such partnerships classroom teachers are valued for their knowledge and understanding of the children and their communities and for their ability to translate the curriculum into units meaningful to the context of the students' lives. College faculty are valued for their knowledge of pedagogical research and subject matter, and for their ability to integrate technology into curricular areas.

To achieve effective and efficient curricular reform, simultaneous change in curriculum must occur within colleges of education where educators are prepared and in school systems where educators serve children. Partnerships between school and college faculties that integrate subject areas at college and school levels hold promise as models for curricula that can be delivered by student teachers and classroom teachers.

There is evidence that many current classroom practices consistently and systematically disadvantage a great majority of our children (Oakes, 1985) and "one can argue that virtually every major effort designed to improve the school's capacity to serve has resulted, at least early on, in improving or extending the options of those already best served" (Goodlad, 1990). Clearly, curricular changes must occur and meet the needs of all schoolchildren. Innovative curricula will be developed when those who care for and about children work together. The chapters in the following section present examples of new ways to think about curriculum.

THREE RESEARCH REPORTS

There are many forms of partnerships and collaboration among school and college faculties. In the three studies in this section of the Yearbook, authors have described several structures for collaboration. Griffin focuses primarily on teacher education and provides a brief historical overview of curriculum trends from the 1930s to the present day. He delivers a dialogue that challenges most current curricula that tend to be fragmented and unrelated to the life of classrooms. Major gaps in education students' preparation are delineated. The chapter concludes with innovative instructional recommendations for using cases or stories, group learning, and experiential learning when preparing teachers. Griffin's ideas provide a plan for enabling teacher education programs to better meet the needs of students who serve the children of the 1990s.

The second study addresses the important and timely study of AIDS/HIV education. Forese and Cleary explore two strategies for developing effective programs for middle grade students in six seventh-grade health classes. Health professionals with school and college faculties collaborated in developing the course content and the instructional approaches. It has become clear that adolescents are becoming one of the most at-risk groups for AIDS/HIV and are also the most difficult to reach with awareness programs. These authors point out that the time spent must be as powerful and compelling as possible. For the content they used films and interviews with AIDS/HIV victims. Students confronted the course content and their beliefs with peers in cooperative groups. One implication of this study is that the future training for health educators should include content related to how an effective AIDS/HIV curriculum might be planned and implemented.

In the third study by Connell, Peck, Buxton, and Kilburn, the reader learns that changing teachers' conceptualization of mathematics is a daunting task. The authors have described an earnest attempt on the part of mathematics education faculty to bring about changes both conceptually and in their teaching practices. The authors have identified the key issue as the teachers' view of the nature of mathematics. A dichotomy between school and the real world of mathematics is defined with the culture of the practicing mathematician and scientist as the one that teachers should emulate as being real. The teacher in this project became a learner, participating in mathematics activities much as her students were doing. This direct learning experience was crucial to the teacher's efforts to reconstruct her own mathematical knowledge and develop new attitudes toward the nature of mathematics. The study indicates that in-depth, long-term collaborative intervention is needed to bring about these changes. A natural part of this collaboration would be to include preservice teachers who can, as a part of the team, be learners of the new world of classroom mathematics along with classroom teachers.

REFERENCES

Goodlad, J. I. (1990). *Teachers for our nation's schools.* San Francisco: Jossey-Bass.

Oakes, J. (1985). *Keeping track: How schools structure inequality.* New Haven: Yale University Press.

CHAPTER 10

Teacher Education Curriculum in a Time of School Reform

GARY A. GRIFFIN
University of Arizona

GARY A. GRIFFIN is currently Professor of Education at the University of Arizona. His experience includes positions as Professor and Director of the Division of Instruction at Columbia University Teachers College, Program Director at the Research and Development Center for Teacher Education at the University of Texas, Professor and Dean of the College of Education at the University of Illinois at Chicago. He has published extensively on the topics of teacher education, staff development, school change, and curriculum theory and development. Griffin is active in the American Educational Research Association, was a member of the founding Board of Directors of The Holmes Group, is a member of AERA National Commission on Research and Practice, and served as ongoing consultant to the NEA Mastery in Learning Project.

In this chapter, I am interested in issues related directly to the curriculum of teacher education. By curriculum, I mean the content and processes of instructional programs designed to prepare teachers for the nation's schools. Although teacher education has been considered a continuum of learning from preservice through the first years of teaching to the end of a teaching career (Griffin, 1988), this chapter focuses directly on college- or university-based preparation programs, although the observations presented and the suggestions made may be applicable to other points on the continuum. Necessarily, the chapter is selective. The proposals I advance are ones that have some practical and theoretical currency, but so do others. The content that appears here was selected primarily because it seems applicable to most teacher-preparation programs rather than useful only in specialized educational settings. Also, the changing organizational and intellectual contexts of public elementary and secondary schools in the United States (Murphy, 1991) prompted me to urge responses from the teacher education community. This is in contrast, for example, to using research findings or policy initiatives as the stimuli for proposing content and process in teacher education.

This chapter on teacher education curriculum has three major sections. The first reminds us of persistent assertions about the weakness of teacher education programs in terms of changing teacher candidates' (and new teachers') perspectives about what teaching is or should be. Purposeful changes in these perspectives are considered here as interventions in the ways intending teachers think about schools and teaching. The second section includes several suggestions for content to be considered for inclusion in a teacher education curriculum. The third identifies several options to consider when making process decisions in teacher education.

TEACHER EDUCATION AS INTERVENTION

Teacher education programs are seldom termed educational interventions. Yet, teacher candidates are engaged with content and pedagogy designed to alter their ways of thinking and acting in relation to teaching and schooling, alterations that higher education faculties believe will help their graduates provide high-quality educational opportunity for children and youth. As is true for other educational interventions, teacher education typically rests on sets of intentions accompanied by opportunities to learn and demonstrate learning. These opportunities are tied, directly or indirectly, to conditions in schools and the society that appear to the college and university decision makers to be important to modify or maintain.

If we give direct and serious attention to teacher education as intervention, we come face to face with the important issue of intention. What do we mean to accomplish? How do we propose to bring about the goal? What evidence do we believe is sufficient to make judgments about the degree to which our purposes are met?

These are curriculum questions (Goodlad & Richter, 1966). When asked (and answered), they provide focus for our work and lead us to action. They help to organize the ways we bring students of teaching in contact with important teaching issues. They help us track our progress, chart our consequences, shift our perspectives, respond to emerging understandings about the human condition, and push us to invent, create, and discover.

When curriculum questions are not asked, when matters of intention are buried in discussions of institutional procedures and regularities, we go through the motions of "doing" teacher education in an often rote and well-remembered way, usually highly organized but without firm foundations upon which to build meaningful intellectual and practical frameworks. Coming to grips with why we choose to engage our students with certain content, and how we make the content present to intending teachers in the ways we do, helps us to strengthen the power of teacher education as intervention. Ignoring matters of intention sets us adrift in ad hoc decision making or working with students in ways that may be comfortable for us but without substantial consequence for teacher candidates.

Historically, teacher education has proved to be a relatively weak intervention. A number of studies have concluded that teachers tend to teach much as they were taught; that teachers prefer to teach students who are much like themselves; that teacher education programs are perceived by graduates as too theory-driven and not helpful in teaching (particularly during the first years of practice); and that school-based officers and staff developers believe they must somehow provide "real" teacher education to teachers in service (Goodlad, 1990). These assertions are persistent threads in the literature on teacher education.

Lortie (1975), in what is now a classic study, called our attention to the cumulative influence of persistent teacher-watching. Coining the phrase *apprenticeship of observation,* he noted that prospective teachers experienced teaching up close and personal day after day during their elementary and secondary-school years and into colleges and universities. Typically, then, a prospective teacher will have had as many as fourteen years (including at least two years of postsecondary general education) of unplanned opportunities to come to understandings about what teaching is and should be. Further, if Lortie and others are even partially correct in their conclusions, the teaching we see today has been passed along through generations of teachers, each generation learning from the one before it. This extended student view of teaching, he and others have concluded, promotes ways of thinking about teaching that are powerful predictors of how the students will eventually teach.

What do students in elementary and secondary schools learn about teaching? With some modest variation, they learn that teaching is relatively simple in terms of intellectual requirements. This view has strong historical roots, planted in a time when knowledge had not expanded exponentially as it has recently. Prospective teachers and their classmates (future parents, patrons, legislators, policymakers, and opinion influencers) learn that knowledge is held externally, is privileged information, and is doled out in some regulated fashion by the holder, the teacher. They come to believe that learning is individual and largely private. They learn that understanding comes only when text can be comprehended, when algorithms can be applied, when there is command over already-developed formulae that are part of one's learning repertoire. And, in many cases, they learn that teaching and learning are dull and lifeless phenomena.

The apprenticeship of observation, then, can be seen as a primary shaping force in everyone's life, at least everyone who spends significant student time in classrooms. And what is observed day after day and year after year has been passed along from one teacher generation to the next. This probably accounts not only for the persistent sameness in teaching, but also for policymakers' resistance to any concerted attempt to redefine teaching, even in the face of a growing consensus that schools are not succeeding in their tasks, on the one hand, and in the presence of thoughtfully designed propositions for change on the other.

Other scholars have argued that recent attention to the growing "knowledge base" for teaching is overblown and that teaching may not be specialized human activity in the ways that doctoring or lawyering are believed to be. This view, simplified for this discussion, rests on the assumption that we've all taught someone something and, therefore, that teaching is pervasive in society, a kind of natural human activity (Buchmann, 1986). It follows, then, that teaching does not rest on anything very special, only on the willingness to do it most of one's time rather than sporadically as other aspects of living call for it.

These views, again rooted in other times with other societal demands, ignore two important interacting phenomena. First, the simple "each one teach one" perspective does not take into account that teaching as we've come to conceptualize it in most cultures involves groups of students, not individuals, groups that come together because of a societally determined mandate. It is probably true that individuals learn skills from one another through imitation, relatively simple interactive dialogue, and trial-and-error work of one kind or another. It is also probably true that individuals who come fresh to a mature group easily learn values and dispositions that are persistently displayed by the group's members. It does not follow, however, that societally mandated groups of students can be taught in the same ways. As society has organized teaching and learning as group activity, it has been necessary to devise ways of teaching that consider both crowd control and intellectual development.

This leads to the second phenomenon that proponents of teaching as simple activity seem to either ignore or not value: the relatively recent research-based understandings of how to proceed when teaching groups. I join others in being cautious about accepting too readily the claims for the robustness of the knowledge base for teaching. I do, however, believe that we are considerably better informed than in previous years about how students learn, about how students' interactions with one another can be productive, about how groups can be managed and sustained for learning tasks, and how understanding (knowing how and why as opposed to knowing what and that) can be achieved with students. In short, although the body of specialized knowledge for teaching is still insufficient to the formidable tasks it is expected to contribute to, it provides some substance to the assertion that professional teaching can be conceptualized as something other than conventional human activity that is pervasive in the larger society (Reynolds, 1989).

Herein, of course, lies a significant part of the discontent about teaching as intervention. We are uncomfortable about findings such as Lortie's regarding the power of the apprenticeship of observation only if, first, we believe that this need not be the case and, second, if we believe that there is knowledge about teaching that is more substantial and important than that which teachers typically demonstrate in their public roles. (It has been argued correctly that teaching is considerably more than what students see [Griffin, 1989]. This perspective suggests that what is special about teaching is made up largely of the ways that teachers think about teaching during their planning, reflection, and other less-obvious aspects of their work, and that it is this intellectual approach to teaching that differentiates the professional teacher from the thoughtful person in other walks of life. But, the argument does not negate the generational sameness of teaching as observed activity. If teachers thought about teaching in more adventurous ways, to use Cohen's (1987) term, I believe that students would see more adventurous teaching activity in elementary and secondary classroom settings.

If we suspect that there are better ways to teach than are typically the case, and that this different teaching rests on specialized knowledge, it is imperative that we identify that knowledge and find powerful ways to present it to prospective teachers. These deliberations and decisions reveal our intentions in teacher education. In other words, we must ask two important curriculum questions: How should teachers teach and how can we prepare teachers to teach in these different ways? In short, we must devise ways to overcome the dominance of the apprenticeship of observation as the prime predictor of the several generations of teacher work.

HOW SHOULD TEACHERS TEACH?

The question of how teachers should teach is a complex one, although both explicit and more tacit responses to the question often mask the complexity. The past several decades in the United States have borne witness to two competing ways of responding to the question. On the one hand, there is the passionate search for a kind of educational silver bullet that, sent on its way with careful aim and a steady hand, will penetrate the layers upon layers of complications that seem to hinder desired student learning. On the other hand, some practitioners and more researchers are caught up in the complications surrounding teaching and learning to the degree that some appear to have given up any sustained search for "best practice" solutions to the tangle of intellectual, societal, cultural, linguistic, developmental, and personal considerations that often seem to blunt teaching effectiveness.

The "silver bullet" theory typically rests on a narrowly conceptualized version of teaching and learning. It aims directly at one observable piece of the teaching-learning puzzle, ignoring most or all others. It doesn't really matter whether the silver bullet is derived from psychological theory, as in the case of Hunter's Essential Elements of Instruction (Stallings & Krasavage, 1986); from observations of teachers whose students are high achievers, as in the case of the many effective teaching studies (Barnes, 1981); or from perspectives on healthy groups, as in the case of some strategies for dealing with disruptive students. What matters is that one piece of the teaching-learning conundrum is seen to change in some positive direction. Policymakers and school officers are very taken with silver bullets.

On the other hand, considerable talk and thought is focused on the complexities of teaching and learning. No silver bullet could find its way through the density of the tightly woven fabric of difficulties that confront teachers in the nation's schools. Students' personal circumstances prohibit engagement with learning. School and district working conditions push back against the most earnest teacher. Societal and local support for schools is lacking. Parents are not engaged with their students' schooling. School curricula are poorly designed and largely irrelevant. And so on.

Neither of these perspectives, taken alone, is helpful to the teacher educator as curriculum decisions, formal and informal, are made. Although there are instances in which silver bullets, usually expressed thematically, are central to programs of teacher preparation, they are rare. It is also unlikely that concentration on the problematic nature of teaching without attention to how teachers might deal with the problems is representative of many teacher education programs.

Teacher educators, of course, do not ignore the question of how teachers should teach, but this observer has found it rare that the *content* of teacher education programs rests on a firm foundation of analysis, experimentation, reflection, and refinement. More likely, the particular predilections of teacher educators prevail, sometimes formally as documented in program descriptions, and more frequently as faculty teach from their pedagogical and content strengths and well-developed belief structures (Griffin, 1990). This observation is exacerbated by the fact that teacher education is most often a university-wide phenomenon involving faculty from liberal arts and sciences, education, and importantly, the elementary and secondary teachers who provide practicum and student teaching supervision (The Holmes Group, 1986).

When one realizes that the curriculum content of teacher education is presented to prospective teachers in general education courses, in professionally oriented courses, and in school settings, the dilemmas associated with the teacher education curriculum become sharply apparent. Returning to the idea of the power of the apprenticeship of observation to shape understandings about teaching, it is not surprising that teaching traditions (rather than teaching innovations) prevail. Higher-education faculty, with some dramatic exceptions, are not known for innovative teaching methods, and teacher candidates spend a good deal of time in their classes. We have already noted the prevailing norms in elementary and secondary schools as conservative and traditional. It is important to remember, also, that prospective teachers working with school professionals are in what is essentially an apprentice mode of learning, as opposed to participating as members of groups in other learning-to-teach situations. This may explain the persistent assertion by teachers that student teaching is the most influential and important aspect of their teacher education programs (Griffin, 1986a). Even with the most innovative content and teaching methods, teacher educators in schools and colleges of education are hard put to challenge prevailing norms in other teaching-learning settings in which their students do their post-secondary teacher watching.

Even in the face of these understandings about the difficulties associated with learning to "teach against the grain" (Cochran-Smith, 1991), it is still important to respond to the question, "How should teachers teach?" The answer to this question becomes the content of teacher education. I propose four bodies of content that appear to me to respond to current school and societal needs. They are curriculum planning, teaching for understanding, inquiry in teaching, and the school as a workplace. Other content candidates, of course, could be advanced. Those proposed here seem to me to be responsive to prevailing conditions in schools *and* the needs of our present-day and future society.

Curriculum Planning

The concept of "teacher as curriculum worker" has gained some modest popularity in the past several years (Zumwalt, 1986). Historically, though, teachers have been seen by policymakers and school district officers as people who carry out the curriculum decisions made by others. The belief was that curriculum planning required specialized theoretical and technical knowledge and skill that were best learned in graduate degree programs, leaving teacher preparation courses to deal with "methods" of instruction and with some modest attention to microcurriculum processes associated with lesson planning. These practices are strongly related to the historical movement toward centralizing schooling. That is, schools were expected to deliver essentially the same curriculum to all students and, therefore, curriculum planning could be accomplished most efficiently at some central point in the state or local educational establishment. Teachers were sometimes a part of this centralized planning process but, typically, were not the major players in decision making about content (Klein, 1991).

Because of the growing understanding that students in schools differ dramatically on several continua of characteristics, such as readiness to learn and cultural background, a shift in thinking has occurred about curriculum planning as a state or district decision-making umbrella, meant to cover all. Recent relocation of curriculum responsibility from a centralized function to a school or classroom responsibility has demonstrated faith in (1) the power of the individual school and/or classroom context to influence what is learned and (2) the curriculum planning sensibilities and skills of teachers. This faith is well-placed; research has demonstrated clearly that distanced curriculum decision making often results in school programs that are irrelevant or trivial to students (Klein, 1991). The faith is also mischievous in that few teachers are well-equipped to engage in thoughtful and serious long-term curriculum planning (Griffin, 1991).

The logic of placing teachers at the heart of curriculum decision-making, it seems to me, is sound, in that student groups differ significantly, school community expectations vary, cultural traditions and mores reflect local rather than more centrally decided values, and so on. Because schools, in large measure, are expected to be responsive to clients and patrons, it seems reasonable that teachers, whose lives are intricately entwined with those of their students, should bear considerable responsibility for deciding what is to be learned and how it is to be taught.

Do teacher education programs typically help prospective teachers to think and act in ways that lead to solid curriculum work? Are teachers prepared to sort through myriad curriculum possibilities? Are most or many teachers equipped to debate philosophical or other theoretical bases for curriculum decisions? For that matter, do teachers think of curriculum as locally produced and enacted, or do they think of their work almost exclusively in terms of pedagogy? (I acknowledge the difficulty in separating curriculum from instruction. For the purposes of this chapter, though, I make the distinction between curriculum as something that is to be learned and instruction as the ways that the content is made present to students.) Do teacher education programs deal with these questions in any detail?

I believe that the answer to all these questions is no. Observations of practice and several decades' worth of sharing stories with other teacher educators suggest to me that there are few exceptions to the rule that curriculum planning in preservice programs is concentrated solidly on planning lessons, perhaps grouped together into units of several weeks duration, and that this planning generally is guided by where the resultant plan might fit into a larger curriculum scheme that has been developed by so-called curriculum experts (Griffin, 1990). Also, studies of new teachers' practice reveal that novice teachers believe they are woefully inadequate to the task of planning a school program of any considerable duration (Hoffman, Edwards, Paulissen, Barnes, O'Neil & Leighty, 1986).

Because it appears that the decentralization movement in schools will not die away any time soon and because there is some intuitive appeal in the notion that teachers should be intimately engaged in planning for the particular groups of students whom they know best, I believe it is worth considering for inclusion in teacher education programs of study theories and models of curriculum planning. Teachers, it is safe to say, are called upon more frequently now than ever before to decide from a bewildering choice of possibilities what should be included in particular student groups' curricula. Notwithstanding the continuing presence of broad-scale curriculum frameworks, teachers' decisions about curriculum intentions and learning opportunities are major forces in shaping students' school lives. Teacher education programs should respond by providing prospective teachers with the conceptual and technical tools necessary to make reasoned choices as they move with students through programs of instruction.

Teaching for Understanding

In years past, teaching for understanding was the underpinning of a large number of teacher education programs. Largely grouped under the rubric of progressive education, these efforts to prepare teachers focused sharply and coherently on the ways that students might be meaningfully and productively engaged with the artifacts of culture and society (Dewey, 1916). "Meaningful" in this intellectual context required understanding. "Productive" meant that there was personal *and* social value associated with what was learned.

The progressive education emphases on meaning and productivity were derived almost exclusively from philosophy. The curriculum question, "Should X be taught," and its answer, were informed by expressions of value, of preference, of expectation (Tyler, 1949). Beyond the basics, seen by progressives as the tools of learning rather than the matter of learning, teachers and students were required to explore together problems, possibilities, dilemmas, unanswered questions. Content decisions were made in no small measure because they represented beliefs that certain phenomena were of greater value and that these phenomena had inherent power to link to students' curiosity, interest, thoughtfulness, and, over time, lifelong concern and engagement.

Students in elementary and secondary schools encountered carefully selected social, intellectual, and cultural artifacts chosen because they represented an aspect of lived experience that was considered to be valuable, had the promise of catching students' minds and hearts, and would lead to important personal and social consequences. Rather than learn *that* certain resources made up the chief exports of a South American country, for example, students might find in their classrooms a wide variety of indigenous plants and locally manufactured goods. They would spend considerable time and intellectual effort "finding out" about these examples, partly through answering teachers' carefully designed questions, questions aimed at arousing interest and eliciting questions rather than only as solicitations of student knowledge. Over time, progressive educators believed that certain habits of mind, centered on fostering inquiry and assisting problem solving, would become natural to students. The habits of mind, then, became the tools with which the students unlocked the secrets of their world. And, these intellectual tools were designed to last a lifetime.

As progressive education philosophy and practice waned in popularity in teacher education programs and as certain school-related societal ills became more obvious, such as poor reading ability and weakly held scientific knowledge, schools became preoccupied with basic skills. Teacher educators, not as concerned with skill development, perhaps, as their elementary and secondary-school counterparts, seemed to drift uncomfortably between attending to prospective teachers' needs for skill development expertise and fragmented and often poorly conceptualized conceptions of "generic" teaching strategies, the latter bolstered to a considerable degree by the effective teaching research carried forward during the '70s and '80s. Gone from most programs were the remnants of progressive education's preoccupation with making meaning, with contributing to student understanding as a requisite for productive citizenship.

Accompanying this shift in teaching and teacher education was the strengthened role that frequent and widespread standardized testing played in the nation's schools. Until recent attempts at broadening the ways of knowing that can be tapped by an assessment of student progress, standardized tests aimed low and hit the mark. Tests taught students and their teachers that what was valued by policymakers, and to some degree the public, was ability to recall and recite and remember discrete factual information. Lost in the shuffle were more complicated-to-discover relational understandings, problem-solving ability, and generalization skills. Questions of "how" and "why," because of their mutability across situations, were not asked. Determining "what" became the norm.

Today, however, there is a resurgence of interest, indeed of excitement, about ways to engage students in elementary and secondary schools with opportunities to understand, to apply understandings, to evaluate critically and systematically (Blumenfeld, Soloway, Marx, Karjcik, Guzdial, Palincsar, 1991). Unlike the progressive education movement, this resurgence is rooted in insights from educational psychology rather than philosophy. It seems that now that we have some marginally scientific comprehension of how minds work in relation to puzzles and dilemmas, we are urged to move ahead and use what we know. It is interesting to note that the earlier push for teaching for understanding was tied to answering the question, "*Should* students learn this in these ways?" Current admonitions to teach for understanding seem to be rooted in positive responses to the question, "*Can* students learn this in these ways?"

Whatever the source of the current interest in renewing commitment to teach for understanding, philosophical or psychological, teacher education programs should be helping prospective teachers develop knowledge and expertise about underlying assumptions, theoretical constructs, pedagogical strategies, and practical considerations related to teaching for understanding.

Inquiry in Teaching

Another shift in the professional consciousness of today's educators is the move from the teacher as worker who teaches according to fairly well-defined proscriptions for practice to the teacher as inquirer into his/her own practice (Duckworth, 1988). Although it can be argued accurately that most teachers deal somehow with the puzzlements of practice, relatively new conceptions of "being a teacher" promote disciplined inquiry as part of a teacher's dispositions and mental habits. To a degree, this change responds to some calls for teachers to be considered as professionals. A hallmark of professionalism is that professionals are preoccupied in thoughtful, ongoing, and systematic ways with the activities and consequences of their work.

Attention to teachers as inquirers is not a new idea, but it should be noted that there are sharp differences between historical antecedents and today's conception of teaching as inquiry. Action research in the 1930s and 1940s involved teachers, working with higher education faculty, in attempts to overcome persistent problems of practice. Teams of teachers and teacher educators, for example, might choose an aspect of schooling that was troubling, puzzling, or otherwise ill-understood. Together, the action research teams would devise a way to create understanding and, most often, improve practice. These early examples of action research, then, were problem-focused, collaborative, and largely local in terms of impact and utility of findings and conclusions.

Later, Interactive Research and Development (IR&D) was devised as one way to reduce the research-practice gap, focused more directly on teacher-like research questions, concentrated on developing products (development) from the research, and served in large measure as a staff/professional development strategy (Tikunoff, Ward, & Griffin, 1981). The IR&D process, as originally conceptualized and implemented, was highly successful in terms of: (1) producing research findings that were considered by teachers to be relevant to their work; (2) linking research findings to development and improvement activities; (3) serving as a powerful professional development opportunity for participating teachers; and (4) yoking the interests and concerns of elementary and secondary schools to the intellectual aspects of the higher-education community.

The most recent proposals related to the teacher as inquirer/researcher are less overtly strategic than action research and IR&D, and more focused on creating what might be called an inquiry orientation in prospective and practicing teachers. That is, instead of giving a great deal of attention to products of inquiry, as in the form of publications, a characteristic of earlier proposals, attention now is given to the processes of self-analysis, reflection, and deliberation as expected ways of thinking by teachers (Duckworth, 1988). Inquiry into practice, now, is seen as a desirable and valued part of being a teacher.

Teacher as researcher, then, is a way of thinking about teachers and thinking that is believed to be important in the contributions it makes to teaching as complex intellectual activity. It is not an isolated set of activities, rigorously carried forward according to a plan of action. Instead, it suggests that teachers who are able to stand outside their own practice as observers and use what is observed as the stuff of reflection, analysis, and refinement, will become better teachers, not novice researchers in the academic sense. It is argued that this habit of mind will help teachers give more serious attention to the consequences of their teaching, to the development and ongoing modification of rationales for practice, and to searches for alternatives when teachers' conclusions about their own work are less than satisfactory. (Focusing on teacher as inquirer also might change future teachers' preoccupation with task at the expense of concerns about impact on student learning as noted by Fuller (Fuller & Bown, 1975).

In an era preoccupied with experimentation, innovation, and reform, it is important that participants in the educational process be disposed toward understanding the consequences of their own and others' professional activity. As teachers are better equipped for thoughtful study of teaching and learning toward the end of improving educational outcomes, it is reasonable to expect that teaching as research will be helpful in creating meaning around reform proposals and interpreting life in classrooms well beyond simple acceptance of business as usual.

Teacher education curricula, with little modification, could include inquiry orientations that begin to build research sensibilities in teacher candidates. Rather than simply consuming research, prospective teachers could learn some of the tools of inquiry and use them in critique and review of conventional academic studies. They could use these same tools to create small-scale studies of their own learning. They could be expected to use their field sites as natural laboratories where their own learning is not simply demonstration of imitated behavior but where teaching and learning are legitimate objects for curiosity, scrutiny, and questioning.

The School As Workplace

Implicit in this discussion so far is the assumption that many of the nation's schools, and by inference teaching methods in those schools, are changing. Although the 1980s, in large measure, were years of considerable conservatism nationally, a large number of proposals emerged aimed at changing the face of American schools (Smylie, in press). Although most of the proposals were aimed directly at the structure of the conventional school, some were promoted as ways to make significant changes in such school components as curriculum, grouping of students, assessment technologies, materials of instruction, and so on. Taken together, these proposals for school change are expressions of deep dissatisfaction with schooling as we have come to know it through our own apprenticeships of observation.

In the same ways that teacher educators are concerned with helping prospective teachers shift their student understandings of teaching to teacher understandings, it is reasonable to propose that they also help novice teachers revisit their conceptions of schools. To be a teacher in a school is dramatically different from being a student in a school. For teachers to be productive members of a school community, to participate fully in the life of the school as current reform initiatives call for, it is necessary for them to understand the school as a workplace.

Most students, I believe, think of schools much as they think of teaching. They do not consider the complexity of schools as organizations, the authority that the organization's normative structure has on teachers, or the ways that schools do or do not change and improve. Serious students of teaching need to be helped to move beyond acceptance of the school as an intractable and simple organization to understanding of the myriad ways that the school organization has to influence what goes on within boundaries.

For example, school have rhythms, rhythms that promote and hinder productive learning activity (Lieberman & Miller, 1884). Schools have histories that press upon present practice in ways that are seldom well-understood.

Schools and school systems go about their business in well-defined ways and according to both explicit and implicit assumptions and values and norms. Members of school faculties share belief structures that bind them together or keep them distanced from one another. Schools have leaders, formal and informal, whose behavior structures how rewards are distributed, how incentives are conceptualized, how new teachers are socialized, and how resources are allocated.

Knowing about schools, rather than just knowing about classrooms, is an important part of being a teacher. Yet, little attention is paid to this in teacher-preparation programs. Teacher educators, probably naturally, are concerned with classroom practice, with teaching methodologies, with lesson planning, with student assessment. These are worthy objects of attention, of course, but teacher candidates must be helped to understand that they will be influenced not just by what the individual teachers know and are able to do but also by the contexts in which they are carried forward. Being able to "read" a school, in terms of its essential elements and structures and norms, can be very valuable to a new or an experienced teacher. Being able to analyze why conditions are as they are, rather than falling back on the organizationally weak argument of "I'm not satisfied here," can help teachers to move their professional workplace toward a more desired state (or, it must be said, move from one school to another).

Teachers who are ill-equipped to understand how their work is influenced by the place in which it is carried forward, it seems to me, are more likely to develop defeatist, angry, or acquiescent postures than are teachers who are sensitive to the organizational structures that affect their work. In teacher education programs, prospective teachers can focus on schools as organizations, draw lessons from their field experiences, reflect together on the reasons that well-known schools look and feel the way they do, and come to grips with what naive school-watchers conclude are mysteries. Tracing experienced teachers' stories back to school context expectations and requirements is helpful. Mapping not just the physical layout of the school, but also its intellectual underpinnings, reveals the reasons underlying otherwise puzzling activity. Understanding how their own ways of thinking are shaped by a school faculty and administration reveals the power of organizations over the individuals in them (Griffin, 1986b).

This section has proposed four atypical bodies of content for inclusion in teacher education programs. The four represent new ways of thinking about teachers and teaching, ways that have intellectual and intuitive appeal in the current context of school reform, restructuring, and change. They also reflect new understandings about teaching and schooling less from a political stance than a knowledge-oriented one.

TEACHING PROSPECTIVE TEACHERS

This section presents a brief discussion of how instruction might be provided to students in teacher education programs. As is true for the preceding section, I include these candidates for consideration because they have some currency in today's debates about professional education and there is research to support their candidacy. They also appear logical in relation to the curriculum content already proposed. Again, this is a selective rather than a comprehensive set of suggested delivery strategies.

Carter and Anders (in press) use the term *program pedagogy* to capture strategies such as these. The term is helpful because it joins conceptions of teaching with programmatic issues. As can be seen, what follows are not narrow pedagogical approaches but attempts at capturing broader conceptualizations of working with prospective teachers. Included in this section are group learning in teacher education, story as instruction, using cases, and making sense of experience.

Prospective teachers, for most of their program of studies, *learn in groups.* In general education and in professional courses, students come together to learn about, and how to do, teaching. Too often, however, I believe that the coming together is seen as simply a time-honored convenience mechanism rather than as an instructional strategy. We teach groups because it is efficient to do so. But, the learning that takes place in these groups tends to be conceived of as individual and personal. Students may be together during instruction, but they might as well be miles apart as they wrestle with their private learning.

Two emerging theories, one about learning and one about schooling, suggest to me that teacher candidates would be well served if teacher educators focused more learning opportunity toward groups than is typically the case. In many of the same ways that students in elementary and secondary school classrooms assemble for instruction only to be expected to learn as individuals, teacher candidates take courses in which their intellectual activity is privately held rather than publicly shared. Learning about pedagogical approaches, theories of student cognition, even classroom management strategies usually are matters for private contemplation and examination.

However, when we think of our learning outside of school places, much of it is socially constructed, the product of interpersonal intellectual pursuit (Richardson & Hamilton, in press). Dialogue, sharing perspectives and viewpoints, interpreting others' meaning, mirroring one's views against someone else's are all aspects of out-of-school learning. Certainly, we learn alone in many instances, but we also learn together in many others.

This conception of learning as the product of intellectual exchange among interested parties fits well with the growing understanding that schools are human organizations that depend for health upon ongoing dialogue, critique, review, shared understandings, and negotiated meaning (Bentzen, 1975). There is in successful school places a strong element of exchange of ideas, exchange that shapes meaning and creates mutual understanding. Schools as places where adults are isolated from one another, where ideas and practices are privately developed and personally held, prove in the long run to be ineffective in terms of both student and teacher learning and satisfaction (Rosenholtz, 1989).

If teacher educators were more self-conscious about instruction that fosters group learning, promotes the value of exchange and negotiation of ideas, and creates opportunities for students to work together to devise responses to complex problems and dilemmas, it appears to me that their students would benefit in at least two ways. First, and directly tied to the conception of learning as socially constructed meaning, teachers would experience the theory in action and might be more willing to apply the theory to their own teaching situations. Second, novice teachers would come to expect and depend upon professional collegiality in dealing with important issues in teaching and schooling (Little, 1990). They would be prepared to participate in the newer conceptions of schools as learning communities. They would expect professional dialogue and push back against teacher isolation and privacy of practice. They could be more influential on school contexts as members of collegial groups.

Few activities in professional sequence teacher education programs can be accomplished as well by individuals as by like-minded people working together. The disposition toward collegiality can be fostered and strengthened in preservice programs in the hope that it will be helpful as teachers become responsible for their own practice and for the shared norms of the schools where they work.

An intriguing proposal is the use of *story in teacher education*. Carter (1992) calls our attention to the growing attention that story is receiving in the research community and how story as a way of thinking and knowing can be helpful in teacher education. Appealing features of story in professional education include the blending of technology with biography, personal theory with grand theory, abstract generalizations with context specificity. When teachers, for example, talk about their work, they mix their views with explanations of how they came to hold those views. They frame their own understandings in nested analyses of what "others may think" and what the situation demands. They move readily and easily through the artificial but often constricting boundaries formed by different ways of knowing.

The teacher-researcher orientation advanced earlier in this chapter lends itself well to thinking about story in teacher education. Inquiry is often designed as a way to discover someone else's story. The academy's traditional inclination to strip the personal from the abstract is an artifice that often undercuts the richness of story. It is precisely the blend of the biography and professional practice that may have tremendous power for the teacher candidate who is searching to find his or her place in the teaching profession. Is it better to talk or read about abstract or even concrete conceptions of classroom management, for example, than to place those conceptions in the experiences of admired teachers? Is it more effective to conceive of cooperative learning as a linked set of strategic teaching behaviors rather than as a story of how a teacher intellectually negotiates the requirements of subject matter, the character of classroom groups, and expectations for learning? Is it helpful for novice teachers to come to believe that teaching expertise is somewhere "out there" to be found, rather than a long and intricate tale involving ambition, disappointment, renewal, hunching, discovering, inventing?

The power of story in everyday lives is well-documented. It seems reasonable to assume that this same power can be applied to learning in a professional context. I suspect that another reason that experienced teachers recall their student teaching experience in such admiring ways is that they shared storying with an important person (Griffin, 1986a). The student teacher's stories intertwine with those of the cooperating teacher. They made meaning together, meaning that may have had abstract theoretical properties but that was also grounded in events, specific verbal exchanges, a particular place in time. This is the stuff of story and this is what makes story important.

Teacher education can help students of teaching develop, tell and retell, and refine their stories. We can legitimate experience, not as the sole criterion against which to measure thoughtfulness or effect, but as a way to bring some meaningful coherence to the dailiness of teaching and schooling. Encouraging prospective teachers to write about their changing perspectives, beliefs, and values can contribute a sense of continuity and progress to the process of learning to teach. Helping novices become self-conscious about their evolving stories can help them sort out the wheat from the chaff in their professional practice and see possibilities that, without attention, might pass from consciousness.

One relatively formal kind of story is the *case*. Although the use of cases in law instruction has a long tradition, it is only recently that teacher educators have seriously considered cases as important ways for novice teachers to understand their chosen field of study (Doyle, 1990). A number of anthologies or casebooks have been produced, typically focused on problems of practice in teaching. Cases might be concerned with issues of classroom management, cooperative learning groups, student assessment, gender equity in classrooms, instructional strategies, and other dilemmas faced by teachers. However, unlike straightforward presentations of strategies or activities or ways of thinking, cases are textured and enlivened by particulars of teaching and learning situations.

Students have names and histories, situations are characterized by conflicting points of view, dilemmas are thickly described, subtleties abound, and simple resolutions may be misleading.

Cases are stories with purposes. *A good case is a case of something of importance* (Doyle, 1990). It is not simply an illustrative vignette with villains and heroes. It is a complex and intricate rendering of an issue believed to have meaning, often concealed, that must be teased out to be understood. A good case engages prospective teachers with the myriad possibilities associated with any given course of action, any persistent or suddenly present problem, any surface solution. A good case successfully represents the intricacies of teaching groups of students in schools.

In addition to responding to cases, teacher candidates can develop their own. Creating a case around an issue of importance, prospective teachers can work together to demonstrate variety and dissonance, rather than conformity and harmony, in teaching. Cooperating on case development, students are called upon to acknowledge the uncertainty and mutability that characterize teaching. Sharing cases across student groups, teacher educators can point to the multiple avenues open to the thoughtful teacher, calling attention to the ways that theories in action influence how we all shape our understanding of what otherwise might be seen as particularistic and simple events and situations.

Story, cases, and group learning can be helpful as teacher candidates engage in *making sense of experience*. As is true for most professional education, the preparation of teachers depends in no small measure upon gradually increasing opportunities to experience, to practice teaching. Typically beginning with focused observations of teaching and moving through mini-teaching opportunities to student teaching, teacher candidates have educative experiences that show what teaching is. Unfortunately, it is also typical that this experiential learning is seldom carefully guided and monitored. In the same ways that elementary school students sometimes systematically practice making errors while doing their arithmetic homework, teacher candidates sometimes mimic and absorb teaching practices that are less than desirable. It is nearly impossible to prepare the numbers of teachers needed by the nation's schools only by using field settings that match some optimal conditions. By default, many teacher candidates' experiential learning takes place in schools and classrooms that may be only marginally effective.

At issue here, though, is not just the kind of experiences, good and bad, that prospective teachers have in schools. Whether the experience is desirable or not, we are also concerned about how preservice students make sense of their experience. How do they make meaning from experience? What intellectual and practical screens do they use to accept or reject their experience? What criteria do they apply when they judge their time in schools?

Again, I believe that students of teaching would be well-served if teacher education programs provided more frequent and systematic opportunities for group learning around experience. Ongoing seminars can connect experience with theory, promote understanding across individuals who have stories to tell and eagerness to hear others' stories, assist in refinement of understanding and perspective, promote clarification of personal theories.

Teacher education programs, because of the sheer numbers of students in them, may never be able to connect all students with exemplary classrooms and schools, but they may be able to help students make sense of experience over time. Connecting experience, from early in the program through student teaching, through the use of strategically designed learning opportunities, is to me an imperative in teacher preparation. Reflective and interactive journals, for example, begun upon admission to a program of study and continued until graduation or certification, may be one way to help novice teachers gain cumulative power over their experiential learning. Ongoing seminars that attend to the connections between contemporary issues in teaching and schooling and ways of understanding those issues in particular situations, the students' field placements, is another. Placing responsibility on students to develop cases or vignettes illustrating practical dilemmas they face and using the cases with other students is another. Insisting on self-consciousness about beliefs, values, and personal theories of teaching over time is another. All are suggested as ways to help prospective teachers make sense of their experiences in classrooms and schools.

CONCLUSION

The program pedagogies, again using Carter and Anders' (in press) term, advanced above are not widespread in teacher education practice. They do, however, complement the curriculum content suggested earlier in this chapter. There is a compatibility among the emerging conceptions of teaching and schooling, considered here as content, and the ways that intending teachers might make sense of those conceptions through teacher education instruction. The search for this kind of harmony of content and pedagogy is one that many teacher educators seek. Instead of harmonious, conventional teacher-preparation programs tend to be fragmented and lacking in theoretically reinforcing content and process. Witness, for example, the recurring complaint about teacher education's emphases on imaginative instruction and the ways that teacher candidates are instructed (Hoffman et al., 1986).

It is obvious that this chapter has a primitive conception of schooling as democratic activity as an underlying theme. Current proposals for teaching, schooling, and teacher education also express this theme, attending most often to the idea of community as a desirable one to put into practice. Achieving community is a difficult task, one that is fraught with the tensions that have resulted from histories of bureaucratic control, burdened with the residue of thinking about teachers as workers rather than as professionals, and fragile knowledge bases from which to construct exemplary practice.

Teacher education, however, can sometimes cut through the frustrations of practice and create communities of learning. Current attempts to create professional development schools, for instance, have the potential to bring together teacher educators, professional educators, and novice teachers for developing shared understandings. Other alliances across historically separate institutions like social-service agencies, schools, universities, and commercial organizations provide opportunities to open the eyes of teacher candidates to vistas of possibility heretofore closed to outside view. School reform activities can focus our attention on realizing the possible rather than only fitting in with the present.

At issue is how teacher education curricula can embrace these new forms, include new conceptions of content, and devise imaginative and thoughtfully implemented ways of engaging prospective teachers with the content. This chapter in this Yearbook is but one set of suggestions about how to move forward.

REFERENCES

Barnes, S. (1981). *Synthesis of selected research on teaching findings.* Austin, TX: Research and Development Center for Teacher Education, University of Texas at Austin.

Bentzen, M. M. (1975). *Changing schools: The magic feather principle.* New York: McGraw-Hill.

Blumenfeld, P. C., Soloway, E., Marx, R. W., Karjcik, J. S., Guzdial, M., & Palincsar, A. (1991). Motivating project-based learning: Sustaining the doing, supporting the learning. *Educational Psychologist, 26*(3&4), 369–398.

Buchmann, M. (1986). Teaching knowledge: The lights that teachers live by. Paper presented at the conference of the International Study Association on Teacher Thinking, Leuven University, Belgium, October 13–17, 1986.

Carter, K. (1992). The place of story in research on teaching and teacher education. Paper presented at the Annual Meeting of the American Educational Research Association, San Francisco.

Carter, K., & Anders, D. (in press). Program pedagogy. In F. Murray (Ed.), *A knowledge base for teacher education.* Washington, D. C.: Association of Colleges for Teacher Education.

Cochran-Smith, M. (1991). Learning to teach against the grain. *Harvard Educational Review, 61*(3), 279–309.

Cohen, D. K. (1987). *Teaching practice: Plus que ça change. . .* East Lansing, MI: Michigan State University.

Dewey, J. (1916). *Democracy and education.* New York: Macmillan.

Doyle, W. (1990). Case methods in the education of teachers. *Teacher Education Quarterly, 17,* 7–15.

Duckworth, E. (1988). *The having of wonderful ideas and other essays.* New York: Teachers College Press.

Fuller, F. F., & Bown, O. (1975). Becoming a teacher. In K. Ryan (Ed.), *Teacher education: Seventy-fourth Yearbook of the Society for the Study of Education.* Chicago: University of Chicago Press.

Goodlad, J. I. (1990). *Teachers for our nation's schools.* San Francisco: Jossey Bass Publishers.

Goodlad, J. I., & Richter, M. (1966). *Toward a conceptual system for dealing with the problems of curriculum and instruction.* Los Angeles: Institute for the Development of Educational Activities.

Griffin, G. A. (1986a). Issues in student teaching: A review. In J. Raths & L. Katz (Eds.), *Advances in teacher education, 2* (239–274). Norwood, NJ: Ablex Publishing Company.

Griffin, G. A. (1986b). Thinking about teaching. In K. Zumwalt (Ed.), *Improving teaching.* Alexandria, VA: Association for Supervision and Curriculum Development.

Griffin, G. A. (1988). Leadership for curriculum improvement: The school administrator's role. In L. N. Tanner (Ed.), *Critical issues in curriculum: Eighty-seventh Yearbook of the National Society for the Study of Education* (pp. 244–266). Chicago: University of Chicago Press.

Griffin, G. A. (1989). Coda: The knowledge-driven school. In M. Reynolds (Ed.), *Knowledge base for the beginning teacher* (pp. 277–286). Oxford: Pergamon Press.

Griffin, G. A. (1990). Curriculum decision making for teacher education. *Theory Into Practice, 39*(1), 36–41.

Griffin, G. A. (1991). Teacher education and curriculum decision making: The issue of teacher professionalism. In M. F. Klein (Ed), *The politics of curriculum decision-making* (121–151). Albany, NY: State University of New York Press.

Hoffman, J., Edwards, S., Paulissen, M., Barnes, S., O'Neal, S., & Leighty, C. (1986). *Teacher induction: Final report of a descriptive study.* Austin, TX: Research and Development Center for Teacher Education, University of Texas at Austin.

The Holmes Group. (1986). *Tomorrow's teachers.* East Lansing, MI: The Holmes Group.

Klein, M. F. (Ed). (1991). *The politics of curriculum decision-making.* Albany, NY: State University of New York Press.

Lieberman, A., & Miller, L. (1984). School improvement: Themes and variations. *Teachers College Record, 86*(1), 4–19.

Little, J. W. (1990). Teachers as colleagues. In A. Lieberman (Ed.), *Schools as collaborative cultures: Creating the future now* (165–194). New York: Falmer Press.

Lortie, D. C. (1975). *Schoolteacher.* Chicago: University of Chicago Press.

Murphy, J. (1991). *Restructuring schools: Capturing and assessing the phenomena.* New York: Teachers College Press.

Reynolds, M. (1989). *Knowledge base for the beginning teacher.* Oxford: Pergamon Press.

Richardson, V., & Hamilton, M. L. (in press). Staff development: The practical argument process. In V. Richardson (Ed.), *Staff development and teacher change in reading comprehension instruction: A new generation of programs.* New York: Teachers College Press.

Rosenholtz, S. J. (1989). *Teachers' workplace: The social organization of schools.* New York: Longman.

Smylie, M. A. (in press). Redesigning teachers' work: Connections to the classroom. *Review of Research in Education.*

Stallings, J., & Krasavage, E. M. (1986). Program implementation and student achievement in a four-year Madeline Hunter Follow-through Project. *Elementary School Journal, 87*(2), 117–138.

Tikunoff, W. J., Ward, B. A., & Griffin, G. A. (1981). Interactive research and development as a form of professional growth. In K. R. Howey, R. Bents, & D. Corrigan (Eds.), *School-focused in service: Descriptions and discussions* (187–214). Reston, VA: The Association of Teacher Educators.

Tyler, R. W. (1949). *Basic principles for curriculum and instruction.* Chicago: University of Chicago Press.

Zumwalt, K. (1986). *Improving teaching.* Alexandria, VA: Association for Supervision and Curriculum Development.

CHAPTER 11

Collaborating to Save Lives: Cooperative HIV/AIDS Education in a Middle School

PATRICK FORESE
Grove City Middle School

MICHAEL J. CLEARY
Slippery Rock University of Pennsylvania

MARIAN D. SUTTER
Pennsylvania Department of Education

PATRICK FORESE is a Health and Physical Education teacher at Grove City Middle School in Grove City, Pennsylvania. Research interests include learning styles and pedagogy.

MICHAEL J. CLEARY is Associate Professor and Graduate Coordinator in the Department of Allied Health at Slippery Rock University of Pennsylvania. Before his present assignment, he instructed health education in school and community settings. Research interests include teacher cognition and curriculum development.

MARIAN D. SUTTER is the Health and Physical Education Advisor and Project SAVE (Stop AIDS Via Education) Coordinator with the Pennsylvania Department of Education Bureau of Curriculum. She is also a Certified Health Education Specialist. Research interests include HIV/AIDS–related knowledge, beliefs, and practices among secondary school students, and teachers' understanding of eating disorders.

ABSTRACT

Collaborative action research is characterized by its focus on practical problems of individual teachers or schools and emphasizes a partnership between teachers and university staff to pursue a common goal. The immediacy of the threat of HIV/AIDS infection among young adolescents has made it imperative that health teachers, allied health faculty, and state education personnel collaborate to develop effective educational approaches that address the learning domains related to reducing HIV/AIDS–related risk behaviors. This study subsequently examined the effectiveness of cooperative learning and traditional (lecture-oriented) teaching upon the acquisition of HIV/AIDS knowledge and attitudes among seventh-grade students in a rural middle school. In addition, the study compared the effectiveness of cooperative learning to traditional teaching along the same measures. Six health classes were randomly assigned to either cooperative-learning or traditional-learning formats. Within the groups, post-tests indicated that both cooperative and traditional learning groups experienced significant improvements on the knowledge and attitude subscales. Post-tests also revealed that cooperative learning groups scored significantly higher on measures of knowledge than traditional learning groups, while no significant differences were found for changes in attitudes. These findings tentatively support cooperative learning as a viable alternative to lecture-oriented teaching for HIV/AIDS education for young adolescents. Implications for professional preparation, curriculum development, and school reform are subsequently offered.

The prevention of HIV (human immunodeficiency virus) infection continues to challenge health-education professionals. Surveillance data report that 20 percent of current U.S. AIDS cases are found among persons between the ages of 20 and 29, while the lengthy incubation period of the virus strongly suggests that initial HIV infection for many infected persons probably occurred in early adolescence (Centers for Disease Control, 1990; Haffner, 1988). Thus, the search for successful school health interventions has led to a rather narrow focus on high school programs as opposed to placing even attention in middle schools and high schools. The narrow focus may limit instructional efficacy, because sexual values and behaviors coalesce during both phases of development.

Recent work by Seigal, Lazarus and Krashovsky (1990) has further substantiated that very young adolescents, particularly minorities, are at considerable risk for HIV infection. Like other investigations (Memon, 1990; Petosa and Wessinger, 1990), this study specifically identified a number of misconceptions held by students regarding transmission mechanisms of the AIDS (acquired immune deficiency syndrome) virus. Subsequent recommendations called for age-appropriate curricula that addressed adolescents' responses in the affective domain in order to enhance acquisition and retention of essential HIV/AIDS-related knowledge. In addition, Allensworth & Symons (1989) believes that AIDS education must emphasize all learning domains, self-esteem, active involvement of the students, and risk-reduction behaviors. Research on the general outcomes of cooperative learning strategies therefore appears to support several of the aforementioned HIV/AIDS curricular objectives.

Cooperative learning is a set of instructional methods in which students of varying abilities work together in small four-to-six member groups to achieve a common goal (Slavin, 1987). Because each group member is an equal participant in this process, cooperative learning is significantly different than peer teaching. The teacher subsequently provides less direct instruction, and it becomes the responsibility of group members to teach each other the assigned material (Slavin, 1987).

Johnson and Johnson (1982) found that cooperative learning not only promotes high levels of information acquisition, but can facilitate critical thinking, cooperative tendencies, constructive student-student relationships and even psychological health. Slavin (1987, 1991) found that cooperative learning often results in increased self-esteem. Specific to the behavioral goals of HIV/AIDS education, Yarber (1987) noted that cooperative learning provides opportunities for practicing negotiating and assertiveness skills. With health education's increasing emphasis on skill development, Dorman, Small & Lee (1989) also recognized the potential of cooperative learning for enhancing behavior change.

Although cooperative learning has proved to be effective in several academic disciplines, its efficacy in AIDS education has not been studied extensively. In fact, Bentrup's (1989) recent evaluation of the Team Pack (1988) cooperative learning techniques versus lecture upon high school students' AIDS-related knowledge is currently the only comparative study of its kind.

The AIDS epidemic has emphasized the need for better ways to present health messages; it has also mandated that evaluation of these new formats continue, albeit with different populations and settings (Rienzo and Dorman, 1988). The immediacy of the threat of HIV infection among middle-school students has made it imperative that classroom teachers, university faculty, and state education personnel collaborate to develop effective interventions targeting very young adolescents. This chapter examines the effectiveness of cooperative learning to traditional (non-group) learning upon acquisition of HIV/AIDS knowledge and attitudes among seventh-grade students in a rural school environment and compares the effectiveness of these two approaches.

METHODS

Participants

The subjects in this study were seventh-grade students enrolled in a small rural western Pennsylvania middle school during the fall of 1991. A total of six health classes ranging in size from twenty-four to twenty-seven students were utilized (n = 250). For purposes of this investigation, the classes were first divided into two general groups of equivalent academic ability and then randomly assigned to the cooperative or the traditional learning groups. The instructional intervention was designed to comply with the 1987 Pennsylvania Curriculum Requirements, which state that all school districts must provide instruction on AIDS in a planned series of lessons to occur once at each level of instruction (elementary, junior/middle school, and high school). Students could be excused if parents/guardians provided a written request based on moral or religious beliefs. The specific cooperative learning strategy employed was Student Teams Achievement Division (STAD), in which students are grouped heterogeneously by academic ability, gender, and ethnicity. The students then proceeded to learn the new material through group discussion, coaching and quizzing each other at various intervals (Slavin, 1990). As per typical STAD procedure, the students in each of the cooperative learning classes were grouped in teams of four, which comprised a high achiever, a low achiever, and two middle-ability students. When an occasional group of three existed, care was taken to ensure that all members were of different academic ability. In addition, all cooperative learning groups included at least one member of the opposite sex.

The traditional learning subjects received the AIDS information through teacher lecture, open-ended discussions, audio-visual presentations, and homework assignments. No group work was performed. Both the cooperative-learning and traditional-learning groups received five (forty-two minute) classroom periods of instruction. To control for variation of teaching styles, all six classes were instructed by the same teacher.

Instrumentation

A survey with two subscales was implemented to assess overall differences in group performance. Sources of test questions included Yarber's (1987) *AIDS Education: Curriculum and Health Policy* as well as materials from the Pennsylvania Department of Education. Basic questions were employed to ascertain general knowledge about AIDS including transmission, treatment, and prevention.

An additional fifteen items presented in a three-point Likert scale format measured attitudes, beliefs, and values related to AIDS and HIV infection. Scores ran from +1 (disagree) to +3 (agree). Both groups of students were pre-tested to determine levels of prior knowledge and attitudes. Group achievement goals were subsequently assigned. A post-test (parallel form) was administered following the five-day unit. Group averages for the knowledge subscales were measured by combining all individual members' scores. The same procedure was supplied to determine group averages with attitude subscales.

Data Analysis

To determine the differences between the cooperative-learning and traditional-learning group post-test means, independent T-tests were utilized at the .05 level of significance. Mean attitude scores were examined separately with the same procedure. In addition, pre-test and post-test differences within the groups were analyzed by a dependent T-test to ascertain if any significant increases occurred.

Results

On the knowledge post-test, the cooperative-learning groups significantly outscored the traditional-learning groups with combined mean scores of 37.08 and 35.32, respectively ($p < .0003$). The combined scores of the cooperative-learning group were also more clustered (S.D. = 2.59 vs S.D. 3.07) indicating that cooperative learning appeared to "pull" group members closer together in terms of academic achievement. The cooperative-learning group also scored higher on the attitude portion of the post-test. The differences however, were not significant.

TABLE 1

Comparison of post-test knowledge and attitudes between cooperative and traditional learning groups

	Cooperative X + S.D.	Traditional X + S.D.	Difference	T-ratio
Knowledge	37.08+2.59	35.32+3.20	1.76	3.72*
Attitude	37.05+3.07	36.56+2.95	0.49	0.97

* Significant at the 0.0003 level.

TABLE 2

Pre-post test comparisons of knowledge and attitude scores for cooperative group

	Pre-test X + S.D.	Post-test X + S.D.	Difference	T-ratio
Knowledge	24.14+3.97	37.08+2.59	12.94	−27.27★
Attitude	35.21+3.45	37.05+3.07	1.84	−5.49★

★ Significant at the 0.0001 level.

TABLE 3

Pre-post test comparisons of knowledge and attitude scores for traditional group

	Pre-test X + S.D.	Post-test X + S.D.	Difference	T-ratio
Knowledge	23.67+4.37	35.32+3.20	11.65	−21.76★
Attitude	34.79+3.01	36.56+2.95	1.77	−5.09★

★ Significant at the 0.0001 level.

General knowledge improvements were found among students participating in either of the instructional intervention styles. With the traditional learning group, for example, pre-test scores rose significantly (p < .0001) from an average of 23.67 (40 points maximum) to 35.32. In addition, desired HIV/AIDS–related attitudes were significantly enhanced among students in cooperative- and traditional-learning groups. Finally, it is noteworthy that gains evidenced from pre-test to post-test scores of the cooperative learning groups were noticeably higher (53 percent) than those of the traditional learning group (49 percent).

DISCUSSION

There are definite limits to the speculations that can be taken from a small pilot study, particularly when the entire sample is drawn from the same school.

Contamination of learning across groups, for example, could certainly have occurred. In addition, extensive analysis on pre-test scores to further assure homogeneity between the groups was not part of the study design. The results of this investigation, however, still revealed several worthwhile outcomes. First, while significant gains were evident across both learning groups from pre-test to post-test, indicating the general efficacy of both approaches, those in the cooperative learning groups scored significantly higher on the knowledge subscale. The circumstances surrounding the cooperative learning groups' superior knowledge gains are also interesting to note. Unlike Bentrup's (1989) study in which the "traditional" learning groups were exposed to a standardized one-period HIV/AIDS lecture, the traditional learning groups here were exposed to five one-period lessons with varied instructional strategies. Surprisingly, significant achievement differences still occurred.

Rienzo and Dorman (1988) have suggested that professional preparation programs must increase HIV/AIDS–specific pre-service and in-service training for health educators. Based on the results shown in this study, training to implement cooperative learning techniques should be considered a valuable and effective component of all HIV/AIDS education professional preparation and continuing education programs.

The outcomes of this investigation are also pertinent to health educators involved in school reform efforts, particularly the restructured schools concept whereby interdisciplinary teams of teachers will collaborate on instructional decisions (Murphy, 1990). Under these new arrangements, however, specific classroom time for health education might be adversely affected (Cleary, 1991). Therefore, use of cooperative-learning strategies such as STAD to investigate issues such as prevention of HIV infection, which are deemed essential learning, may prove to be efficacious in strengthening positive outcomes from limited instructional time.

The results of this study are also relevant to school reform efforts seeking to increase research collaboration between schools and universities (Clift, Veal, Johnson, & Holland, 1990). Too often, the university defines the constructs of research, expects the schools to implement them, and subsequently finds that practicing teachers deem much of the educational research to be irrelevant (Bracey, 1990). Through collaborative action research, however, teachers will not only add to the professional knowledge base but can construct their own programs based upon solutions *they* have elicited (Clift et al., 1990). This particular study involved a research team composed of a classroom teacher, a methods professor, and a state department curriculum director.

Collaborative action research is characterized by its focus on practical problems of individual teachers or schools, emphasis on professional development, and construction of an environment that provides time and support for teachers and university staff to work together on a common goal. Research findings are often used in seeking solutions, and teachers and researchers sometimes co-author reports of their findings and the process of collaboration (Oja & Smullyan, 1989). Whitford, Schlechty & Shelorm (1987) believes that collaborative action research will eventually help schools become recognized as centers of inquiry, which in turn will contribute to and increase the professionalism of teachers—a major goal of educational reform.

CONCLUSION

Although cooperative learning is not a panacea for the HIV/AIDS epidemic or the myriad of other health problems facing American youth, it does appear to be one effective educational intervention method for younger adolescents. By engaging students in the instructional process, cooperative learning assertively addresses the issues surrounding "passive" secondary students (Watkins, 1990). Thus, students cooperatively learning about AIDS are not just actively acquiring necessary facts, but are also acquiring interpersonal skills beneficial to adolescent developmental tasks.

Because education is the primary defense against the spread of HIV/AIDS, it is more crucial than ever that educational interventions be suited to the learning needs of the population to be served. The challenge to classroom teachers, university faculty, and state curriculum personnel is to continue to recognize special vulnerabilities of young adolescents and to collaborate in action research endeavors.

REFERENCES

Allensworth, D. D., & Symons, C. W. (1989). A theoretical approach to school-based HIV prevention. *Journal of School Health, 59*(2), 59–65.

Bentrup, K. (1989). AIDS education using cooperative learning technique for high school students. Unpublished masters thesis, University of Florida, Gainesville.

Bracey, G. W. (1990). Rethinking school and university roles. *Educational Leadership, 47*(8), 65–67.

Centers for Disease Control. (1990). *HIV/AIDS Surveillance Report.* Atlanta, GA: Centers for Disease Control.

Cleary, M. J. (1991). Restructured schools: Challenges and opportunities for school health education. *Journal of School Health, 41*(4), 50–58.

Clift, R., Veal, M. L., Johnson, M., & Holland, P. (1990). Restructuring teacher education through collaborative action research. *Journal of Teacher Education, 41*(2), 52–62.

Dorman, S. M., Small, P. A., & Lee, D. D. (1989). A cooperative learning technique for AIDS education. *Journal of School Health, 59*(7), 314–315.

Haffner, D. W. (1988). AIDS and adolescents: School health education must begin now. *Journal of School Health, 58*(4), 154–155.

Johnson, D. W., & Johnson, R. T. (1982, August). Having your cake and eating it too: Maximizing achievement and cognitive-social development and socialization through cooperative learning. Paper presented at the meeting of the American Psychological Association, Washington, DC.

Memon, A. (1990). Young peoples' knowledge, beliefs, and attitudes about HIV/AIDS: A review of research. *Health Education Research, 5*(3), 327–335.

Murphy, J. (1990). Helping teachers prepare to work in restructured schools. *Journal of Teacher Education, 41*(4), 50–58.

Oja, S., & Smullyan, L. (1989). *Collaborative action research: A developmental approach.* London: Falmer.

Petosa, R., & Wessinger, J. (1990). The AIDS education needs of adolescents: A theory-based approach. *AIDS Education Review, 2*(2), 127–136.

Rienzo, B. A., & Dorman, S. M. (1988). Ten consequences of the AIDS crisis for the health education profession. *Journal of School Health, 58*(8), 335–338.

Siegal, D., Lazarus, N., Krashovsky, F. (1990). AIDS knowledge, attitudes, and behavior among inner city, junior high school students. *Journal of School Health, 61*(4), 160–165.

Slavin, R. E. (1987). Cooperative learning and the cooperative school. *Educational Leadership, 45*(3), 7–13.

Slavin, R. E. (1990). *Cooperative Learning: Theory, Research, and Practice.* Englewood Cliffs, NJ: Prentice-Hall.

Slavin, R. E. (1991). Synthesis of research on cooperative learning. *Educational Leadership, 48*(12), 71–82.

TEAM PACK (1988). Instructional methodologies developed by the Center for Cooperative Learning for Health Science Education. Gainesville, FL: University of Florida.

Watkins, B. T. (1990, November 7). An education professor tries to put his "fantasy school" into effect. *Chronicle of Higher Education,* A3.

Whitford, B. L., Schlechty, P. C., & Shelorm, L. G. (1987). Sustaining action research through collaboration: Inquiries for intervention. *Peabody Journal of Education, 64*(3), 151–169.

Yarber, W. L. (1987). *AIDS Education: Curriculum and Health Policy.* Bloomington, IN: Phi Kappa Delta Foundation.

CHAPTER 12

True Collaboration: An Analysis of an Elementary School Project in Mathematics

MICHAEL L. CONNELL
DONALD M. PECK
WILLIAM F. BUXTON
University of Utah

DIANNE KILBURN
Granite School District

MICHAEL L.CONNELL is an Assistant Professor in the Department of Educational Studies at the University of Utah. His interests include mathematics education, evaluation, teacher education, and the uses of technology in instruction.

DONALD M. PECK is Professor in the Department of Educational Studies at the University of Utah. His interests include mathematics education, teacher education, and the uses of technology in instruction.

WILLIAM F. BUXTON is a graduate student in the Department of Educational Studies at the University of Utah. His interests include mathematics education, teacher education, and development psychology.

DIANNE KILBURN is a fifth grade/special education teacher for Granite School District in Salt Lake City, Utah. Her interests include mathematics education, the use of technology in teaching, and school improvement/reform.

ABSTRACT

For change to occur in mathematics instruction, teachers need to control significantly different instructional sequences, evaluation schemes, and curriculum

255

and to think beyond procedural views of mathematics. Two-week in-service and course work separate from classroom experience are *not* sufficient to achieve these goals. In-service and support must bring about conceptual understandings and parallel actual classroom implementation via extensive co-teaching and modeling. Sufficient time must be spent to integrate these new and desired understandings into teachers' routines. This chapter describes implementations in which such change took place and the model that led to joint ownership in project and outcomes.

INTRODUCTION

For a meaningful change to take place in the mathematics instruction of our young people, teachers must be in charge of a significantly different instructional sequence, evaluation scheme, and curriculum. Merely stating the need for these items, however, is not enough to ensure it will take place. A major barrier to implementation is that elementary teachers are simply not in a position to implement such changes (Peck & Connell, 1991b). Teachers first must be able to reach beyond procedural views of mathematics to grasp essential conceptual constructs.

It is important to note, however, that neither are simple two-week in-service, or additional course work separate from actual classroom experience, sufficient if these goals are to be reached (Fenstermacher & Berliner, 1983; Hart, [in press]; Little, 1984). Teacher in-service and support must bring about conceptual understandings on the part of the teachers and parallel actual classroom implementation via extensive co-teaching and modeling by master teachers throughout the intervention. Sufficient time must be spent to ensure that the new and desired understandings are thoroughly integrated into teachers' normal routines.

A case in point is that of elementary mathematics education. It is currently plagued by various conceptions regarding mathematics as held by practicing mathematicians and those within the school environment where mathematics is taught. These diverse belief systems have lead to the creation of a dichotomy in which there is the world of "school mathematics" of the teacher and that of the "real mathematics" of the mathematician and scientist (Hess, 1991). This dichotomy causes severe problems for education because practicing teachers are aware only of the world of school mathematics.

To see how this dichotomy plays out in the daily life of students, consider the following characteristics of "school" versus "real world" mathematics.

For our students to be adequately prepared for the demands of the evolving society, there must be a significant change in the view of "school"

TABLE 1
"School" versus "Real World" Mathematics

School	Real World
Based upon association and behaviorism	Constructivist in nature
Values computational accuracy and efficiency	Values problem-solving persistence and resourcefulness
Emphasis on memorizing algorithms and equations	Emphasis upon using mathematics to reason from external situations and objects
External determination of "right" or "wrong" is made by teachers or textbooks	Internal determination of "right" or "wrong" made by the individual based on actual situations and mathematical conceptions
"Problem solving" means decoding word problems that apply a single well-defined skill	"Problem solving" requires an active synthesis of knowledge and skills along with creativity and experience
Only one correct method leading to one correct solution is possible for each problem	Many methods exist for solving problems that may have one solution, many solutions, or no solutions
Technology and other resources are not to be utilized in school mathematics; that would be "cheating"	Technology and other resources should be fully utilized in problem solving
Supported by the structure of the curriculum, textbooks, and standardized texts	True competency in mathematics is achieved by immersion in meaningful problem solving

mathematics to enable an induction into "real mathematics" as envisioned by mathematicians and scientists. Yet, for change to occur, practicing teachers must be aware of and be members of the "real world" culture of mathematics as recognized by the practicing mathematician and scientist. This induction cannot occur without the active and willing participation of the teachers themselves.

Although most teachers cannot specify the exact nature of this dilemma, many are nonetheless aware that it exists and would like to do something to remedy it. It has been a common occurrence in our work to be invited by classroom teachers to work with them to "do *something* to help my class." This chapter will describe the results of one such invitation, the program that it helped to generate, and the subsequent impact this program had upon the classroom teacher and the students this teacher served.

DESCRIPTION OF THE VALLEY CREST PROJECT

The original invitation was facilitated by an existing working relationship with a Professional Development School (PDS) at which school faculty were already serving as adjuncts to university faculty. However, as in the case of each successful intervention in our experience, the invitation was initially at the teacher level. Once a working arrangement had been achieved with the teacher involved, administrative support was obtained. This is in marked contrast to traditional top-down reform efforts.

The collaborative nature of this project affected the curriculum, evaluation, and implementation at many levels. Researchers provided materials, lessons, and much of the instruction. The classroom teacher selected topics and concepts in accordance with the district and state guidelines for fifth- and sixth-grade classes and contributed to the instructional effort. All decision-making was a team effort with the researchers and the classroom teacher working in concert. To provide an overview of the resulting project, a brief summary will be provided of the curriculum, instructional focus, and implementation procedures used.

Curriculum Focus

The curriculum used in this project was conceptually based and utilized a five-phase approach that allowed students to construct mathematical intuition via physical materials (Peck & Connell, 1991a). In this approach, the initial two phases used physical materials in a much different way from traditional approaches. Rather than using manipulatives to demonstrate procedures or rules, problems were posed that required active student involvement with physical materials to model mathematical situations, define symbols, and develop solution strategies via actions with the materials. As the children used these physical materials to solve problems, they actively constructed the operations and principles of arithmetic. The third phase required sketches of the physical materials and situations experienced by the students to encourage a move toward abstraction. The sketches then served as the basis for additional problems and as tools for thinking. In the fourth phase, the children constructed mental images through imagining actions on physical materials. The experiences with mental images provided a basis for the fifth phase, in which students constructed strong mathematical generalizations and problem-solving skills.

The computer was another tool available to the students in their ongoing efforts to construct meaningful methods of dealing with the problems they encountered. The nature of this tool, which was provided for the students to "think with," came to shape their performance and cognitive styles. When a computer was available, the problem-solving situation shifted toward the identification and selection of what data to include in the problem, identification of the problem goals, and choice of appropriate procedures and control statements to obtain and verify the desired results. As a consequence of the instructional sequence outlined above, the children constructed a series of related mathematical concepts. When these concepts and applications were overlearned, the students instructed a Macintosh via Hypertalk to carry out the necessary instructions and operations that they had derived (Peck, 1989). The computer played a pivotal role in this project, albeit a much different role than that usually associated with Computer Assisted Instruction (CAI). Rather than using the computer for its speed, the study utilized the computer's patience and need for exactness of logic and clarity of expression. The computer assumed the role of an active listener that would do exactly what it was told, as opposed to a pre-programmed instructor requiring a specific type of answer.

Throughout the project, a major curriculum goal was to enable the successive internalization of abstraction which represented the preliminary physical experiences the children shared. Each of the outlined phases was viewed as a step along the path toward eventual mathematical abstraction. For example, the sketches drew much of their power from earlier experiences with objects. In a similar fashion, the mental images reflected the sketches and manipulations performed by the students. The interrelated nature of these experiences set the stage for abstractions and the intuitive foundation upon which the abstractions could safely rest. These abstractions, rather than being based upon a single demonstration of rules, rested upon a tightly woven network of understandings.

Instructional Focus

An explicit instructional objective was to help each child find a way to answer the question, "How can you tell for yourself?" for all portions of the mathematics they were learning. The instructors shared the common belief that children must be allowed to figure things out and be responsible to themselves, not a teacher or answer key, for their results. It was felt that if children are to think about and solve problems for themselves, they must have a "place" to go in order to be able to determine whether they are making sense. Physical objects in this instructional model served this purpose. These beliefs, coupled with the earlier described curriculum focus, led to the following principles:

1. The instructor did not explain. The instructor served as a problem poser, skeptic and question asker focusing upon *student* explanations.

2. Manipulations with physical materials defined meanings that were associated with arithmetic symbols and operations. Problems were developed requiring an appeal to those objects and meanings.

3. The instructor attempted to enable the children to internalize and abstract their experiences by requiring them to work problems in the absence of the physical materials.

4. The instructor used a meaning-centered evaluation scheme (Peck, Jencks, & Connell, 1989).

Evaluation Focus

Evaluation as used in traditional instruction often appears designed to identify and reward "winners" over "losers" using information acquired from measures of success or failure on narrowly prescribed sets of cognitive tasks (Corrigan, 1990). When every child is given the chance to construct the understandings necessary to make them a "winner," however, this approach is not particularly helpful. The authors certainly did not want the designated "losers" opting out of further mathematics education.

A shift was needed toward evaluation methods that could be used to guide instruction aimed at maximizing the number of "winners." To accomplish this, a two-step evaluation scheme was used to guide classroom instruction involving the use of Sato's Student-Problem Chart (Sato, 1990; Switzer & Connell, 1990) and a follow-up teacher interview (Peck, Jencks, & Connell, 1989). Each of these techniques is quite effective alone, but when used together they provide a very efficient methodology in assessing student understandings.

The information provided in Sato's reporting format quickly identifies problems and also identifies students with unusual response patterns, indicating potential sources of difficulty and identifying key questions to ask selected students. At a simple level, a Student-Problem Chart (see Table 2) is a systematic ordering of student item responses to teacher-selected sets of problems (Sato, 1990). First, the problems and their associated student responses are ordered from left to right beginning with the easiest (as determined by those problems having the highest number of students responding correctly)

TABLE 2

Example of a Simple Student Problem Chart.

			Problem Number
Student Number	Test (Raw)	Score (%)	0 0 0 0 1 1 0 1 1 0 0 2 1 1 2 0 1 2 2 1 0 2 1 1 9 2 3 5 3 4 6 8 9 1 7 4 2 5 2 4 0 0 1 7 8 3 6 1
Answer Key	──────►		4 4 2 1 2 1 2 3 1 3 4 4 2 1 1 3 2 3 1 3 1 1 3 5
5011	23	95.8	+ 1
4064	23	95.8	+ 5 + +
4105	22	91.7	+ 4 1
2111	22	91.7	+ 2 + 5 + +
5094	21	87.5	+ + + + + + + + + + + + 3 + + + 3 + + + + + + 3
2170	20	83.3	+ + + + + + + + + + + + + + + + + + 3 + 5 5 2 +
5055	20	83.3	+ + + + + 3 + + + + + + + + + + 3 + + + 4 + + 1
2034	19	79.2	+ + + + + 3 + + + + + + + + + + 4 + + + 3 4 4
5115	19	79.2	+ + + 3 + + 1 + + + + + + + + + + + 4 + 3 4 +
5131	19	79.2	+ + + + + 3 + + + + + + 3 + + + 3 4 + + + 5 + +
1016	17	70.8	+ + + + + + + + + + + 1 + + + 1 3 + + + 3 3 1 4
2105	15	62.5	+ + + + + + + + 3 + + + + 4 3 + + 1 + 2 3 2 1 4
2182	14	58.3	+ + + + + + + 2 + + + + 3 2 + + 3 4 3 4 + 3 4 3
3225	13	54.2	+ + 4 + + + + + 2 4 1 + + 4 3 1 + + 4 + 2 3 + 4
2226	11	45.8	+ 2 1 + + + + + + 1 2 + + 2 2 4 + 4 4 4 3 + 4 3
2246	11	45.8	2 + + 3 1 + + + + 1 + + 3 4 2 1 + 4 + 4 3 + 4 4
1046	10	41.7	+ 2 + + + + + + + + + 2 2 + 4 4 4 2
1232	10	41.7	+ + + + 3 2 + + 3 4 1 2 4 3 + 2 4 4 + + 2 + 4 2
1102	09	37.5	+ 2 + + + + + + 1 4 1 3 1 + + 4 2 + 4 4 4 2 3 2 3
2163	06	25.0	2 3 + + + 3 1 + 2 4 2 1 3 4 4 2 3 4 4 2 + + 4 3

to the most difficult (those problems with the least number of students answering correctly). Once this is done, the students are ordered from top to bottom by highest total score to lowest total score.[1]

Each row of the Student-Problem Chart contains the responses of an individual student. The sum of "+"s in each row corresponds to the raw score (total score) for each student. In Table 2, "+" indicates a correct response. Incorrect responses are indicated with either a blank if the student did not attempt the problem, or the value of the response if the problem was answered

---

1. The computer program, *SPCC,* which creates Student-Problem Charts and additional statistical information is available for IBM compatible computers from:

   The Office of Educational Testing, Service, and Research
   51 Gerty Drive
   Champaign, Illinois 61820.

incorrectly. Each column corresponds to an individual item on the test. Reading down a column reveals how students responded to that item.

Examining a Student-Problem Chart made it a simple matter to determine which students to interview and what questions to ask in order to pin down conceptual understandings. To see how this is done, consider student number 5094 from Table 2.[2] This student performed very well on the test. A score of 87.5 percent identifies him as a "winner" and little further concern would typically be given regarding the developing understandings. Looking across the row of item responses (see Figure 1), however, we make a disturbing observation. The student has missed problems 12 and 10. These problems as indicated by classmates' performance are significantly easier than other problems to which the student had responded correctly. There may be a potentially dangerous gap in understanding. A talk with this student about these problems is in order.

This method of looking at student data can also provide information showing unsuspected strengths of students. For example, consider student 2163 (see Figure 2), who despite a very poor overall performance has correctly answered problems 23 and 8, two of the more difficult problems.

This approach enabled us to determine with whom we should talk and what questions to ask to maximize our effectiveness in the interview. Student interviews were then conducted to evaluate student explanations and problems. These follow-up interviews with these key students and problems provided meaningful feedback about the results of instruction and the construction of any nonproductive conceptualizations. In short, they provided a closer examination of what the students were *thinking* and not just what they were *doing*.

To see the impact of this combined approach consider student 5094 (Figure 1). As a result of examining the Student-Problem Chart, the teacher decides to interview student 5094 concerning problems 10 and 12. The student did not yet know whether his answers were right or wrong. Both problems dealt with a common concept: multiplication of fractions. Taking a clue from this information, the teacher presented the student with a problem similar to the test problem and raised questions about it. In the course of the conversation, the student's thinking was described while doing the problem.

. . . Well, multiplication makes things bigger, see. Like 12—I mean 3 × 4 is bigger than 3 or 4. So 1/3 × 1/4 has gotta be bigger than 1/3 or 1/4 and the way I did it first, it wasn't.

---

2. This Student-Problem Chart is taken from an actual classroom set of responses. The student names for this example have been replaced with ID numbers to protect student privacy.

			Problem Number	
Student	Test	Score	1	1
Number	(Raw)	(%)	2	0
Answer Key ⟶			2	2
5011	23	95.8	+	+
4064	23	95.8	+	+
4105	22	91.7	+	+
2111	22	91.7	+	+
5094	21	87.5	+ + + ++ ++ + 3 + + + 3	

FIGURE 1

Example of Student-Problem Chart use.

The experienced success was due to familiarity with a procedure that applied only part of the time—not on a useful understanding of the meanings surrounding fraction multiplication. Further discussion with the child revealed that this view of multiplication as "making things bigger" was interfering with the development of adequate understanding.

DESCRIPTION OF TEACHER IMPACT

At the beginning of the project, the participating instructor showed many of the characteristics identified earlier as those typical of "school" mathematics (Hess, 1991). In particular, the instructional posture was behavioristic and associationistic, with emphasis on correct answers and consistent forms of problem solution. In keeping with this orientation, the instructional emphasis was placed upon memorizing algorithms and equations for later application. When problem solving was presented, it generally referred to the decoding of

			Problem Number
Student	Test	Score	0 2
Number	(Raw)	(%)	8 3
Answer Key ⟶			1 1
.			++
.			++
2163	06	25.0	2 3 + + + 3 1 + 2 4 2 1 3 4 4 2 3 442 ++43

FIGURE 2

Additional example of Student-Problem Chart use.

word problems provided from the text, where there was only one correct answer and one correct method of solution.

For the first year of the project, the university team took over much of the classroom instruction, with the classroom teacher serving as a monitor and supporter. During this period a shared language was developed to facilitate communication. It became extremely common to hear them discussing a student's performance as being "kind of like a 4 (referring to the Structured Interview Groups) but I don't really think he understands that much" or "good scores, but she seems to miss some of the easiest questions—like a B (referring to the Sato's SP Groups), I guess." Soon this language was extended to groups as well as individual students as evidenced by comments such as, "This activity will be great for my 2's, but I don't know if the 4's will get it" and "these 4's are going to drive me nuts."

With time and experience, the tentative nature of the communication became less tentative with statements such as "definitely a 4" or "A responses for sure" becoming increasingly common. An important aspect of this developing language was to promote a continuing and conscious examination of student processing and conceptual understanding. The vocabulary described in the previous paragraph allowed the expression of a richer understanding of students' performance and convenient discussion of differential effects of the curriculum.

Model of Staff Development Provided

In attempting to introduce the participating teacher into the "real" mathematics culture, the university faculty began with discussions of the underlying mathematical framework and how it could be articulated in her class. Differences of perceptions and possibilities were then discussed and worked through. Once the ideas required were identified, a staff development plan covering these topics was identified.

In doing this, the teacher was required to become a learner, with all of the associated learner characteristics. Teachers already possess knowledge and beliefs about the content to be learned. This perspective provides a filter through which new information is processed and understood. Accordingly, the process of learning for teachers involves more than a simple adding on or replication of content. It involves the development of new conceptual perspectives through which content—facts, principles, instructional practices—can be personally mediated and understood.

Believing that a teacher cannot teach using a method in which there is no experience as a learner, the staff development followed the *same* five-phase instructional plan outlined above that would later be used with the students. Treating the teacher as learner, then, involved creating a commonly understood set of definitions and terms with which problem solving could take place. Just as with the students, problem solving followed using concrete materials to develop new problems and problem representations. The staff development process proceeded to develop abstract representations using graphics, leading to the creation of mental images serving as a bridge to the formalized mathematical symbols. Through this process, the teacher was able to generate physical, graphic, and symbolic representations of mathematic problems in the same fashion as that which would be presented later. This treatment of the teacher as learner is viewed as a crucial aspect of the intervention. Without personal understanding from experience of this kind of learning, it is unlikely that later teaching could be impacted.

A training and modeling period followed this staff development process, during which the university faculty co-taught with the school faculty in the classroom. In this manner, university faculty became part of classroom instruction and served as models to which the teacher could relate. The university faculty provided support, and served as a scaffold (Collins, Brown, & Newman, in press) from which the teacher developed independent strategies and methods.

The student growth and progress observed by the teacher led to a refinement and stronger adoption of the project ideals and goals. Her own teaching characteristics shifted by the end of the second year toward the "real world" mathematical culture. The following characteristics were observed: instruction became student-centered and constructivist; the instructor's role became that of question-asker and problem-poser; and problem solving, persistence, and resourcefulness on the part of the students became highly valued.

The long-term support of the instructor continued long after this study. This true collaboration created a lasting support system within the school and district and an impact on instruction outlasting the daily presence of the researchers. The project is being disseminated to other schools within the district by the initial instructor.

DESCRIPTION OF STUDENT IMPACT

This study included a wide variety of qualitative and quantitative measures. Although other data were gathered, the description of student impact will focus on two strands of evidence, one quantitatively and one qualitatively based. The mixed methodology discussed in previous sections utilizing S-P Charts and structured interviews were carried out during this study to guide instructional focus.

Quantitative Findings

The Valley Crest Mathematics Inventory was used to gather student pre- and post-test data.

This assessment had been used in earlier studies by the authors and mapped nicely to the curriculum of the school. For this study, validity controls were constrained to face validity and content validity. It should be noted that an earlier extensive cooperative effort with a district-level evaluation team (from another state) had been undertaken in test construction in which extensive item analysis was performed to select the best items and establish the item to objective mapping used in this study. Reliability estimates using Cronbach's Alpha were calculated for both pre-test (alpha = .74) and post-test (alpha = .84).

An initial examination of the pre- and post-test total scores as shown in Figure 3 illustrate that growth was indeed achieved during the course of the year. A T-test on these scores found a mean difference of 13.95 and a value for T of 7.93, which was significant beyond the .001 level.

Although heartening, this finding must be tempered by the realization that this intervention took place over the course of a year. Had a significant difference *not* been found, it would have been cause for alarm on the part of

Assessment Performance

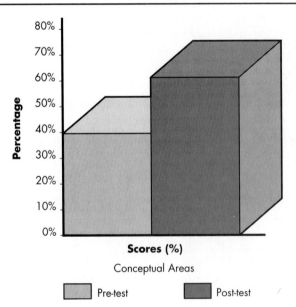

FIGURE 3

Pretest vs. Post-test total scores.

the investigators and the local school authorities. In looking at the content areas measured (see Figure 4) it is possible to make additional observations.

There are several noteworthy increases in performance. Although geometry and statistics were not formally presented, performance increased in these two areas. In extended mathematics (pre-algebra) problems, miscellaneous problems (which required a variety of problem-solving strategies), and estimation (which although not formally discussed was inherent in all student work) the greatest increase in student performance was observed. The near doubling in student performance in each of these areas provides strong evidence that the instructional emphasis upon student problem solving was effective for this group.

An additional support for this may be found in examining the Modified Caution Signs computed for the students using the pre- and post-test assessment. This index may be interpreted in the following manner: An A type response indicates high levels of performance and consistent patterns of item response; B indicates high performance and inconsistent response; C indicates

Assessment Performance

by Content Area

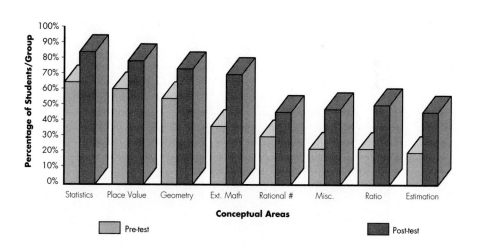

FIGURE 4
Pre-test v. post-test total scores by content area.

low levels of performance and consistent responses; D represents low performance and inconsistent patterns of response. In looking at Figure 5, the number of students identified as having type A responses (high and consistent) nearly trebles over the course of the intervention while the number of students in B increases. This is accompanied by a corresponding decrease in the number of students showing a C or D response pattern.

Qualitative Findings

The reported qualitative findings derive from two sources collected during the first and second years. The first is the interviews conducted throughout the year. The second is the notebooks in which the students wrote a five-minute reflection of their work at the end of each session.

Student Performance Groups

(Based upon MCI)

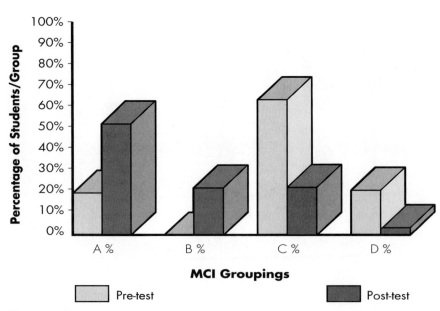

FIGURE 5
Pre-test vs. post-test modified caution signs

One of the major observations from the student interview lay in the student perceptions of the problem and the associated problem-solving efforts that they attempted. In particular, the students showed a consistent "reversion to form." As long as the problems made sole use of newly constructed information, the students could utilize their developed understandings. They were able to demonstrate effective problem-solving strategies that required both conceptual and procedural understanding. This situation shifted dramatically, however, whenever prior knowledge was required as part of the problem-solving efforts.

One case in particular illustrates this tendency. During the course of the interview, the student had been asked to "share" seventy-two counters with nine people as shown in Figure 6.

In working this problem, the student successfully completed the exchanges necessary and achieved the correct answer. Self-generated procedures, which were highly effective for this student, were used. In the subsequent explanation the student was able to describe numerous situations in which such "sharing out" would be desirable. The student was then presented with the problem shown in Figure 7.

The student's response was immediate and discouraging.

Student: This is a *Dear Miss Sally Brown* problem! We learned how to do these ages ago . . . see, you just divide, multiply, subtract, bring down . . . Dear Miss Sally Brown.

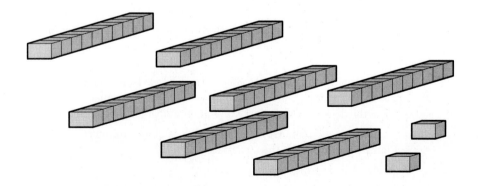

FIGURE 6
Sharing problem posed to student.

$$9\,\overline{\big)\,72}$$

FIGURE 7
Follow-up problem posed to student.

In applying the steps of divide, multiply, subtract, and bring down, however, the student failed to perform a single step correctly, with the resultant answer of 720! Furthermore, the attention to sense-making and reality checks used in the first problem situation were nowhere to be found. The strength of Dear Miss Sally Brown and its associated "right procedure" proved unhelpful to the student.

This reversion to an earlier, simpler, and for the most part inaccurate level of functioning occurred most often whenever time pressures came into play (such as those associated with a test) or when an overlearned piece of prior procedural knowledge was involved in dealing with the problem situation. The strength and persistence of this observation leads the authors to urge great caution in using only procedural guides during children's initial mathematical experiences.

The student notebooks provided an interesting insight into student perceptions and difficulties presented in this procedural approach. To illustrate, selections from four students follow in sequence.

Student 1 (Female):

10-22.   Today was easy and hard. First it was hard because I didn't know what to do. When he wrote the problems on the board . . . I looked at the board and thought "I can't do these" but once I got started it was easy but it took time because I had to use counters then I figured out how to do them without counters then I was going fast.

10-24.   Today we worked with egg cartons it was very confusing I couldn't seem to do it. it looked easy but then I tried to do the next problem but I couldn't. It's just to hard.

10-25.   We used the egg cartons again today. I learned alot today. I found a pattern to all of the problems when the answer (share with number) is 6 it's always half of the denominator I did 19 in 3 minutes that's super for me!!

11-27.   Today we did these those and altogether (division and addition of fractions) I figured a short cut so then it was easier.

1-3.   Today I learned to multiply fractions. they are very easy last year I learned to do them the hard way. I think I learned how to in third grade. This class isn't boring anymore.

1-5?.   Today I went to computer I tried to multiply fractions it wouldn't work because all my fields were on background fields. I had to delete all of my fields and make new ones I tried it and it worked!! It was time to go but I had to try it one more time so I could see for sure it worked

Student 2 (Male):

10-2.   I really like using the blocks because it helps me learn it better, and its fun . . . I think working with people smarter than me really helps me learn because they explain it very well

10-9.   Today was complicating I didn't understand anything at first but after halfway K. explained it I still didn't understand a word she said. When she finished explaining I understood. C was kind of wacky today

10-18.   I really liked working today because I know I did good. One of the hardest problems was one that I made up.

10-23.   Today all we did was play around wich (sic) was exiting (sic) because we discovered many different things . . .

11-4.   Today I did 15 problems (wich(sic) is good for me!) I started doing more problems after I had finished with out being asked.

11-8.   Today I was at computer. There was three ladies here that watched us. We had fun. I feel like a genius (I like it). We got into buttons.

1-13.   We did cakes on a piece of paper. What I mean is we drew a cake and shared it with a certain number . . . I feel smart. Almost as smart as C.

12-5.   Today we did test review problems, it was fun! One of the problems I liked was 2/2/3 divided by 1/4. I liked it because I had to draw 4 cakes Today was one of the funnest days I've had *all* year in math. I have many reasons why One I sit by C. Two I made *tons + tons* of progress! It was awesome. One of the problems was 1 1/2 + 2 3/5. I did it different than K but I got the same answer

1-16.   Today we had a substitute. her name was Miss H. She confused us (C and I) because she did it the old fashioned way! but then I got better

Student 3 (Male):

10-2.   I worked by myself. I finished my paper. I learned about share with. I cleaned up my work area. This math is easy.

10-3.   We worked as a group. I don't really understand todays math the problems are too hard. I don't know if I got my answers right. I don't like this class its to hard

10-8.   I used the counters which made it easy I don't like this very much I don't like this math

10-10.   I worked with T. The math was a little hard. Then I understood it. Then it was easy. T. helped me I don't like this math much. I finished all the math I was supposed to do I don't like writing in this book

10-16.   I understood *some* of the math today. I don't see what the big deal is. there's no big secret. I got finished. it was easy. K. confused me about some secret. Which I don't know. I hate those circles.

10-25.   I worked on the computer. I learned to use the button and field I have my own stack I got lost a lot. I made a mess I always do but I clean it up. I made a formula today it was D*4-4=C. It is easy But thats what I think. We did seven problems they were pretty much easy. I thought it was fun using formulas . . . we might use them another day!

11-6.   I finished the paper. I did most of it by myself. T and I worked todgether. I disliked problem 3/5 (?) I hated problem 2/13 (?) it was hard too. It was fun cutting the yard stick up.

11-8.   I finished my work I cut 6 clocks it was fun. I made up two problem it was 3/6 and 2/4 they were easy. It was easy too! I learned what 15*4 was again. It is 60. I don't know why I forgot it. I bugged A. because of my counting but I was supposed to count the centimeters.

11-27.   We learned WHAT? I understand the relationship between what and how many. It's easy now. I did extra work that I didn't have to do

Student 4 (Female):

10-8.   entry journal today I figured out a really hard problem and I mean it was really hard I like to work in this class and I helped people out on there problems this math group is really fun the really hard problem was 4 counters and share with 37 and the answer was 27/37 it took me 5 days and I finaly figured it out (Smiley face drawn in margin).

10-10.   today I did some of my math problems and I got some of them wrong so I had to go through (self-enforced) every single problem and see I got them right and lucky I did because I would have missed almost every single one of them. I worked really hard today but thats okay

10-16.   im trying to figure out this really hard problem because she (??) wants me to have six covered up and then make up problems and I'm trying to figure out a hard problem that no one can figure out and Dr. X. thinks he can fix me he thinks he can give me a hard problem and I can't figure it out but ill (I'll) show him!!!

Several observations seem in order about these student notebooks. First, in almost every case the students show a marked increase toward self-posed problems as opposed to teacher-directed problems. This shift took place at different times for different students, but occurred for nearly all students. These self-posed problems became a driving force in the instruction and a source of student pride as evidenced by the notebooks.

The appearance of a substitute, as evidenced in many notebooks, was a trying event for the children. Many of them dealt with this by doing it "the old way" on paper and then "talking about it" with their friends. Others merely "did it (the problems) the old way" and then complained about having to do worksheets. Time became a problem, not because of the time necessary for conceptual development, but because time would run out. The children's enthusiasm is evidenced by the frequent comment "It was time to go but I had to try it one more time so I could see for sure it worked."

In short, the students were actively engaged in solving their own problems based upon group-constructed meanings and procedures. The motivation came from the problem situation itself, and the computer was viewed as a tool to verify independently achieved results, not to dictate instruction. The result was a marked shift toward successful independent problem solving as indicated by the quantitative analysis and by the interviews and observations.

SUMMARY

The framework for this cooperative effort began with the teacher as the initiator of the collaborative effort. (We have found our work seldom has a positive impact if the principal calls.) The researchers considered themselves as guests and as hands-on workers with the children. The commitment was, and is, daily as well as long-term (1–3 years for this project) for all parties involved. The result of this endeavor was a transition of control to the teacher and a viable implementation of effective mathematical change at the school level. In this case, the teacher not only became indoctrinated into the culture of "real world" mathematics, but was pivotal in disseminating this culture and the project to the students and to other teachers within the school and district.

REFERENCES

Collins, A. L., Brown, J. S., & Newman, S. E. (in press). Cognitive apprenticeship: Teaching the craft of reading, writing, and mathematics. In L. B. Resnick (Ed.). *Cognition and instruction: Issues and agendas.* Hillsdale, NJ: Erlbaum.

Corrigan, D. (1990, October). Keynote address. Address presented at the meeting of the Far West Region of the Holmes Group, Seattle, WA.

Fenstermacher, D. G., & Berliner, D. C. (1983). *A conceptual framework for the analysis of staff development.* Santa Monica, CA: Rand.

Hart, A. W. (in press). Instruction-based teacher work redesign in schools. In S. B. Bacharach & B. Mundell (Eds.), *Organizational behavior in educational administration.* Boston: Allyn & Bacon.

Hess, N. M. (1991, August). An analysis of MARS and RNS scores of professional scientists and in-service teachers. Unpublished master's thesis, University of Utah, Salt Lake City, UT.

Levine, S. L. (1987). *Promoting adult growth in schools: The promise of professional development.* (pp. 57–117). Boston: Allyn & Bacon.

Little, J. W. (1984). Seductive images and organizational realities in professional development. *Teachers College Record, 86,* 84–102.

Peck, D. M. (1989). Children derive meaning from solving problems about physical materials, *Proceedings of the Second International Seminar on Misconceptions and Educational Strategies in Science and Mathematics, 3,* 376–385, Cornell University, Ithaca, NY.

Peck, D. M., & Connell, M. L. (1991a). Using physical materials to develop mathematical intuition. *Focus on learning issues in mathematics.* SUNY: NY.

Peck, D. M., & Connell, M. L. (1991b). Developing a pedagogically useful content knowledge in elementary mathematics. Paper presented to the Annual Meeting of American Educational Research Association. Chicago, IL.

Peck, D. M., Jencks, S. M., & Connell, M. L. (1989, November). Using tests to improve instruction. *Arithmetic Teacher,* 15–17.

Sato, T. (1990). *An introduction to education information technology.* Harnisch, D. L., & Connell, M. L. (Eds.). NEC Technical College, Kawasaki, Japan.

Switzer, D. M., & Connell, M. L. (1990, Summer). Practical applications of student response analysis, *Educational Measurement: Issues and Practice, 9*(2), 15–18.

Curriculum: Implications and Reflections

JANE STALLINGS
DONNA WISEMAN
GERALD KULM
Texas A&M University

ROLES OF PARTNERSHIPS IN MAKING TEACHER EDUCATION MORE RELEVANT

Some agencies of government and Independent School Districts consider colleges of education as insignificant players in the reform agenda and "out of the loop" in making a difference in education (Fenstermacher, 1991). Teacher educators are often characterized as producing meaningless products and unrealistic research. It is imperative to the well-being of colleges of education that the work of teacher education be regarded as vital and important in relation to schools and society. Teacher education research and curriculum development must address real societal problems, especially issues of children and families. Partnerships between schools and universities are one way to achieve this goal. Teacher education faculty are more likely to address relevant issues when working with school-based faculty to confront problems facing today's children and families.

The measure of relevance in teacher education is the degree to which transmitted information can be applied to real settings. Curriculum developed and implemented in collaboration with school-based professionals has a greater chance to meet the "applicability" test. When university and school-based faculty collectively embark on curriculum and instruction work, there is a high probability they will focus on issues that are important for schools and children. An added benefit of these cooperative ventures is that they often lead to more rapid dissemination of results. Educators at all levels are quick to embrace solutions that have been developed in the light of a practical understanding of schools and learners.

The complex nature of our societal problems suggests that educators should become involved in broad systemic changes in approaches to providing health care and social services as well as schooling. Today, a few school-university partnerships are attempting to connect schools more intimately with homes, communities, health and human service agencies through a single provider system that integrates all social agencies. This network of educational, health, and human service makes the requisite care more available to families and children in our schools. It is important that colleges of education restructure programs to prepare our teachers, administrators, counselors, psychologists, and health care workers in the context of these integrated services.

THE THREE PAPERS AND THE ISSUES

The three curricular studies in this section of the Yearbook focus on collaboration in restructuring the curriculum in colleges of education and schools. Chapters 11 and 12 in this division are examples of partnership research, and Chapter 10 addresses ways to make teacher preparation curriculum more relevant. Each of these papers has something to say about the roles of learners, teachers, teacher educators, and future teachers. Each of the papers focuses on the importance of collaborating with others to become a more reflective teacher and learner.

The two school-based curricular studies, Chapters 11 and 12, not only illustrate extremely important societal topics, but also demonstrate the impact of school-university development of research agendas. In "Collaborating to Save Lives: Cooperative HIV/AIDS Education in a Middle School" the researchers combine a socially relevant topic with an investigation into the exemplary practice of cooperative learning techniques. The study compares the best practice of cooperative learning with more traditional approaches to instruction. The results suggest that there is not a great deal of difference between the two approaches as far as knowledge acquisition, but there is a difference in the student's self image when cooperative instructional techniques are employed. Attitudes of children in this study were affected as they used interactive and collaborative skills to investigate sensitive issues. The study reminds us that any instructional approach should be aligned with the goals and objectives of the materials. In choosing the cooperative learning approach, the authors identified key features of the strategy that can be used to promote the learning goals of the lessons and promote discussion among students. In addition to instructional implications, the study suggests a collaboration model in which the curriculum development team is a mix of professionals who design effective and powerful instruction.

"True Collaboration: An Analysis of an Elementary School Project in Mathematics," is an example of one teacher being willing to become a learner and place herself in the hands of a college team of mathematics educators. This is not a partnership in developing curricula. Instead, it is a partnership in researching how best to prepare and retrain mathematics teachers. The study uses a case study approach focusing on actions of one teacher. The case study demonstrates the importance of preparing mathematics teachers to be problem solvers so that they can in turn teach their students to be problem solvers. This study found that this program resulted in active learning by the teacher as well as the students. As the teacher gained more mathematical knowledge, she became a model of learning for her students and other teachers in the district. The mathematics teacher in this study learned about exemplary teaching by reflecting on her practices and discovering the best approaches for her classroom. The teacher in the project became a learner, participating in mathematics activities very much as her own students were doing. This direct experience was critical as the teacher began to reconstruct her own knowledge and develop new attitudes toward the nature of mathematics.

Finally, "Teacher Education Curriculum in a Time of School Reform" suggests that "teaching is considerably more than what students see." This chapter describes curriculum as something that is to be learned and more important, to be questioned. The author strongly suggests that the restructuring of teacher education must focus on the teacher as an inquirer and must provide relevant experiences to incorporate the results of the inquiry into practice. Further, teacher preparation programs are expected to provide future teachers with a clear view of schools. Some of the ways the author suggests that teacher preparation programs might accomplish this task is to assign students to settings where they can develop collegiality. Part of the preparation program should feature the use of teacher stories and case studies. The paper establishes a need for professional development schools to integrate the strengths of the professional educators and novice teachers. In the natural school setting these partners reflect on their problems and practices and develop understandings of child learning as it occurs in school contexts.

APPLICATION

The health AIDS curriculum study demonstrated that using the cooperative learning strategy, children learned facts and acquired interpersonal cooperative skills necessary to the development of middle school children. The mathematics curriculum study demonstrated that the teacher learned to solve mathematical problems based upon her newly constructed meanings and procedures and the children learned by engaging in similar activities that allowed them to solve their own problems. The Griffin study argues that teaching is more than what students can observe. "What is special about teaching is made up largely of the ways that teachers think about teaching during their planning, reflection, and other less obvious aspects of their work, and that it is this intellectual approach to teaching that differentiates the professional teacher from the thoughtful person in other walks of life. But, the argument does not negate the generational sameness of teaching as observed activity. If teachers thought about teaching in adventurous ways, . . . I believe students would see more adventurous teaching activity in elementary and secondary settings."

All three chapters suggest partnerships as a way to encourage change and reform in schools and colleges of education. It is imperative for colleges of education that these partnerships provide avenues for faculties to design research and curricula that have a demonstrable connection to "real world" problems. The goal is for teacher educators to become involved in real life settings and they will model adventurous teaching and learning activities to future teachers.

SUMMARY

The emphasis on school–university partnerships influences the manner, roles, and participants of school renewal and restructuring. Curriculum development and inquiry in schools and colleges of education will become more relevant as collaborative relationships are formed. Partnership activities require that schools and universities jointly participate in the designs of curricula and the implementation of the programs. While there are some barriers to partnerships, the efforts to work together are well worth the costs. One result may be the development of curricula that more realistically respond to the needs of our complex society. Informed integrated curricula that respond to the problems of schools and society have the potential to improve the quality of our children's school learning experiences.

REFERENCES

Cole, A. L. & Knowles, J. G. (in press). Teacher development partnership research: A focus on methods and issues. *American Educational Research Journal.*

Cuban, L. (1992). Managing dilemmas while building professional communities. *Educational Researcher, 21*(1), 4–11.

Fenstermacher, G. D. (August, 1991). Where do we stand on America 2000? *AACTE Briefs,* 3.

Goodlad, J. (1988). School-university partnerships for educational renewal: Rationale and concepts. In K. Sirotnik & J. Goodlad (Eds.), *School-university partnerships in action: Concepts, cases, and concerns* (pp. 3–31). New York: Teachers College Press.

Lasley, T. J. (1984). Editorial. *Journal of Teacher Education, 35*(6), inside cover.

Schlechty, P. & Whitford, B. (1988). Shared problems and shared vision: Organic collaboration. In K. Sirotnik & J. Goodlad (Eds.), *School-university partnerships in action: Concepts, cases, and concerns* (pp. 191–204). New York: Teachers College Press.

Smith, S. D. (1992). Professional partnerships and educational change: Effective collaboration over time. *Journal of Teacher Education, 43*(4), 243–256.

Future Directions of Partnerships in Education: Schools, Universities and Human Service Systems

DEAN CORRIGAN
Texas A&M University

DEAN CORRIGAN is Professor and holder of the Harrington Chair in Educational Leadership at Texas A&M University and chair of the new ATE National Commission on Interprofessional Education to Create a Collaborative Education, Health, and Human Services System.

The time has come for leaders in the educating professions to re-examine the ways in which we deliver education, health and human services to America's children and their families. We must reinvent the system in ways that help all of our young people and their parents cope with the challenges associated with becoming well educated and healthy citizens in 1993 and beyond.

THE CHALLENGE

There have been rapid changes in the fabric of our society that have signaled the need for changes in our social institutions and in our professional practices.

- Communities and neighborhoods no longer function as systems of support within which children can safely grow into adulthood and become self-sufficient. Violence has permeated the social environments of families at all socioeconomic levels.
- Our country is still split by the divisiveness of racism, prejudice and polarization. In far too many places, individual differences are mocked and ridiculed rather than viewed as a source of richness.

281

- Poverty is ever-present and is on the increase. In the last ten years the rich got richer, and the poor got poorer. More than 12 million of America's children, the equivalent of half the population of Canada, are poor (about one in every five children).
- There are significant changes in traditional family structures and roles. Today, over half of all new marriages end in divorce, leaving 15.3 million children living with one parent, the mother in over 90 percent of the cases. Also, 23 percent of all children born today are born outside of marriage.
- Our service delivery systems are not organized in ways that are responsive to the needs of single parent families, aggregate families and families with two working parents. A critical need is the development of adequate child care services that help parents to meet the enormous responsibilities involved in child rearing and full-time employment.
- Homelessness is reaching epidemic proportions in this country. Families are the fastest growing segment of the homeless population. Moreover, one of every five homeless children is school-age. Currently there is a shortage of affordable housing. The stock of four million low income housing units subsidized by the federal government has stopped growing. There are eight million low income renters competing for four million housing units.
- Forty-two million children aged ten to 19 experience serious problems. Substance abuse is increasing and creates serious disruptions in the lives of children and families as well as threats to their health and safety. Teenage suicides and violent deaths are increasing at an unprecedented rate.
- Value systems are being transformed as children see materialistic rewards coming from dealing drugs and other illicit activities rather than from the kinds of jobs that they can obtain as a result of their schooling. The relationships between education and crime are striking, in that 82 percent of America's prisoners are high school dropouts.
- Schools and medical facilities are faced with serving children they never had to deal with before. AIDS has become a serious threat to our children. The number of teenage pregnancies is escalating and the consequences of inappropriate care are being felt in the rise of infant mortality and morbidity rates. Today, 37 million Americans have no health insurance or coverage, and 12 million of these are children.
- America's schools are presently set up to produce winners and losers. Many children are doomed to fail before they start and they are dropping out at an alarming rate. Because of the relationship between poverty and access to equal educational opportunity, it is usually the children from poor families who find themselves at the bottom of the heap.

- The most rapidly growing age group in America is people over 85. 2.2 million people are over the age of 85; 34,000 citizens are one hundred years of age or older. Twenty-four million people are over the age of 65. In 1983, we crossed a major watershed in the United States. We had, for the first time, more people over age 65 than we had teenagers. Young families will now spend as many years taking care of dependent parents as they will taking care of dependent children.
- The student dropout situation takes on a new sense of urgency when viewed beside the data on the shortage of youth and the increase in the elderly. In 1950, there were 17 workers to pay the benefits of each retiree. By the year 2000, only three workers will provide the funds for each retiree and one of those three will be a member of a minority group. We are a society with a shortage of youth and rapidly increasing senior citizen population.
- The future of the aging white middle class will be determined in part by the successes of young minorities in getting a sound education and a good job. If 50 percent of the students flunk out of school before the tenth grade and stay on welfare until they are 65, no one will be able to retire. For the first time, due to demography, we are interdependent— our futures are all inextricably interlocked.

For further amplification of the conditions of America's children and their families see *The Forgotten Half* by W. T. Grant Foundation (1988), *Within our Reach: Breaking the Cycle of Disadvantage* by Schorr (1988), *The Same Client* by Hodgkinson (1989), *Savage Inequalities* by Kozol (1991), *When the Bough Breaks* by Hewlett (1991), and *The Vanishing Dream,* and *Leave No Child Behind* by the Children's Defense Fund (1992).

As the education and human service needs of children and families have expanded and become more complex, it is more and more apparent that boundaries of professional responsibility as reflected in our existing service delivery system are often dysfunctional and uncoordinated. There are several populations of children and families currently being served independently by multiple education, health and human service providers. Up to now, at policy and political levels we have responded with single issue or categorical programs as each education, health and human service concern has been brought into focus. This approach will no longer suffice. Services must be coordinated and partnerships between educational and community agencies must be created in order to be responsive to the needs of children and families today.

A New Response

State and national policy makers now recognize that we must develop new organizational relationships at the family and community level among schools, universities, health agencies and other human service organizations. This collaborative reform strategy is central in the new direction proposed by President Clinton's education, health, and human services team: former Governor Richard Riley, Secretary of Education, and Dr. Donna Shalala, Secretary of Health and Human Services. (The integrated services concept is already included in the Kildee Education Bill.) *Together We Can: A Guide for Crafting a Profamily System of Education and Human Services* (1993) was developed jointly by the U.S. Department of Education and the U.S. Department of Health and Human Services to help communities improve coordination of education, health, and human services for at-risk children and families.

Many states, at least fifteen at last count, have passed legislation fostering the coordination of health, social services, and education, for example, the far-reaching Kentucky legislation, H. B. 940, that created Family Resource Centers and Youth Service Agencies throughout the state. Communities in Schools Programs and Human Service Children's Programs have been established in places as far apart as New Jersey, California, and Texas. Many other states are considering variations of the Kentucky plan and in many states education, health, and human service agencies are writing five-year coordinated strategic plans together and creating sites where multiple agencies are located for easy access. For example, Texas House Bill 7, entitled "Providing Client Access," will provide funding for pilot studies to enhance proximity and intercommunication across human service providers.

Commitment to the concept of collaboration and partnership is also reflected in many newly established entities such as those being supported by Dr. Ernest Boyer of the Carnegie Foundation and Dr. C. Everret Koop, former Surgeon General; for example, the new National Ready to Learn Council, the Carnegie Task Force on Meeting the Needs of Young Children, and the Safe for Kids Programs. Numerous collaborative ventures are being funded by other foundations such as the New Futures Programs of the Annie Casey and Hogg Foundations, and the School/University/Community Projects supported by the Danforth Leadership Program. Another excellent resource is *The One Place: A New Role for the American School* by the Young and Rubicam Foundation (1991). A summary of these new ventures titled, *Putting it Together: Redefining Education and Family Service for Children,* is available from the Education Commission of the States.

Interprofessional Preparation in a Time of Collaboration

As on past occasions in the history of professional education, the policy makers seem to be way ahead of those of us who work in universities. Even though we know that interprofessional education is the key to reforming the system, very little attention has been given to it in policy formulation. It seems that policy makers and politicians need to be reminded again, and again, and again, that trying to reform professional practice without reforming training and development will not work. The two actions must take place simultaneously.

At the present time, there are few interactions or partnerships between education, health, and human services faculty in the development and implementation of their respective professional curricula. Those of us who work in universities must confront a most vivid truth—if we do not model collaborative behavior in the training and research arm of the education, health, and human services professions, it is unlikely that future providers will understand the importance of such coordination, or be prepared to function in the new unified system that is emerging. The education profession, in conjunction with the other human service professions, must identify the particular knowledge, skills, and values needed by teachers and administrators in order to be effective collaborators with health and human services providers, and vice versa. They must insure that the aforementioned knowledge, skills, and values become part of the curriculum in each field of specialization and that they are infused appropriately into interprofessional programs.

Tomorrow's colleges of education must connect pre-service and in-service education with multi-purpose professional preparation programs oriented toward a variety of education and human service professions to prepare leaders who are able to work together to provide integrated services for children and their families (health, social work, and the like). The range of personnel educated by the reformed interdisciplinary programs will be as broad as the needs of the communities served.

In addition to reforming university preparation on campus, we must develop creative ways to make appropriate knowledge and related skills a part of continuing education efforts. This will require significant interactions and partnerships between practitioners and their respective professional associations and collaborating universities because it is unlikely that there will be adequate staff in schools and health and human service agencies who are prepared to offer such training. New leaders will need to be trained so that they can serve as trainers and mentors in their respective professional roles "on site."

Central to the conceptualization of interprofessional education as a means for reforming education, health, and human services is recognition of the fact that colleges of education, schools, and community agencies are interrelated and interacting components of *one* system. In this system we will have to legitimize schools as a locus of advocacy for all children, the poor and deprived not just the rich and powerful. Since schools are the only community institution that see every child every day, school leaders will need to accept the responsibility for helping to mobilize community resources.

When one steps into a schoolhouse today it doesn't take long to realize that the "persistent life situations" of many of today's students will need a multiple agency, multiple profession response—drugs, suicide, AIDS, teenage pregnancy, crime, jobs, poverty, etc. Talk to pediatricians about any of these problems and they will tell you that education is the key. In order for educators to accomplish the primary job of intellectual development—creating humane centers of intellectual inquiry, creating communities of learning—we will need to work with our professional partners in the rest of the human service delivery system on their piece of the action.

Interprofessional Development Schools

I am convinced that tomorrow's schools will be the hub of a community network for facilitating access to various components of the human services delivery system. They will be "Full-service Schools"—"Interprofessional Development Schools." Already in many schools we have social workers, psychologists, child care workers, health clinics, tutors, mentors from business and industry, adult literacy specialists, etc. Now that the professional development movement is well underway, perhaps we can add this interprofessional dimension to the design of future professional development schools. In fact, interprofessional development schools may be the best setting in which to start interprofessional training and research because that is where the interface across professions is taking place and where it will take place in the future.

Interprofessional development schools possess great potential as school-focused pre-service and in-service professional education centers as well as vehicles for enhancing collaborative education, health, and human service delivery systems. An "inquiry mode" is the basic characteristic that defines a professional development school—inquiry pervades the environment. In such a school there is inquiry by students to learn the knowledge that will help them to make important decisions facing them as a free people; inquiry by teachers and administrators to find better ways of teaching the relevant curriculum to their students and inquiry by teacher-educators and other leaders searching for ways to improve knowledge of their students, the content of the curriculum, and the pedagogical skills and knowledge necessary to provide each student success experiences. A school is a professional development school not because of its structure, but because of its purpose. It has changed its substance not just its form. It has become a humane center of intellectual inquiry where everybody is somebody; where everybody is both learner and teacher.

Conceptualizing the interprofessional development school as a center of inquiry that will lead its community in developing a system of integrated services that will help children and families meet the intellectual, economic, demographic, and social challenges of the 21st century is a significant enough purpose, with important enough consequences, to be a powerful motivator. The most severe shortcoming of past reform movements at all levels is that we have concentrated on means rather than ends. We have been so enamored with organizational changes (longer days, year-round schools) and technological changes (testing, computers, and television) in the means of education, that we have failed to examine the fundamental purposes of education—the ends of education.

The first priority for all of the partners involved in designing interprofessional development schools and other education and human services collaborative efforts today is the construction of purposes. So many past reform efforts have not lasted because the purposes of the reforms were not clear enough and the consequences of the reforms were not powerful enough to sustain the reforms over the long haul.

The most important lesson learned from my thirty years of involvement in developing collaborative and partnership efforts is that we need a comprehensive, systemic, national strategy to change American education. The primary strategy for change in the past has been to set up model programs—"projects" that last only as long as the government or private sector funding keeps flowing. When the money runs out, or the political advocate for a particular model program dies or moves on to other priorities, the reform fades into the night. It will take a big idea to match the enormity of the problems facing education and society as we face the 21st century. What we must create is a collaboratively-designed, community-based, family-oriented integrated infrastructure that involves professional leaders in all of the education, health, and human service agencies in communities across this great country.

In the future I envision a cadre of leaders in each of the participating professions who will function as "human service educators." In addition to being prepared and licensed as specialists in their respective professions, these "human service educators," whether teacher, school principal, physician, social worker, psychologist, child care worker, health care provider, urban planner, family counselor, etc. will possess the knowledge skills and values that make them competent to view problems and issues from each other's perspective. Colleges and departments of education must be in the forefront of this Interprofessional Education movement.

ASSOCIATION OF TEACHER EDUCATORS' ROLE: FOSTERING LEADERSHIP IN INTERPROFESSIONAL EDUCATION

In this context, what is the responsibility of the Association of Teacher Educators, which represents the training and research arm of the largest of the educating professions? Without a doubt the response of ATE lies in developing the capacity of future leaders in the education, health, and human services to view education and social problems in a broader, community-based, collaborative interprofessional services perspective.

We need leaders in the educating professions who possess vision and can manage cooperation—leaders who realize that collaboration in education, health, and human services today is not an option—it is a necessity and an obligation of leadership. In order for leaders from the various professions to interact effectively, an understanding of the "professional cultures" of each must be acknowledged. This can only occur as dialogue among groups is fostered. Only as leaders view today's education, health, and social problems from each other's perspective and walk in each other's shoes can barriers be replaced with partnership and bridges of understanding.

Since the Association for Teacher Educators has had years of experience with school and university collaboration (membership includes educators in schools as well as in universities) it is uniquely suited to take the lead in establishing a national interprofessional dialogue which focuses on the study of ways to produce a new generation of leaders in teaching, administration, social work, health, and other human services who can create collaboratively-developed education, health, and human services delivery systems.

This is the rationale that undergirds the recently established Association of Teacher Educators Commission on Leadership in Interprofessional Education. The Commission includes forty members who represent all of the professional partners working in the emerging collaborative system (social work, public health, law, psychology, extension, medicine, theology, education, etc.) At its first meeting, held during the 1993 annual ATE conference in Los Angeles, the Commission framed the following questions and issues to guide its work.

1. What is the condition of America's children and their families today? What are the demographics, needs, and threats to children and families today, and into the 21st century?

2. What are the ideal education and human services components of a new delivery system built to respond to the conditions identified?

3. How can the current system be restructured through collaborative action?

4. What will be the specific roles and role relationships of each of the professional partners in the reinvented education, health, and human services delivery system?

5. What can we learn from activities currently underway such as the "full-service" school concept and other coordinated efforts across the fields of education, social work, allied health, medicine, nursing, law, psychology, urban planning, extension, etc.?

6. What policies and legislation are being developed at the local, state, and national level to enhance and support the coordinated services concept and what policies need to be developed at each level?

7. What are the implications of the aforementioned issues for redesigning professional preparation to produce a new kind of leader for the 21st century; one who can move with confidence in a wide variety of education, health, and human services settings and link the various parts of the system? What must this leader know and be able to do? What changes will be needed in leadership development programs in "on site" settings as well as in collaborating universities to produce a new generation of education, health, and human services community leaders?

8. Can we broaden the definition of the professional development school and conceptualize it as the hub of the network connecting various parts of the education, health, and human services delivery system as well as a humane center of intellectual inquiry—a "community of learning" where everyone is both learner and teacher?

9. What kind of collaborative interprofessional research and evaluation should we undertake to insure that we are able to identify and implement the best of the untried ideas? What research and evaluation designs are appropriate for the studies that are needed? What is the most effective way to disseminate the best we find in research and practice so we can all learn from each other across the aforementioned participating professions?

There was unanimous agreement at the meeting that recommendations regarding (1) the structure of the new collaboratively developed delivery system, (2) the roles and role relationships of partners from multiple agencies, and (3) the type of interprofessional education needed to create and deliver services more effectively should be client-based. Therefore, it was agreed that all recommendations coming out of Commission meetings would be given a client-based reality check.

Four committees were established. First was a committee to collect and make available client-based data from each of the professional groups represented on the Commission, including case studies, critical incident information, and summaries of focus group sessions. It was interesting that many of the professions have already collected client-based feedback.

Second, a committee was designated to collect descriptions of collaborative programs already in operation, as well as copies of research and policy statements related to these programs. In addition, the committee will prepare a bibliography of theoretical pieces that propose new policies and programs to guide the future. However, the primary emphasis of the committee will be on collating and sharing "the lighthouses of innovation" that are already underway so networks of "doers" as well as thinkers can be developed to share problems and barriers as well as successes.

A third task was assigned to Dr. Ed Ducharme who will write a visionary statement on what an "ideal" collaborative interprofessional setting would look like. Roles and role relationships of the participating professional partners will be described. The statement will then be critiqued by members of all the professions involved, and changes will be added to the statements reflecting their perceptions of what their particular role ought to be and what the roles of the other professional partners ought to be to make a collaborative system work.

The fourth committee will prepare a proposal to be submitted to potential donors for funds to support the work of the Commission. Thirty members attended the session in Los Angeles on their own budgets. This kind of demonstrated commitment to the goals of the Commission should help in discussions with funding agencies.

Down the road, the Commission will make recommendations on the knowledge, skills, and values that should be included in the respective training and research programs of the participating professions to produce leaders who can create a collaborative education, health, and human service system. The design of the interprofessional education programs including what, where, and when appropriate curriculum and field experiences should be offered will emerge from joint examination of the perceived role and role relationships in a multiple agency collaborative system.

The Commission will disseminate its recommendations and various products through national and state meetings of the participating professions. Sessions will be planned the day before or the day after the national conferences of the participating professions. In addition, multi-disciplinary teams will present their ideas through a panel format at the various professional association conferences. Policy makers, politicians, and clients will be included as partners in this extended dialogue.

Each Commission meeting will be organized as a "think tank," or an "inquiry seminar." Since many of the Commission members have authored papers, books, or articles on one aspect or another of education, health, and human services, they will be asked to highlight the ideas in these materials that relate to the "issues in focus." All participants will come to the Commission meetings ready to respond to the nine issues identified by the Commission to guide its work. Concept papers and articles regarding the nine issues will be disseminated through the publication offices of the professional associations represented on the Commission.

The comments of several members of the Commission capture the "tone" and challenge of the Commission's work.

Merle McPherson of the Bureau of Maternal & Child Health & Resources Development said:

> We must change service systems so they serve children. Collaboration must take place at the family and community level. First and foremost we must convey a sense of urgency to all of the participating professions.

Al Buccino, dean of the College of Education at the University of Georgia, said:

> New conditions in the environment (e.g. demographic, social, economic changes) require a new analysis of the role of the community in child development including responsibilities of new or existing institutions (including collaboration among institutions and professions) in fulfilling the community's role.

Vince Hutchins, Executive Director of the National Ready to Learn Council, said:

> We must seek collaboration. Collaboration goes beyond coordination, consensus, or compromise; it implies new help in achieving a common vision. Collaboration in this venture means that one group, in a sense, becomes the other's agents in developing an expanding network of partners who are committed to the futures of children over the long haul.

Martin Haberman, professor of urban education at the University of Wisconsin at Milwaukee, reiterated that:

> The starting point in defining what leaders need to know and be able to do to create a new collaborative system should be the actual needs,

problems, and conditions facing America's children and their families. Training and research should be viewed as means for discovering and implementing better ways to serve those most in need. Professional education must be connected to the lives of practitioners and their clients and the settings in which they live, learn, and work.

All of the members of the group agreed that the Commission should seek to:

Capture and command the high ground in enticing all relevant professions to focus on and provide services to the *whole* child in a broad family/educational/community/societal context.

Because of its knowledge and experience in developing partnerships, ATE is strategically situated to *lead* this new direction.

REFERENCES

Children's Defense Fund. (1992). *Vanishing dreams: The economic plight of America's young families.* Washington, D.C.: Children's Defense Fund.

Children's Defense Fund. (1992). *The state of America's children: Leave no child behind.* Washington, D.C.: Children's Defense Fund.

Education Commission of the States. (1992). Putting it together: Redefining education and family services. Washington, D.C.: Education Commission of the States.

Hewlett, S. A. (1991). *When the bough breaks.* New York: Basic Books.

Hodgkinson, Harold L. (1989). *The same client: The demographics of education and service delivery systems.* Washington, D.C.: Institute for Educational Leadership, Inc.

Kozol, J. (1991). *Savage inequalities.* New York: Crown Publications.

Schorr, L. (1988). *Within our reach: Breaking the cycle of disadvantage.* New York: Doubleday.

United States Department of Education and United States Department of Health and Human Services. (1993). *Together we can: A guide to crafting a profamily system of education and human services.* Washington, D.C.: U.S. Government Printing Office.

William T. Grant Foundation Commission on Work, Family and Citizenship. (1988). *The forgotten half: Pathways to success for America's youth and young families.* Washington, D.C.: The Commission.

The Young and Rubicam Foundation. (1991). *The one place: A new role for American schools.* New York: St. Martin's Press.

Name Index

SUBJECT INDEX